Indigenous Medicine among the Bedouin in the Middle East

Indigenous Medicine among the Bedouin in the Middle East

Aref Abu-Rabia

berghahn
NEW YORK • OXFORD
www.berghahnbooks.com

First published in 2015 by
Berghahn Books
www.berghahnbooks.com

First paperback edition published in 2020

Library of Congress Cataloging-in-Publication Data

Abu-Rabia, Aref.
Indigenous medicine among the Bedouin in the Middle East / Aref Abu-Rabia.
pages cm
Includes bibliographical references and index.
ISBN 978-1-78238-689-6 (hardback : alk. paper) --
ISBN 978-1-78238-690-2 (ebook)
1. Bedouins—Medicine. 2. Traditional medicine—Arab countries. I. Title.
DS36.9.B4A38 2015
615.8′80899272—dc23

2015002049

British Library Cataloguing in Publication Data

A catalogue record for this book is available from the British Library

ISBN 978-1-78238-689-6 (hardback)
ISBN 978-1-78920-851-1 (paperback)
ISBN 978-1-78238-690-2 (ebook)

This book is dedicated to the Bedouin people
and healers in the Middle East;
may it help preserve their heritage.

Contents

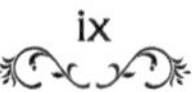

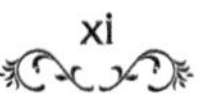

List of Illustrations

Preface

I was six years old when I became seriously ill. It was the middle of a very cold winter and I was put to bed on a small mattress near the hearth in the tent. My parents called a healer, but before he arrived my condition began to deteriorate rapidly. There were no physicians in the area. Thinking I was going to die, my parents took my brothers and sisters far away from me and turned my face to the south, toward Mecca. I sensed the gravity of my state and began to imagine that good and bad angels were quarreling over my life. The bad angel wanted to take my soul, while the good angel wanted me to survive. I comforted myself that children would not be punished by God on the Day of Judgment, and I would go directly to Eden. Suddenly, when I felt myself between the earth and the sky, the tent flap flew open, and the dervish-healer Sheikh 'Isa Hamd entered. He shouted and chanted verses and pushed a finger covered with yellow powder into my throat. He took a large tent needle and heated it in the embers. He put some of his saliva on the center hair whorl of my head (*fatilat al-ras*) and cauterized me twice, in the shape of an X. I heard an explosion, felt a sharp pain and cried—the first sound I had uttered that day. He gave me tea with herbs and I fell asleep. The next day when he came to visit I had recovered. My parents gave him a gift of a kid for curing me. I kept in touch with him from time to time, and saw him treat many people afflicted with disease, snakebites, and scorpion stings. Eighteen years later, when I was a master's student in public health, he taught me the secrets, the skills, and the art of Bedouin medicine. Through him, I was introduced to other healers in the Negev. I owe him my life.

The data for this book are derived from a broad study of traditional and folk medicine conducted among pastoral, nomadic, seminomadic, and settled Bedouin tribes in the Negev, Galilee, the Gaza Strip, Sinai, and Jordan during the last thirty years. This book is based on interviews

with healers, clients, and key informants who are active participants in treatments. Most of the material was recorded in field logs, and some was tape recorded. Unstructured interviews and observations of participants were carried out in the homes of the informants and the traditional healers. Most of the healers (men and women) were aged from thirty to eighty. Most of the informants were married and over the age of thirty. Samples from all the plants used in healing were collected and identified by healers, patients, and university botanists.

This book is based on primary and secondary sources as well as on a review of archival and documentary material and a review of published and unpublished materials, books, and scientific journals. It is usually difficult to gain more than a superficial knowledge of intimate life in other cultures, as anthropologists know. However, being a native Bedouin anthropologist, I maintained close personal ties among the Bedouin tribes in this region before and during the field work I conducted for my master's degree in public health and my PhD in anthropology. Informants felt relaxed and were generally glad to share information with me. The collection of this material over the last thirty years has been a lifetime task for me.

My training in anthropology has given me the tools with which to collect material systematically and analyze it professionally. I do not intend to claim that traditional medicine should replace modern medicine, yet I would like to contribute to renewed thinking about a synthesis between the two and their reciprocal enrichment, and to a holistic/comprehensive therapy that, I believe, can only benefit those who seek relief from diseases and other medical conditions. Among Bedouin tribes in different locations, there are similarities and common conceptions of disease, health, and the treatment of medical problems. At the same time, different tribes have unique treatment techniques for certain illnesses. I have collected and described these treatments, which I discovered during my many years of fieldwork.

I do not claim that the treatment methods presented in this research exist today among Bedouin throughout the Middle East, or among all generations (adults and educated young people), particularly since modern medicine has penetrated Bedouin tribes in the course of rapid urbanization and education. But when serious illness strikes, particularly in the case of incurable diseases, even educated people turn to traditional medicine for a remedy.

The daily hearth or sheikh's coffee-gathering is their education, a university for every man grown enough to walk and speak. —T.E. Lawrence, 1921

Acknowledgements

This manuscript would not have been completed without the help of the following: the Bedouin people, who accompanied my research; the Soroka Medical Center and the Veterinary Hospital in Beersheba; Ben-Gurion University of the Negev, Tel-Aviv University, the Hebrew University of Jerusalem; the Department of Anthropology and the Welcome Centre for the History of Medicine at University College London, and Huron University in London.

Many thanks for their comments and suggestions go to Emanuel Marx, Tom Selwyn, Violet Kimani, Allan Witztum, Younis Abu-Rabya, Mali Smutz, Clinton Baily, Gideon Kressel, Vardit Rispler-Chaim, Ann Gardner, Anita Nudelman, my students, and the healers.

Many thanks also go to all those who assisted me in compiling the manuscript. There is not enough room to mention all their names here, but I remain forever grateful for their assistance.

This work was supported by the National Geographic Society, the Jerusalem Center for Anthropological Studies, Ben-Gurion University of the Negev, the Israeli Ministry of Science, and Huron University in London. I am grateful for their assistance.

My father, Ibrahim, encouraged me to obtain higher education; and my mother, Sālmih, was a local healer. Her *baraka* directed and protected me during my field work. My parents' souls are moving between earth and sky. God have mercy on them.

Introduction

The purpose of this book is to describe the indigenous healing practices, health situation, and environmental and cultural origins of perceptions of disease among the Bedouin tribes during the twentieth century. In addition, it discusses access to state health services among the Bedouin, and examines their beliefs and attitudes towards healers and Western medicine.

In order to understand Bedouin medicine in the twentieth century, one must first gain an understanding of ancient Arabic medicine in the pre- and early Islamic periods. The Bedouin of Arabia in the pre-Islamic period were influenced by many cultures and civilizations, among them their neighbors and kindred: the Nabateans, Palmyrens, Ghassanids, Lakhmids, and the Byzantine and Persian cultures. Areas of contact between the Arabs and other civilizations included commerce and trade as well as political, military, religious, and intellectual fields (Judaism and Christianity) (Amin 1969: 1–35; Hitti 1951: 23–25; al-Najjar 1994: 2–53). Beyond these realms, the influence of neighboring cultures was felt in the practice of medicine, health, and hygiene.

Ancient Arabic medicine was also influenced by Greece and Rome. The Greco-Roman system of medicine developed based primarily on the writing of Hippocrates (460–360 BC), Dioscorides (circa AD 54 to 68), and Galen (AD 130–201). Alexandria, Rome, Constantinople, Antioch, Edessa, Amida, and Gundishapur flourished as centers of scientific and medical activity (Mursi 1966; Savage-Smith 1996). A combination of political and religious events caused many Greek and Syriac-speaking scholars to move eastward to Persia and establish a center of learning, including a medical school, in the city of Gundishapur in the sixth century AD (Murad 1966; al-Said 1997; Savage-Smith 1996: 907–8; al-Shatti 1970).

The Arab medical system grew out of the works of physicians who were contemporaries of the Prophet Muhammad (AD 571–632), including al-Harith b. Kilda[1] and Ibn Abi Rimtha (Hawting 1989). The sayings (hadith) of the Prophet Muhammad on health and illness were systemized and became known as Medicine of the Prophet (*al-Tibb al-Nabawi*) (Hawting 1989; Savage-Smith 1996). In the early period of Islam, a number physicians or traditional healers practiced, among them al-Nader b. al-Harith (the son of al-Harith b. Kalada), Zuhayr b. Janab al-Himyari, Zaynab al-Awadiya from Bani Awd, al-Shamardal b. Qibab al-Ka'bi al-Najrani, Ibn Hudhaym from Tim al-Ribab, Hammad b. Tha'labah al-Azadi, Abd al-Malik Abjar al-Kinani, Um 'Attyya al-Ansariyya, and Rafidah (al-Labadi 1992: 80–81).

Ancient medical works began to be translated during the Umayyad rule (661–750 in the East).[2] Over the course of the following five centuries (750–1258), the Abbasids dominated the sociopolitical life of the greater part of the Muslim world. The ten caliphs of the period were generous in their promotion of knowledge and medicine, and medical translations and writings flourished under the Abbasids. Particularly notable in this regard were al-Mansur (754–775), Harun al-Rashid (786–802), and al-Ma'mun (813–833). A hospital was built and became the cradle of the Baghdad School of Medicine. Countless manuscripts, particularly those written in Greek, were collected and stored in Bayt al-Hikmah (House of Wisdom, established in Baghdad in 830, by Caliph al-Ma'mun),[3] where scholars labored at translating them into Arabic. One of the early translators was the Nestorian Christian Yuhanna b. Masawayh (d. 857), a pupil of Jibril b. Bakhtishu' and a teacher of Hunayn b. Ishaq. Al-Ma'mun appointed him superintendent of his library/academy and he was responsible for all scientific translation into Arabic (Hitti 1951: 310–16). One of his pupils was Hunayn b. Ishaq[4] (810–877), physician of the caliph al-Mutawakkil. His treatise *al-Masa'il fi al-tibb li-lmuta'allimin* (Questions on Medicine for Students) was extremely influential, as was his *Kitab al-'Ashr Maqalat fi al-'Ayn* (Ten Treatises on the Eye). Another translator was Thabit b. Qurra (d. 901).[5] 'Ali b. Sahl Rabban al-Tabari,[6] a physician, translator, and author, dedicated his book *Firdaws al-Hikma* (Paradise of Wisdom) to the caliph al-Mutawakkil in 850. Qusta b. Luqa al-Ba'albaki (d. 912) a physician and translator, wrote on various topics, including blood, phlegm, yellow bile, and black bile.[7]

It was during this period, too, that the philosopher Ya'qub b. Ishaq al-Kindi (d. 873) authored several works on medicine. (His *Formulary* of compound medicines was translated from Arabic to English by Martin Levey in 1966.) Another scholar, Abu 'Abd Allah b. Sa'id Al-Tamimi (d. 980), from Jerusalem, went to Egypt to work as physician for the Vizier Ya'qub ibn Killis. He wrote a guide on foods and medicines and a book about plague, *Maddat al-baqa' bi-islah fasad al-hawa'*. Ishaq ibn Sulayman al-

Isra'ili (855–950) was both a physician and a philosopher. He first worked as an oculist in Cairo, and later emigrated to Kairouan in Tunisia, where he studied medicine under Ishaq b. 'Imran and became court physician to Ziyadat Allah III (reg. 903–909), the last emir of the Aghlabid dynasty. His finest work was *Kitab al-Hummayat* (The Book of Fever). One of the most highly regarded ophthalmological manuals was *Kitab Tadhkirat al-Kahhalin* (The Oculist's Notebook), by Sharaf al-Din 'Ali b. 'Isa al-Kahhal (d. 1010), who practiced as an oculist and physician in Baghdad. This text covered 130 eye ailments.

Within a century of the birth of Islam, Muslim physicians and scientists were making original contributions to medical and botanical knowledge. One of the greatest and most well-known Islamic doctors was Ibn Sina (Avicenna, 980–1037),[8] who compiled the *Kitab al-Qanun fi al-Tibb* (Canon of Medicine) (Foster and Anderson 1978: 58; Gruner 1930; al-Shatti 1970). Another leading Arabic philosopher/physician was al-Razi (Rhazes, 865–923),[9] who compiled the *Kitab al-Hawi fi al-Tibb* (Comprehensive Book on Medicine).[10] It should be noted that the works of Ibn Sina and al-Razi were later translated into Latin, and continued to influence medical practice until as late as the nineteenth century (al-Said 1997; Johnstone 1998; Murad 1966; al-Shatti 1970). Most physicians in Andalusia were herbalists, and most herbalists served as healers. The *al-Jami' li-Mufradat al-Adwiya wa'l-Aghdhiya* (Compendium of Simple Drugs and Food), by Ibn al-Baytar (1197–1248), describes more than 1,400 medicinal drugs, including 300 not previously described. This is probably the best known of all Arabic herbal books (Johnstone 1998: xxxi–xxxii).

The medicinal use of plants was a popular topic in Arab medical writings. Among the well-known physicians who wrote on the uses of plants was Sulayman b. al-Hasan b. Juljul (d. 994), who worked at the court of 'Abd al-Rahman III and assisted in the translation of Dioscorides' herbal into Arabic. He was the author of *Tabaqat al-Atibba' wa-l-Hukama'* (History of Medicine and Physicians) (Johnstone 1998: xxxi). Hamid Ibn Samajun (d. 1010) compiled a large volume on herbs, *al-Kitab al-Jami' li-Aqwal al-Qudama' wa'l-Mutahaddithin min al-Atibba' wa'l-Mutafalsifin fi'l-Adwiya al-Mufrada* (The Comprehensive Book of Sayings of Ancient and Modern Physicians and Philosophers Concerning Simple Drugs) (Johnstone 1998: xxxi). Abu Ja'far Ahmad b. Muhammad al-Ghafiqi (d. 1135), originally from Ghafiq, near Cordoba, compiled a large text on herbs and drugs *Kitab al-Adwiya al-Mufrada* (Book of Simple Drugs) (Johnstone 1998: xxxi). 'Abd al-Malik b. Zuhr (Avenzoar 1113–1162) was the first of a five-generation family of prominent Andalusian physicians. A native of Seville, he achieved widespread fame as a physician in Spain and North Africa. He wrote *Kitab al-Aghdhiya* (The Nutrition Book), but his best-known book was *Kitab al-Taysir fi'l Mudawat wa'l-Tadbir* (Facilitation of Treatment in Therapy and Diet) (al-Said 1997: 697; Johnstone 1998: xxxii; Savage-Smith 1996: 925–26).

Significant contributions to medical science were also made by Al-Zahrawi [Abu al-Qasim Khalaf b. 'Abbas al-Zahrawi] (Abulcasis or Albucasis, 936–1013), born in Zahra, near Cordoba, who laid the foundations of modern surgery. He authored three books that remained standard textbooks for nearly a thousand years. The most famous one of these was *Kitab al-Tasrif li-man 'Ajiza 'an al-Ta'lif* (Manual for Medical Practitioners/The Arrangement of Medical Knowledge for One Who Is Not Able to Compile a Book by Himself). Its primary contribution to the field of medicine is that it contained 278 illustrations of equipment used for surgery.

During this fruitful period of medical writing, Ibn al-Jazzar (d. 980), an Arab physician and member of a distinguished medical family in Qayrawan, the mediaeval capital of Tunisia, authored several works that added much to the medical knowledge of the time. His writing earned him renown in medieval Western Europe. Some of his books were translated into Greek, Latin, and Hebrew: *Kitab al-Adwiya* (Treatise on Simple Drugs), *Tibb al-Fuqara' wa-al-Masakin* (Medicine for the Poor), *Risala fi al-Nisyan wa 'ilajihi* (On Forgetfulness and Its Treatment), *Kitab Siyasat al-Sibyan wa-Tadbirihim* (On the Education and Regimen of Children), *Kitab fi al-Ma'idah wa-Amradiha wa-Mudawatiha* (On the Stomach, Its Diseases, and Treatment). His *Zad al-Musafir wa-qut al-Hadir* (Provision for the Traveler and Nourishment for the Sedentary) is, contrary to what its title suggests, an excellent medical text on sexual diseases and their treatment. This book was translated into Greek, Latin, and Hebrew, and featured among the standard texts for medical instruction at Salerno, Montpellier, Bologna, Paris, and Oxford (Abu-Rabia 2000: 224–29; Bos 1997: 1–18). Another significant contributor to medical sciences was Muhammad b. Ahmad b. Rushd (Averroes 1126–1198), born in Cordoba, whose main medical work is *Kitab al-Kulliyyat* (lat. Colliget).

The influence of Arabic medicine, which is so interwoven with the Greco-Latin legacy, has proved to be of critical importance to Western medicine. The Arabic texts became available mainly through two successive waves of translations into Latin. The first of these became available in southern Italy in the second half of the eleventh century, while the second became available in Spain about a hundred years later. In the middle of the thirteenth century, the three great medical faculties of Paris, Montpellier, and Bologna gradually integrated the fundamental works of Ibn Sina and al-Razi and the surgical part of the *al-Tasrif* of al-Zahrawi (Jacquart 1996: 963–71).

During the Fatimid rule (909–1160), Cairo became a center of learning, attracting physicians such as Musa ibn Maymon (Maimonides, born in Cordoba, 1135–1204), who served as a personal physician for Salah ad-Din's son al-Malik al-Afdal Nur ad-Din 'Ali in Egypt. His most famous work is *Kitab al-Fusul* (Aphorisms). Other famous physicians included Abd al-Latif al-Baghdadi (1162–1231) and Muhadhdhab al-Din 'Abd al-Rahim ibn 'Ali, known as al-Dakhwar. Ibn al-Nafis (Ali abi al-Hazm al-Qurashi, d. 1288), born in Damascus, was a physician-surgeon. His most famous writings are *Kitab al-Mujiz* of the Canon of Ibn Sina, and a large commentary on the Canon, in which he developed his theory of pulmonary circulation, the first to accurately explain the minor circulation of the blood (Ullmann 1978: 48) before the Spaniard Michael Servetus (Miguel Servede, 1509–1553) (al-Najjar 1994: 148; Khan 1986: 19; Nasr 1968: 213).

Among Arab physicians, music was a prominent mode of healing. Music is a means of communication and can be a powerful therapeutic tool. The idea of using music as a healing technique, or as the background for the healing process, is prevalent in many cultures. The basic objective of the healer is to establish communication with the spirits through music. One of the well-known Arab doctors who used music for healing was Abu-Nasr al-Farabi,[11] who lived in the tenth century. Al-Farabi invented a musical instrument on which he played melodies that strongly affected people, causing them to laugh or cry, wake up, or fall asleep (al-Farabi 1967; al-Shatti 1970; Shiloah 2001: 81–95).

In the early eight century, Muslims established hospitals and hospices[12] that were free of charge regardless of the gender, social status, or age of the patient. These Islamic hospitals provided patients with systematic treatments based upon humoral medicine (*al-akhlat*). These included exercises, baths, dietary regimens, and a comprehensive materia medica, in addition to bone-setting, cauterizing, venesection, and eye surgery (Reynolds and Tanner 1995: 249–50). While Islamic medicine was supported and sponsored by the courts, mystical medicine served urbanites in large towns, and healing systems associated with the Zanj[13] movement catered to slaves, peasants, and some artisans (Baer, Singer, and Susser 1997: 208).

At the dawn of Islam, hospitals were built for old people and the mentally ill (Melling and Forsythe 1999).[14] Caretakers would wash patients, dress them in clean clothes, help them pray, and have special chanters with pleasant voices read them verses from the Quran. Sometimes the *Mu'adhdhin* (the announcer who calls the faithful to prayer in the minaret of the mosque) would recite prayers and supplications (*ibtihalat*) before sunrise to relieve patients of their insomnia and pain. The custom of reading verses from the Quran for healing was practiced by the Prophet as part of the healing process for sick people who appealed to him for help. In addition to the daily provision of song and instrumental music in the hospital, it was also customary to invite groups of dancers, singers, and entertainers to perform for the patients. The healing atmosphere was further enhanced by the burning of incense (*bakhkhur*). Sometimes the floors of the hospital were strewn with branches of pomegranate (*rumman*), the mastic tree (*mustaka*), balsam of Mecca (*balsam Makka*), henna (*hinna*), and pleasant-smelling spice trees (al-Shatti 1970).

The main achievements of medieval Arabic-Islamic medicine lay in five areas: systematization, hospitals, pharmacology, surgery, and ophthalmology. The development of Arabic medical literature can be described as a constant reshaping and rearranging of the Greek heritage by shortening, expanding, commenting on, and systematizing ancient source material. Ibn-Sina combined the legacy of Greek medical knowledge with the Arab contribution in his massive Canon of Medicine, which is the masterpiece of Arab systematization. The basis of pharmacology, the *Materia Medica* of Dioscorides, was enlarged by numerous Arab authors, who added some 500 names of simple and compound drugs to the ancient stock (Burgel 1976: 44–62; Haddad 1975; Meyerhof 1931: 311–55; al-Shatti 1970).

Beliefs and Therapies

The Arabs in the pre-Islamic period practiced preventive and curative medicine that some of them learned from neighbors and nations with whom they came into contact. Some ancient Arab medical practices depended on amulets, charms, sorcery, and witchcraft (Amin 1969: 1–35; Mursi 1966; al-Najjar 1994: 2–53; al-Said 1997; Murad 1966; al-Shatti 1970). Among the methods of treatment were divination (*sihr*), magic (*sha'wadha*), talismans (*talsim*), and astrology (*tanjim*). They believed, for example, that the blood of a king or prince was an effective antidote against rabies, and a few drops mixed with water were administered to a person bitten by a rabid dog. They treated a man crazed by love for a woman by cauterizing his buttocks. A boy who developed pustules on his lips was made to carry a sieve (*munkhul*) on his head and go from house to house asking for food; women would throw pieces of bread, dates, and meat into the sieve, which the boy fed to dogs. They believed that this act would cure the pustules, and that another dog/human eating the scraps would be similarly afflicted. When a Bedouin entered a town he would bray ten times at the gate like a donkey to make the epidemic diseases[15] think he was an animal and not human, in the hope of being spared from disease (al-Shatti 1970: 5–10; Ullmann 1970: 185–89; 1978: 1–6). When the Arabs believed that dis-

ease was caused by evil spirits, they would put a bird in a cage for several days and note whether it flew to the left (a bad omen) or the right (a good omen) when it was freed.

Medical treatments in pre-Islamic times were administered either by people themselves, who used herbal drugs and drinks prepared from plants and minerals, or by diviners and fortune tellers whose armamentarium included cauterizing (*kayy, kaii*), cupping (*hijama*), and bleeding (*fasd*). They believed, for example, that squinting could be cured by staring at revolving grindstones. They treated mad people by hanging unclean objects, such as the bones of a dead person taken from a cemetery, around them, or by making them wear the ankle bone of a rabbit (al-Najjar 1994: 52–53). Jewelry and bells were hung on victims of stings or bites to keep them awake, based on the belief that venom spreads through the body of a sleeping person and kills him (al-Shatti 1970). They tied small bags of wheat, barley, and dates on toy clay camels, and placed them at the opening of a westward-facing burrow hole just before sunset. Finding the food undisturbed the next morning meant that their payment for the sick person had not been accepted. Finding the food disturbed signified that their payment had been accepted and the sick person would be healed (Sharif 1970: 3–30).[16] Arabs used gems, crystals, beads, and stones as medicine. They believed that precious stones were useful to wear as ring-stones, since they bore magic powers for healing, preventing diseases, and bringing omens (al-Najjar 1994: 52–53; al-Shatti 1970).[17] Bedouin medicine also made a major contribution to Islamic medicine through the *Sahih* of al-Bukhari, the most famous of the collections recording the Prophet's sunna and sayings on all spheres of daily life, including illness, health, and healing. One of the rules in al-Bukhari's cover chapter on healing originated in Bedouin folklore and advances the basic theory of Bedouin pathology that all diseases are ultimately caused by a disorder of the stomach, by improper nutrition, or by indigestion (Burgel 1976; Elgood 1962: 33–192).

The Islamic medical tradition, established by the *al-Tibb al-Nabawi* (Medicine of the Prophet) in the seventh century, was molded in the tenth century, developed in the eleventh and twelfth centuries, reached its peak in the thirteenth to sixteenth centuries, and later declined in the seventeenth to nineteenth centuries (Hamarneh 1991; Lev 2002: 177; Mursi 1966: 2–39). Medical literature and healing methods that had been the focus of traditional medicine for over a thousand years were marginalized in the nineteenth and twentieth centuries by the advent of Western medicine, becoming the exclusive domain of traditional medicine and folk healers (Abu-Rabia 2005f: 404-407; Lev 2002: 167–79; Lev and Amar 2000: 191–205). Folk healers continued to consult medical texts originally written in the Middle Ages (Lev 2002: 178). Medicine came to be practiced mainly

FIGURE 0.1 Kuhl container; Bedouin women prepare *kuhl* for medical and cosmetic purposes.

by folk healers. Professional healers wandered from place to place pulling teeth, operating on kidney stones, and treating cataracts. Some barbers practiced surgery using methods that included cupping and bleeding, while other healers used cauterizing, medicinal herbs, written charms, and amulets. Among them were healers who also dealt with sorcery and witchcraft (*sihr*) (Abu-Rabia 1983; 1998).

Bedouin Medicine in the Twentieth Century

The use of traditional medicine, particularly herbal medicine, was widespread throughout the Middle East in the twentieth century (Abu-Rabia 1999a; Ali-Shtayeh, Yaniv, and Mahajna 2000; Bailey and Danin 1981; Krispil 2000; Palevitch and Yaniv 2000; Pillsbury 1978: 1–25; Tal 1981: 15–17). The philosophy of traditional Bedouin medicine draws its strength from the belief in fate, the conviction that all things that happen to man, both good and evil, are the will of Allah. It follows that man must accept his fate with strong faith, courage, and patience. According to the Bedouin, both health and illness are caused by Allah, with the help of natural and supernatural powers created by Him. These powers are the source of healing. Most illnesses are a direct punishment by Allah for our sins[18] or for the transgression of Bedouin moral or religious codes. Allah acts through the mediation of man, and therefore cures illness by means of a doctor or folk healer. Health-preserving principles include the practice of the basic rules of hygiene, public health education, and religious behavior and devotion. These include abstinence from carrion, spoiled food, and contaminated water sources, and the avoidance of places where there are dangers and diseases such as plague and cholera. The maintenance of proper relationships, good neighborliness, and regular observance of the rules and commandments of tribal codes of behavior all form part of the healthy basis of human society as perceived by the Bedouin (Abu-Rabia 1983; Bailey 1982: 65–88). In general, studies have shown that the older and the more traditional the Bedouin, the more likely he is to attribute illness to the supernatural and the greater his tendency to view illness in this manner, and the higher the rate of appeal to folk healers and the lower to Western medicine. Moreover, as the rate of reported successes by folk healers rises, the rate of reported healings by Western medicine drops. If, however, the Bedouin is not satisfied with folk medicine, he may turn to Western medicine. In some cases he may appeal to both simultaneously (Abu-Rabia 1979; Ben-Assa 1974: 73–76). Bedouin patients used to refer first to home remedies and traditional medicine, but now they often rely upon Western medicine initially or first after home medicine; if these fail, they finally resort to traditional healers, including religious healers.

Bedouin healers use a range of techniques and medications in their work. Illnesses are cured by means of remedies taken from vegetables, minerals, and animals. Various plant parts are used, including flowers, fruits, leaves, juices, roots, seeds, bulbs, tubers, and pulps. One of the most famous medicines in use among the Bedouin in the Middle East is the *arba'yn*, which consists of a mixture of forty different types of plants and is considered to be a cure for all aches and pains. In traditional and folk medicine, the Bedouin appeal not only to the herbalist, but also to the dervish, the *khatib*, the amulet writer, the cauterizer; the *mujabbir* (for setting broken or fractured bones); midwives; the *'Attar* or local pharmacologist and vendor of medicinal spices; holy tombs (of ancestors or prophets); the sea, rivers, holy springs; and so on. In addition, Bedouin healers use techniques that stimulate physiological processes, including bathing, sweat-bathing, massage, cupping, emetics, burning/cauterizing, incision, and bloodletting (Abu-Rabia 1999a, 2005).

Traditional Bedouin healers are familiar with the conditions of the Bedouin's life, his way of thinking, and his fears. With such healers, a Bedouin is likely to feel free and at ease, because the treatment they offer is simple and accords with his worldview. Furthermore, the traditional Bedouin healer does not charge a fixed fee; the patient pays whatever he or she can. In most cases, the cost of the treatment is whatever the patient wishes to leave, whether money or gifts (sugar, coffee beans, lambs, or sheep). There are healers who refuse to take money, saying: "This is [my profession as a healer] a gift, a *baraka*[19] from God, I cannot be paid for it."

There are Bedouin healers who cooperate with modern medicine by sending patients to a particular physician who, they assure him, will bring them relief. In many cases, this is a good combination, since the patient has complete faith in it, takes his medicine and the advice given with absolute seriousness, and often quickly recovers. Many traditional healers insist that the patient's desire to recover is as important as the healer's desire to cure him. Treatment by traditional healers has established a relationship of psychological-therapeutic dependence on the part of the Bedouin with regard to the healers. This dependence is deeply rooted in their psyches and reinforced and legitimized by Bedouin culture (Abu-Rabia 1999a: 17–25).

Most Bedouin healers learn from their fathers or mothers during their practice of a healing trade. There is no time limit for acquiring the profession, but it is not uncommon for famous healers to have apprenticed for ten years or more. Most healers work in other professions in the tribe, but usually when they become old or very famous and the people of the tribe appeal to them, they devote most of their time only to healing. In the Middle East, the healer's role is perceived as a religious skill related to proximity to saints, which enables the healer to fight the forces of evil that cause illness. Proximity to saints can be more easily attained within a family blessed with many religious healers—dervishes—who treat mental and physical illnesses using a variety of religious and cultural rituals. Men and women usually become dervishes by virtue of having received a *baraka*—a blessing gift from God (al-Krenawi and Graham 1997: 213) or by virtue of birthright (from father/mother), through family members renowned as wise or righteous people, or purported to have special visionary powers, and so forth.

Illness is said to be ultimately determined by the will of Allah. Illness is defined holistically as a deviation from states of normal health, manifested by changes in social, psychological, and physical states. Traditional therapies are not only means for curing sickness, but also means by which specified types of illness are defined and given culturally recognizable forms. While in Western medicine the criteria of proof demand more than plausibility, in traditional medicine the condition of plausibility seems to be sufficient. When healing fails, a patient remains with his disease until he discovers the correct cure from another healer. Healers and patients explain that this is the will of Allah. For the patient, a failed therapy may be considered important because it offers diagnostic information that points to a more appropriate type of healer. That is, some spirits are more powerful than others, just as some healers may be more familiar with and effective in treating a particular problem than others.

Illness is ascribed to the invasion of the body by excessive heat or cold, and the saying *al-bard sabab kul 'illih*, meaning "cold is the main reason for illness or body disorder," is widespread. Cold enters the body under many circumstances, causing common colds and other illnesses. But this illness, which was caused by cold, may lead to increased heat in the afflicted person. For example, drinking cold water may cause toothache, and continuous toothaches may cause headaches and raise the heat of the body.

Bedouin healers examine the facial expression and the eye color of the patient as part of their attempt to diagnose the disease and prescribe treatment. Their reputations as good healers result from of their attitudes toward patients; healers are always warm, friendly, and supportive, and offer good hospitality to those that they treat. Usually their treatments are successful, and patients recover from a majority of their illnesses. Recovering from illnesses regardless of the treatment is well known among the Bedouin in the Negev (Ben-Assa 1974: 73–76) and in other traditional societies (Clark 1959: 208).

Generally, treatments are based on knowledge and on approaches such as causality, classification, and diagnosis of the illness.[20] Actually, the traditional healer functions as a botanist, pharmacist, psychologist, and tribe or group leader in his treatment of various illnesses. Dervishes (*darwish*, pl. *darawish*) in particular are good psychologists, imbuing patients with confidence and having a positive effect on those who believe in them. There are cases in which the dervish hosts the patient for several days in his own (the dervish's) home, where he has a supportive atmosphere filled with expectation, faith, and hope that impart the willpower to get well (Ben-Assa 1974: 75). In general, traditional Bedouin medicine can be divided into two types: preventive and therapeutic medicine (Abu-Rabia 1983).

The aim of preventive medicine is to deter the causes of illness by hanging amulets or talismans on a person, making vows, visiting the tombs of saints, or using stratagems to mislead the sources of the disease, such as the evil eye. The influence of the evil eye is counteracted by devices designed to distract its attention and annul its power through the practice of magic. The concept of the evil eye appears to be a psychological idiom for the fear of misfortune. It may relate to fear of outsiders and their envy (Abu-Rabia 2005b: 241–54). Adhering to the rules of social ethics, religion, and hygiene can also help to prevent illness.

Therapeutic medicine commences with the onset of illness, that is, when a person feels ill or when his family feels he is ill. Since the physical or mental well-being of the person was undermined by another person, who employed some means to make him sick, therapeutic medicine employs traditional methods to remove the harmful agent from the sick person's body so that he may function again as previously. Curative medicine deals with methods used when illness, either physical or mental, has already struck (Abu-Rabia 1983). The sources of the preternatural forces that cause illness are in man's evil impulses, covetousness, jealousy, and the like.

When a Bedouin is ill, or wants to take protective measures for himself, his children, or his property, he beseeches Allah to help him through His saints. Ceremonies surrounding visits to saints' tombs and the traditional rites related to ancestors and the making of pledges engender a psychological-therapeutic dependency of the Bedouin on the saints. This dependency is deeply rooted in faith, and augmented and legitimized in Bedouin culture. Interestingly, belief in saints and the tradition of pilgrimage to the tombs of saints is prevalent among Bedouin even in the areas of the southern Sinai that are isolated from the rest of the peninsula. A Bedouin will not just appeal to one saint. Just as a sick person in modern society will seek several medical opinions, so too the Bedouin will appeal to different saints, each of which has a certain degree of specialization. Among the Bedouin of the southern Sinai, such a pilgrimage can foster any of three kinds of rites: those between members of the tribe, those between the tribes of southern Sinai, and those between members of all the tribes and Islam (Marx 1977: 14–22). Notably, the Bedouin of Jabaliya near St. Catherine's Monastery (Sinai) have developed a unique form of folk medicine, designed to overcome the diseases and mishaps that typify their desert environment (Ben-David 1981: 107–28).

Attitudes towards Doctors and Western Medicine and the Effects of Modern Life

The Bedouin view the Western doctor and Western medicine as intermediaries between the patient and Allah. Therefore, the doctor's attitude towards the patient during the examination and his interest in the patient's general health are of the utmost importance for the success of the treatment. A Bedouin always prefers an injection to pills when visiting a Western doctor; an injection, he believes, is quicker and more efficacious. The Bedouin believe that medical equipment such as X-ray machines, stethoscopes, and blood pressure gauges help to diagnose illness and cure it. That is why they always allow themselves to be examined by them.

Blood tests are a different matter, however. The Bedouin loathe, and often refuse to undergo, such tests. Ben-Assa (1964: 451) notes that the Negev Bedouin usually refuse to give blood for a sedimentation test or even for a hemoglobin test; and when they do agree to such a test they complain about weakness and pain in the area of the puncture for years. The Bedouin claim that the doctor or nurse is taking more blood than necessary. In order to understand this attitude, one must bear in mind that blood is viewed as a special value related to faith. Not only does the Bedouin refuse to take blood tests, he refuses to donate blood, even to relatives. He prefers to buy blood when necessary. This view derives from the belief that the blood [21] that leaves him will never return, and is something for which he may never be recompensed.

The Bedouin are terrified of hospitalization, because in their view a hospital is a place for those on the brink of death.[22] When hospitalized, they experience anxiety and disappointment. Relatives and friends will come to visit, despite long travel distances, to make them feel better and boost their morale. For this reason, visiting the sick is a social and religious mandate. One of the most frightening things to a hospitalized Bedouin is the need to undergo surgery. Anesthesia is viewed as a kind of temporary death, as non-inclusion in this world. They are also frightened by the idea of a postmortem. There are also cases of family members at the bedside of a dying person disconnecting him from intravenous lines and taking him home, so he can die there. In this way, they can grant the deceased the respect due him and ask forgiveness (*samah*). Each family member and relative approaches the dying person in turn and says, "I forgive you and ask your forgiveness." To which the dying person replies, "I forgive you and ask your forgiveness." This ceremony is extremely important to the Bedouin, and is perceived as the purification of sins before death (Abu-Rabia 1992: 8–19; Ben-David 1981: 119–21).

According to Ben-Assa (1974: 73–76), the transition from traditional to modern patterns of life and coming face to face with modern society have influenced life among the Negev Bedouin. Some of the young people have gone to work in kibbutzim and moshavim, in factories, and in construction. Changes in eating habits (e.g., foods rich in cholesterol) and changes in the way the modern Bedouin acts in his adaptation to the rhythm of the high-pressured Israeli workplace have led to a high incidence of heart attacks. While the incidence of traditional diseases has declined, Bedouin have begun to suffer from ailments they had not suffered from in the past, such as diabetes, high blood pressure, asthma, ulcers, and breathing difficulties (dyspnea). Despite this fact, certain aspects of desert life are salubrious; walking long distances develops muscles and proper breathing.[23]

Traditional medical practices and social life were described by Arab scholars as well as Western scholars and travelers during the nineteenth century and early twentieth century. Among these scholars were Bertram Thomas, Anne Blunt, John Burckhardt, Tewfik Canaan, Harold Richard Dickson, Charles Doughty, Hilma Granqvist, Jibrail Jabour, Edward William Lane, Thomas Edward Lawrence, George William Murray, Alois Musil, Edward Henry Palmer, John Philpy, Amin Rihani, Na'um Shuqayr, Robertson Smith, Wilfred Thesiger, Karl Raswan, as well as others. God bless all of them.

Notes

1. Al-Harith b. Kalada (Kilda) (d. 634) traveled to Jundishapur in Persia and studied medicine prior to the advent of Islam. He returned to Ta'if (in Arabia), where his medicine became renowned among the Arabs. He is said to have been a relative of the Prophet Muhammad. The Prophet would send sick people to consult al-Harith. One of these was Sa'd b. Abi Waqqss (Hawting 1989: 127–37). Al-Harith was very familiar with the doctrine of the four humors (*al-Akhlat*) (Ibn Abi Usaybi'ah 1965: 13–17).
2. The first Umayyad caliph, Mu'awiya b. Abi Sufyan (r. 661–680), employed the physician Ibn Uthal. The grandson of Mu'awiya, Prince Khalid b. Yazid (d. 704) had a passion for medicine. He instructed a group of Greek scholars in Egypt to translate Greco-Egyptian medical literature into Arabic. The physician of Caliph 'Umar b. 'Abd al-'Aziz (r. 717–720) was 'Abd al-Malik b. Abjar al-Kinani, a convert to Islam who had studied at the surviving medical school in Alexandria (Savage-Smith 1996: 909).
3. Many physicians were brought to Baghdad. One of these was Jurjis b. Jibra'il b. Bakhtishu'. For eight generations, well into the second half of the eleventh century AD, twelve members of the Bakhtishu' family of Nestorian Christians would serve the caliphs as physicians and advisors, sponsor the translation of texts, and compose their own original treatises (al-Najjar 1994; Hitti 1951: 311–12; Savage-Smith 1996: 910).
4. A Nestorian Christian, originally from al-Hira in southern Iraq.
5. He was a member of Sabian sect of Harran in northern Mesopotamia.
6. He came from Marw, south of the Caspian Sea, and was the son of a Christian scholar. Later he converted from Christianity to Islam.
7. Thus, by the end of the ninth century, the humoral system of pathology as outlined by the Greco-Roman physician Galen in the second century AD had been completely accepted and integrated into the learned medical thinking of the day (Hitti 1951: 311–12; Savage-Smith 1996: 912; Ullmann 1978: 7–40). This system was based upon the notion of four humors: blood, phlegm, yellow bile,

and black bile, derived from the earlier Hippocratic writings. Parallels were drawn with the four elements (air, water, fire, and earth), while the four qualities were aligned in pairs with the humors in the following manner: blood is hot and moist; phlegm is cold and moist; yellow bile is hot and dry; black bile is cold and dry. The four seasons of the year were important, and climatic and geographical conditions were also considered significant (al-Azraq 1948: 2–7; Khan 1986: 37–50; Ullmann 1978: 55–62). Hippocrates, Galen, and the Arab physicians, particularly Avicenna, were the principal authorities for medical theory and practice (Foster and Anderson 1978: 59) at the time.

8. He was born near Bukhara in Central Asia into a family devoted to learning. Known as the Prince of Physicians, he combined the legacy of Greek medical knowledge with the Arab contribution in his *Canon of Medicine,* which is the epitome of Islamic medicine and the culmination of Arab systematization. It was translated into Latin and taught for centuries in Western universities, becoming one of the most frequently printed scientific texts in the Renaissance. In several medical faculties, it was a textbook until 1650. The Canon focused Greek and Islamic medical knowledge, which included medicine, anatomy, physiology, pathology, and pharmacopoeia (al-Said 1997: 695–98).
9. Born in Rayy, Persia, he studied in Baghdad, lectured, and practiced medicines. His most celebrated work was *Kitab fi al-Jadari wa al-Hasba* (On Smallpox and Measles), which was translated into Latin and later into other languages, including English. Another famous book is the *Kitab al-Tibb al-Mansuri* (Book of Medicine), a short general textbook of medicine of considerable influence, dedicated by al-Razi in 903 to the Samanid prince Abu Salih al-Mansur b. Ishaq, governor of Rayy.
10. The material in al-Hawi is arranged under the headings of different diseases, with separate sections on pharmacological topics. This book (24 volumes) was one of only nine books used in the Medical Faculty of the University of Paris.
11. Abu-Nasr al-Farabi, d. 950 (Alpharabius Avenassar), philosopher and musician.
12. The first hospitals were established during the reign of al-Walid ibn 'Abd al-Malik (705–715) in Damascus (al-Shatti 1970).
13. Zanj (also transliterated as Zenj or Zinj, in Arabic "Land of the Blacks") was a name used by medieval Arab geographers to refer to both a certain portion of the East African coast and its inhabitants and is the origin of the place name "Zanzibar."
14. See also Dols (1987: 367–90).
15. The Greeks believed in the divine origin of epidemic diseases.
16. For more comparative details about this topic among the Indians and the Maya see Salazar 1992: 44.
17. For more details about uses of beads among the Arabs in different centuries, see Tifashi 1977; Kunz 1915: 131–33, 281–324, 360–78; Ibn Zuhr 1992 (*Kitab al-Aghdhiya*).
18. This belief exists in other societies. Foster and Anderson note that "illness is attributed to sin, taboo violations, and other forms of wrongdoing. In the Judeo-Christian tradition illness historically has been explained as God's pun-

ishment of man for his moral lapses, for his sins. Individual illness represented personal transgressions, while great epidemics signified major social moral failures. In either case, repentance and adherence to God's law was the way to recovery and the avoidance of future affliction" (1978: 43). Roemer states that "God has revealed his law. Whoever follows it piously will be blessed in this world. Whoever breaks the law will be punished. Every disease is a punishment. Every suffering is a suffering for sin—for the sins of the individual himself, for those of his parents, or for those of his relatives" (Roemer 1960: 14).

19. *Baraka* is divine goodness, blessings bestowed on a man/woman by God (Abu-Rabia 1999a: 20–24, 75–76); *baraka* is the divine blessing bestowed on man/woman by virtue of his/her birth and origin, and it is made manifest in the good works of its possessors (Peters 1990: 279).
20. In anthropological terms, "[t]o name an illness is important for two reasons. First, since the known is less threatening than the unknown, it is easier to live with a named than an unnamed illness. And second, naming an illness determines its etiology, its cause, which in turn provides the doctor with the information he needs to carry out treatment" (Foster and Anderson 1978: 158). Among populations in the Middle East, "the healer, when summoned to the bedside of the patient, identifies the illness. To do this is to immediately define it, circumscribe it, tame it, weaken it. The diagnosis provides the patient with a sense of relief that the unknown pain has been mastered and provides the practitioner with a medical treatment" (Shiloh 1961: 277–88).
21. It is worth comparing this point with Jehovah's Witnesses' views on blood and blood products: they refuse blood products because it is their religious conviction that God (Jehovah) will turn his back on anyone receives a blood transfusion. Rather than risk eternal damnation, Jehovah's Witnesses avoid transfusions for themselves and their children (Jehovah's Witness case 1964; Koenig 2002: 81; Miller 1984: 174–88; Rosen 1998: 69–73).
22. The Bedouin patient is never left alone at home or in hospital. It is important to note that "sometimes people resist hospitalization, not only because hospitals have been perceived historically as places people go to die, but because hospital practices often conflict with traditional patient care" (Foster and Anderson 1978: 229). Foster and Anderson note that "[t]he number of well-wishers pressing into the room varies directly with the gravity of the patient's condition to the point where, to an outsider, it seems a miracle that a dying man's departing soul can fight its way clear of the press of humanity" (1978: 117). This is much like the situation among the Navaho, where the presence of family and friends is assuring to the patient, who feels they are all working to restore his health (Adair et al. 1969: 83–110). Similarly, in lower Zaire, the patient is likely to be supported by a therapy managing group—a set of kinfolk, friends, acquaintances, and community members who confer with the traditional healer and representatives of his/her support structure in the healing process (Janzen 1978).
23. For more on this topic see Chapter 1.

Chapter 1

Health and Health Services among the Bedouin in the Middle East

This chapter discusses the health situation, the environmental and cultural origins of the prevalence of diseases, and other matters of health and illness among the Bedouin tribes in Middle Eastern countries during the twentieth century. It also examines the topic of access to state health services in contemporary times, country by country.

Historically, the state has traditionally dominated indigenous peoples. This is also largely true in the contemporary world. They may displace or eliminate them, integrating them into the state or compelling them to pay tribute. In countries where documentation is available—even in contemporary times, indigenous people who have been integrated into the state have lower life expectancy, lower income, and poorer health than nonindigenous inhabitants (Kunitz 2000: 1531).

Health policymakers should be responsive to the diverse needs within the population of their country. Health systems should adapt to changing demographic patterns, such as ageing populations in industrialized countries and the movement of migrants between countries (Healy and McKee 2004). In other words, health services should not be the province of the dominant population group only. The right to good healthcare is inalienable and universal, and implies equitable access and use, based on the premise that some people will need more healthcare than others and that inequalities in health outcomes should be kept to a minimum. The primary components of a just healthcare system are universal access, access to adequate and responsive care, and fairness in financing (Benatar 1996; World Health Organization 2000). Health disparities are measured in terms of variances in morbidity, mortality, and access to healthcare among different population subgroupings that are defined by factors such as socioeconomic status, gender, place of residence, and especially race or ethnicity (Dressler et al. 2005: 232). Despite efforts by international health agencies to reduce global health inequalities, indigenous populations around the world remain largely unaffected by such initiatives (Hurtado et al. 2005: 639).

The right to medical services has been recognized as an essential element of "the right to health" by the international community (CESC 2000: 43). State legislation and policies that ensure the right to health in practice must take into account four core elements: availability, accessibility, acceptability, and quality. *Availability* is defined as the presence of sufficient health and public health facilities, goods, and services. The concept of *accessibility* to facilities, goods, and services is based on nondiscrimination, physical and economic potential, and access to information. *Acceptability* relates to issues ranging from respect for medical ethics to respect for cultural differences. *Quality* refers to the level of medical and scientific services and their suitability to a given population's needs and culture (CESC 2000: 12).

There are objective obstacles to providing these core elements to pastoral peoples. The long distances between nomadic groups make delivery of healthcare services relatively expensive (Imperato 1974: 443-457). Sedentarization is considered an important catalyst for different types of change (Salzman 1980: 1–20). Indeed, policy advocating permanent settlement of the Bedouin has been pursued by various countries in the Middle East, largely motivated by two goals: (1) the desire to subordinate the Bedouin to the needs, laws, and ordinances of the state, and (2) the desire to improve the Bedouin's economic, social, health, and educational status (Abou-Zeid 1979: 283–90; Abu-Rabia 2006: 865–82; Awad 1959: 27–60). Bedouin throughout the Middle East, who in the past lived nomadic lives, are now either seminomadic or live in permanent settlements planned by the authorities, or in unplanned, spontaneous settlements composed of temporary dwelling of various types. The permanently settled Bedouin have adopted modern patterns of life, while the seminomadic continue to migrate seasonally with their flocks, returning to their permanent dwellings at the conclusion of the migration season (Abu-Helal, Shammut, and Naser 1984).

Many studies have shown that improving healthcare accessibility to pastoral nomadic communities is problematic due to their movements, mobility, and the fact that some of them live in geographically marginalized, sparsely inhabited areas, while modern health services are located in urban towns and cities (Swift, Toulmin and Chatting 1990; Hampshire 2002); sometimes these services serve relatively wealthy communities while excluding rural and marginalized communities (Philips and Verhasselt 1994). From the 1950s onward, organizations such as the WHO, FAO, ILO, and UNESCO have recommended sedentarization of nomadic Bedouin in order to promote their health, education, and socioeconomic development and integrate their economy into national trading networks (Bocco 2006: 302–30) and in particular to eradicate diseases such as malaria and tuberculosis.

Research on the health of nomadic pastoral communities presents mixed results. Most studies on the health and nutritional consequences of nomadic pastoral sedentarization in Kenya, for example, have reported negative effects including poor nutrition, inadequate and unhygienic housing, lack of clean and sanitary drinking water, and high rates of infectious diseases including anthrax, bilharzia, and malaria despite better access to primary education and healthcare services (Duba et al. 2001; Nathan et al. 1996). Other studies have found, on the other hand, that children and women living in nomadic pastoral communities had significantly lower levels of malnutrition and morbidity than those in settled communities (Roth, Nathan, and Fratkin 2005: 173–208).

Since ancient times, the unique geographic position of the Middle East has affected its development in a host of domains. Throughout history, inhabitants of the region have been influenced by their sociocultural, economic, and political contacts as well as military ties with neighboring civilizations to the north and the south. At the same time, the Middle East has served as a land bridge between the east and the west in the movement of traded goods. As a result of these contacts, from a health standpoint, Middle Eastern peoples have traditionally been unduly exposed to communicable diseases originating beyond their borders (Abu-Rabia 2005c: 383–401). Within this context, pastoral nomadic Bedouin lived difficult lives, and their health and life expectancy were low (Bhattacharya and Harb 1973: 266–69). They suffered from poor health due to diseases and environmental health conditions, inadequate hygiene, malnutrition, and the effect of a herd culture that exposed them to a host of parasites and disease-carrying mosquitoes.

Public health theories claim that poverty leads to poor health (Smith 1990: 349–50). For example, in a self-help settlement in Cairo, studies found that the tighter the household resources, the more disadvantaged the female children were (Tekce 1990: 929–40).

The role of environment in health among pastoral peoples of the Middle East is significant. Ecology in the broadest sense denotes the dynamic interrelationship between a community and its total environment. According to Weiner, "[t]he environment represents the totality of the surroundings in which the community finds itself, and includes physical and living elements, that is, the geology, topography, and climate of the terrain and its communications; the vegetation cover and the insect, animal, and bird life" (1977: 389).

As a result of environmental conditions, the Bedouin in Palestine have suffered from various diseases during the last centuries (Abu-Khusa 1976: 70–71, 1979: 106–13; Levy 1998: 478–512; Karakrah 1992; Reiss 1991; Singer 1996: 189–206). For example, the incidence of eye diseases among nomadic pastoral Bedouin was high (Kay 1978: 29–32; Lipsky 1959: 262–66). Many local climatic factors and environmental conditions favored the spread of trachoma: intense sunlight, high temperatures, and low precipitation, all of which creates a dusty, semiarid-to-arid environment with a limited supply of fresh water, conditions that are exacerbated in spring and fall by seasonal searing-hot southeasterly winds (*khamsin*) that bring dust from surrounding deserts as far away as the Sahara (Abu-Rabia 2005c: 390). The Bedouin of the Negev and Sinai call this the eastern wind (*shargiyih, am-Salih*). Among the Rwala[1] tribes (Musil 1928: 10–18) during the winter season, the east wind (*shargiyih*) generally blows for only three or four days. Towards the end of spring and early summer seasons the east wind is especially strong, blowing for as long as seven days and nights. It is called *semum*.[2] It is exceedingly dry and hot, and causes much suffering, especially among women and children. They would all perish if it blew for more than seven days. The debilitating power of such winds is reflected in martial arts: Among the Rwala (Musil 1928: 542) when the first riders arrive the attacked herds must, together with the herdsmen, repel the enemy's first attack. Which direction the wind blows is a crucial factor in this endeavor: if they have to fight against a wind blowing dust and sand in their faces, they are at a great disadvantage relative to the enemy. But once the cavalry is engaged at close range, they can attack the enemy from the rear as well, and the direction of the wind no longer matters.[3]

There are cases where there is abundant summer rain, but while this rain can fill both natural and artificial reservoirs, such water soon swarms with frogs, and all kinds of larvae that render it foul smelling and undrinkable within a short time. When winter and spring rain is abundant, everyone bathes, clothes are washed, and parasites of all kinds are destroyed. Young people hasten to the waterholes (*ghudran*) for their ablutions. Girls and boys bathe in separate locations (Musil 1928: 14–15). Watering of the camels is carried out at various rain pools and reservoirs in the same way as at the wells—at drinking troughs. Only at the large pools (*khabra,* pl. *khabari*) can whole herds go right into the water and drink, but the camels defecate while drinking, and consequently such pools are quickly contaminated. Along the edges of the pool, a layer of manure forms; the water smells of urine and turns yellow and brackish (Musil 1928: 340). Musil (1928: 666) tells of diseases that the Rwala suffered from primarily in the months of July and August. The places where they camped, such as Kerayat al-Meleh, were notorious for their ague[4] (*hemma*) and malaria. In al-Juba the flies were a real annoyance, likewise the strong winds that blows blew continuously, whirling up fine sand and dust that is injurious to the eyes and nose. Therefore the Rwala prefer to camp in either the Nefud or al-Hamad where the air is both clear and more hygienic.

In the early twentieth century, due to shortages of water or limited water use due to great distances of houses or tents from water sources, hygiene and sanitary conditions among pastoral nomads were very poor. During the British Mandate period in Palestine (1917–1948) and Jordan, the British government made efforts to secure water supplies by drilling wells, but when ample water was found, it was highly saline, and when fresh water was found, the flow was too meager to be useful in changing lifestyle patterns (al-'Aref 1934: 269–83; 1944: 184–86; Shimkin 1936: 315–41). Thus, pastoral nomadic Bedouin continued to rely on and maintain their traditional water sources: wells, cisterns, or *thamila*[5] (al-'Aref 1934: 22–34), all of which played a role in the spread of disease.

Historically, pastoral nomadic Bedouin of the Middle East have been highly dependent on their herds for food (Abu-Rabia 1994a: 107–27, 1999b: 22–30). The primary source of protein is their livestock. Low milk production or insufficient herd size due to drought, disease, or economic circumstances constitute a threat to the availability of essential protein (Roboff 1977: 421–28). Malnutrition makes children more vulnerable to whooping cough and measles. Bedouin of all ages during the twentieth century were more susceptible than sedentary populations to parasites and malaria, anemia and vitamin-deficiency diseases, trachoma, venereal disease, mental illness, diarrhea, dysentery and cholera, tuberculosis, and broncho-pulmonary infections (Roboff 1977: 421–28).

In the early twentieth century in Arabia the diet of the Bedouin was tied to socioeconomic status, which ranged from wealthy sheikhs to the very poor (Dickson 1951: 190–200). Diet was based on the following foods and dishes: rice cooked with sesame (*semsen*), sour milk (*leben*), dates (*tamr*), camel, sheep or goat milk; flat bread (including bread prepared from wheat grown locally in the Najd region), okra (*bamia*), locust,[6] edible monitor lizards (*dab*), and wild game of all sorts—from birds to foxes. Seedless sultana raisins (*zabib, zibib*) are used in cooking. A sweet milk pudding (*mahallibi*) was made of ground rice or arrowroot cooked in milk, and flavored with cardamom and chopped pistachio nuts or mixed with saffron.

Main meals consisted of crushed corn and meat porridge (*haris*)—a very nourishing dish, and, on rare occasions, rice and a bit of meat. Mushrooms (*ftur*) and truffles (*fagah*) were eagerly sought after and eaten in the rainy season, but these were a luxury.

Cooking fires in the early twentieth century used dry camel dung (*jallih*) or brushwood (*'arfaj*).[7] Bedouin traditionally drank coffee well laced with cardamom (*hayl*) prepared in coffeepots; a piece of hemp or palm tree fiber (*lifa*) is stuffed into the spout to act as strainer. Usually the host pours a small quantity of coffee into a cup for himself first and drinks it to demonstrate it has not been poisoned. The best and most expensive coffee beans come from Yemen (Dickson 1951: 200–201). According to Dickson (1951: 416), the hump is the most edible part of the camel, and this is also the Arab opinion. Camel milk is drunk throughout Arabia, and it is extremely nourishing and low in fat content and therefore yields no butter.

Most of the research literature assumes that nomadic populations are generally healthier than neighboring sedentary populations. During periods of drought, however, some nomadic groups become increasingly vulnerable to health problems due to the depletion of their food stores (Greene 1975: 11–21; Seaman et al. 1973: 774–78). Studies that compared health of nomadic, seminomadic, and settled Bedouin in Saudi Arabia have revealed a significant variation in the health status of children under age five. In a study of the Turaba in Saudi Arabia, Sibai (1981) noted that nomadic and seminomadic peoples received little or no healthcare. Nomadic children were more prone to malnutrition and parasitic as well as communicable diseases. When nomadic peoples migrate to urban centers, they face difficulties in acclimating to new patterns of hygiene and sanitation that run counter to "natural methods" of dealing with waste through migration practiced by nomadic peoples. Nomadic peoples are also more prone to epidemics due to overcrowding in the poor neighborhoods and are highly vulnerable due to poor nutrition and low resistance to disease. Low population densities and frequent mobility, on the other hand, significantly reduce the occurrence of epidemic diseases, and natural selection develops high levels of disease resistance. Healthy people are those who survive. Tribal societies maintain public health by emphasizing prevention of illness rather than treatment (Bodley 1994: 124). When pastoral nomadic peoples are forced to leave their homes to adjust to new environments and new livelihoods, they face psychosocial stress that is often amplified by the absence of support groups—close kin and friends who can ease a difficult adjustment—a situation that can result in an increase in health problems (Roboff 1977: 421–28; Sadalla and Stea 1982: 3–14).

During the twentieth century the population of the Middle East changed significantly in terms of urbanization, social development, political structures, economic development, and ethnic borders, as well as the diversity of Middle Eastern ecology due to advances in arid and semiarid agriculture. These changes are reflected in nutritional and health outcomes. While urbanization is usually associated with better health and better food supply, in fact poor urban dwellers in the Middle East may face a worse quality of life than rural dwellers. Health in the Middle East is closely associated with the availability of safe water and sanitary conditions (Galal 2003: 337–43). Health dynamics in the Middle East have shifted, parallel to similar global health trends, towards lower mortality rates and longer life expectancy. At the same time, poor diet patterns during childhood and adulthood continue to expose individuals to illness and premature death due to various types of morbidity. Lack of health services for children in the Middle East is a contributing factor to malnutrition, more than poverty or food insecurity. Lamb is the primary source of meat, but mutton is traditionally consumed only on special occasions, when it is slaughtered and consumed immediately, before the meat spoils. The mainstay of protein and the chief component of the traditional Bedouin diet is, therefore, fresh milk and milk products used for cooking and drinking (Dahl 2004: 6–8). Improvements in food surpluses have led to a 1 percent drop in child malnutrition per year in the Middle East, in the twentieth century. In areas that are extremely arid and subject to political instability, child malnutrition is still high and adults are increasingly exposed to a variety of chronic diseases due to a poor diet.

Among pastoral nomadic peoples, the health benefits of an active lifestyle are not fully exploited due to social and cultural barriers (Galal 2003: 340–43). Moreover, the urbanization of seminomadic and agrarian communities in the Middle East has been accompanied by decreased physical activity, drastic dietary changes, and the prevalence of chronic diseases. It is important to analyze how urbanized seminomadic peoples have developed effective disease prevention and health promotion strategies for diet-related chronic diseases.

Many factors connected with the modern world have changed the lives and health situation of the Bedouin throughout the Middle East. For example, the use of radios, particularly transistor radios, brought the Bedouin into contact with the outside world, affecting Bedouin life. The oil industry, particularly ARAMCO, has employed Bedouin at various stages of their operations, from oil exploration and the drilling of wells to oil production and marketing (Salah al-Din Basha 1965: 279–92). This trend has enabled the Bedouin to enjoy the benefits of salaried labor that employment in the oil industry brings, as well as access to education and health services, and sedentarization. All of these changes have ramifications on the health of Bedouin populations.

The Status of the Bedouin in the Twentieth Century: A Country-by-Country Survey

A survey of the literature reveals that the amount of information, statistical data, and anthropological research regarding Bedouin health issues varies greatly from country to country.

Jordan

The Emirate of Trans-Jordan was established in 1921 by British Mandatory authorities. In the 1930s, authorities encouraged settlement of the nomadic Bedouin by providing and expanding dependable water supplies (digging artesian wells, drilling new wells and repairing old ones in the steppe region, building small dams, and improving old reservoirs) to develop agriculture projects, establishing schools in new "Bedouin villages," and teaching the rudiments of modern Western healthcare and hygiene to at least one member of each tribal section (Bocco 2006: 315–16).

In the early twentieth century, arid conditions and constant movement from place to place helped prevent the spread of disease since garbage and human and animal waste—hotbeds for disease-carrying microbes—were left behind every time the tribe pulled up stakes. Nomadic patterns are fueled not only by the need to find fresh grazing and water but also by the need to maintain a clean environment, an issue that is very much a part of Bedouin consciousness (al-Sayyad 1965: 409–24). The sanitation practices of food-foraging peoples—their toilet habits and methods of garbage disposal—are appropriate to contexts of low population levels and some degree of residential mobility. These same practices, however, become serious health hazards in the context of large, fully sedentary populations (Haviland 2002: 48). For example, the health of hunting-gathering peoples was positively affected by their nomadic habits; a people few in numbers and constantly on the go is less likely to reinfect itself from its excrement than is a large, settled population where, once infection is endemic, it is almost impossible to eradicate it, short of the most modern environmental sanitation practices (Foster and Anderson 1978: 16). Settled life and the problem of sanitation in settled communities must certainly have increased the rate of parasitism, since opportunities for repeated reinfection and contamination with human wastes is increased (Underwood 1975: 59). Attempts made by health educators to persuade desert-dwelling villages to construct sanitary latrines have been known to backfire, as was the case in Iran in the early 1950s, in the face of visible evidence that countered assumptions that defecation in the open air produces flies. In fact, the dry atmosphere quickly dries fecal matter, and flies do not breed. The latrines were poorly maintained and became fly breeders (Foster 1962: 180). Many traditional peoples keep their living areas scrupulously free of fecal matter. Although they do this because of the fear that enemies may practice sympathetic magic against them with their excrement, the reduction in flies resulting from the practice is almost certainly beneficial (Foster and Anderson 1978: 42). This practice is widespread among peoples who have a strong belief in witchcraft.[8]

The Bedouin, who suffer from malnutrition that weakens their constitution, not only have difficulty integrating into the workforce; they are also more susceptible to disease (al-Sayyad 1965: 409–24). At the outset of the twentieth century, one of the reasons for sparse settlement of the Jordan Valley was the state of sanitation and constant presence of malaria (World Health Organization 1954: 765–84),[9] except during the winter months. Therefore, one of the adaptive strategies to alter these negative environmental factors was use of goat hair tents that were suitable to transhumance and a pastoral nomadic Bedouin lifestyle (al-Taher 1965: 10).

In the 1930s, two Western physicians, Dr. Shelly Avery Jones[10] and Dr. Maclennan (1935: 227–48), served in the Jordanian medical services and treated the Bedouin population (al-Taher 1965: 10). In his writings from the 1930s, (1935: 227–48) Maclennan noted that some Jordanian Bedouin witnessed a decline in their prosperity, increased poverty, and even starvation. Such depressed conditions lowered resistance to disease—particularly to tuberculosis, anemia, syphilis, ophthalmic diseases (trachoma, conjunctivitis, keratitis, leucoma, pterygium, cataracts, corneal ulcers, trichiasis, pannus, blepharitis), contagious diseases, other illnesses such as fever (*humma*, pl. *hummayat*). Despite antimalarial measures carried out by the Trans-Jordanian Department of Health, certain groups and individuals, due to their migration patterns, were more susceptible to malaria. Those among whom malaria was reported had resided for a period in the Jordan Valley (*al-Ghur*). It is surmised that those Bedouin with certain diseases notoriously associated with civilization, such as tuberculosis, syphilis, and gonorrhea, contracted the diseases directly from contact with non-Bedouin society. A more sedentary lifestyle pattern, however, took its toll—primarily due to sanitation problems resulting from decreased movement and the build-up of animal and human contaminants around encampments that caused frequent outbreaks of enteritis mainly among children—contributing to high morbidity and mortality rates, as well as debilitating parasites such as intestinal worms. The constant inhalation and contamination of eyes by dry pulverized manure was paralleled by various respiratory infections spread by spitting, accelerating the spread of tuberculosis. Water sources also became contaminated due to the proximity of herds, poor sanitation, and extended usage. Lice served as vectors for the spread of typhus, and outbreaks were frequent. Head lice often irritated the scalp, leading to gross septic infection, resulting in enlargement of the posterior cervical glands. Since water, whether sourced from springs, wells, or cisterns, often had to be carried long distances, the use of water for washing was tightly restricted and Bedouin sought to rid themselves of the lice by washing their hair in camel urine. Poverty and the shortage of water left many underclad, and clothes were seldom laundered. Nomadic tents left dwellers exposed to the elements, resulting in frostbite during the winter, and pneumonia was a frequent cause of death (Maclennan 1935: 227–48). Water could not be wasted, as there was hardly enough for drinking and cooking. Some rubbed their hands and faces with clean, dry sand. Their clothes were washed and a bath was taken only when they camped near a large rain pond. Lice resided in their clothes, scratching their bodies. Occasionally a wife deloused her husband and her children, helped by their daughters; and women deloused other women. Soap was kept only by chiefs for their guests. For themselves they gathered *shenan/shinan*,[11] drying, pulverizing, and then using it for washing. The boys made their ablutions in the daytime, the girls in the evening. Young women took good care of their hair; in the morning, a maiden would wait for the female riding camel to get to its feet and catch its urine in a small dish. She would wash her hair with the urine, which killed the lice eggs, rejuvenated the scalp, and prevented itching, and gave the hair a particular gloss (Musil 1928: 117–18).

Low rainfall has indirect repercussions on the health of the Bedouin. Due to the poverty and isolation of the Bedouin, their diet consisted of bread, milk products, and some vegetables and fruits (grapes, figs, melon, dates, and tomatoes), and very little meat. The destitute subsisted on a diet of bread alone—approximately 400 and 500 grams daily or 1,000 calories—a third of the average adult intake. Most suffered from malnutrition, resulting in lowered resistance to disease in general, and particularly depleted energy levels due to nutritional deficiency diseases such as anemia that made them incapable of sustained labor. This situation was exacerbated by nutritional deficits that led to scurvy-associated swollen and bleeding gums, particularly among children. The comparatively low incidence of scurvy is poorly understood, since the Bedouin diet has no sources of vitamin C. It has been postulated that perhaps aquatic plants that often contaminate springs frequented by the Bedouin may secrete some vitamin C into the water.[12] Yet, children often had rickets, evidenced in enlargement of the epiphyses of the wrists and ankles and potbellies. Breastfeeding, which was and continues to be universal and prolonged, provided a good resource of vitamin D. The prevalence of vitamin D deficiency is significantly higher in Arab women and children than in the white population.

Many studies suggest that rickets is more common in Arab countries than in the West (Dawodu 2004: 15–22).

Health problems among the Bedouin in Jordan were varied. Dental caries and pyorrhea occurred to some extent in more advanced age groups, but was extremely rare in children. Pyorrhea—inflammation of the gums and the tooth sockets—was not associated at all with dental cavities, and frequently occurred in patients who had a perfect set of teeth. Among the ear, nose, and throat problems, Bedouin suffered from chronic hypertrophy of varying degrees of severity resulting from enlarged tonsils and frequent throat infections; however, enlarged adenoids and cervical glands, and chronic otorrhea (a discharge from the ear) were rare. The practice of traditional folk remedies including cauterization of wounds under unsanitary conditions often resulted in severe sepsis. Pastoral nomadic Bedouin were also susceptible to a host of communicable diseases resulting from close contact with livestock such as dogs, cattle, horses, donkeys, and fowl, including goat and camel tuberculosis, and rabies. The many parasitic infestations of the intestinal tract reported among Bedouin included ascaris (intestinal worms that stunt growth), oxyuris (nematodes/pinworms), taenia (tapeworms), hydatid (a tapeworm carried by dogs that causes cysts in the liver and lungs), and urinary schistosomiasis. Poor hygiene made worm infestation as well as infantile diarrhea common maladies (Maclennan 1935: 227–48).

The eradication of illiteracy and the introduction of modern education, including advancement through military service that provided both general and military education in Jordan and abroad, prompted Bedouin military career personnel to encourage their sons, other kin, and other tribal members to follow in their footsteps. This process led increasing numbers of Bedouin to settle down, bringing exposure and access to a formal education system (Abu-Helal, Shammut, and Naser 1984: 57–67; al-Maddy and Musa 1959: 309–11), orderly health services and employment opportunities, and rural and urban lifestyles in general—leading Bedouin to adopt modern amenities such as homes with running water and electricity (al-Taher 1965: 38–40). In addition, the paving of roads throughout the Hashemite Kingdom and roads leading to neighboring countries—Syria, Iraq, and Saudi Arabia—encouraged Jordan's nomadic population to engage in income-generating work that went beyond the traditional Bedouin economy: raising goats, sheep, and camels on a commercial scale and agriculture that included planting fruit orchards.[13] Despite these benefits, road construction also plays a major role in the dissemination of certain diseases: "Modern roads built for economic development consequently constituted a major health hazard in endemic regions, their very purpose being to encourage movement and mixture of peoples and goods but having, as implicated effects, the facilitation of man-vector contacts for several different kinds of insect-borne diseases" (Hughes and Hunter 1970: 452–53).

The Jordanian Ministry of Health played a central role in healthcare, particularly treating malaria in the country's valleys and controlling contagious disease—steps that brought a drop in mortality that prompted Bedouin to settle in the valley regions. One of the primary factors encouraging settlement was the establishment of clinics in most parts of the kingdom for the population at large, including remote Bedouin locations.[14] In addition to stationary clinics, mobile clinics operated on behalf of special populations such as the nomadic Bedouin (al-Taher 1965: 47–49). Opportunities to use marketable skills learned at school and growing numbers of Bedouin in military careers led more Bedouin to settle down. This phenomenon was not limited to rural settlement; Bedouin also migrated to the cities and were integrated into urban Jordanian society, where their socioeconomic and health status improved (Abu-Jaber and Gharaibeh 1981: 294–301; Lewis 1987: 131–92). Bedouin pastoral households in Wadi Araba were highly dependent upon livestock products for energy and protein; diminishing cash incomes from livestock sales limited household access to purchase of foodstuffs that supplied essential nutrients, vitamins, and carbohydrates (Tsikhlakis 1997). Livestock (meat, milk, and milk products) provided the Bedouin with fats, carbohydrates, and vitamins. In the course of settling down, opportunities for education have given young Bedouin, women as well as men, skills that are in demand within the Jordanian economy's expanding service sector—in schools, hospitals and clinics, and marketing centers (Layne 1994: 90–91). Settled life has become more attractive to the Bedouin themselves (Chatty 1990: 133). Work in the health domain has not only impacted on the health of the population but has also enhanced their sense of security, encouraging the Bedouin to settle down in one place.

Operations in the Bedouin sector of Trans-Jordanian ministries other than the Health Ministry have also contributed to improvement of health, education, and nutrition among the Bedouin. This has been particularly so in the drought years when the Ministry of Welfare, for instance, serves as a "safety net." Other ministries dug wells and built dams to create reservoirs for rainwater and runoff, established public services such as schools and police stations alongside health clinics, and provided veterinary services for herds—mitigating the factors that cause Bedouin to migrate from place to place and enhancing the process of sedentarization (Jabbur 1995: 282; al-Taher 1965: 49–52).

Employment of Bedouin in projects initiated by government ministries has improved the economic, health, and nutritional status of the Bedouin population by enhancing Bedouin production capabilities. Agricultural training has taught Bedouin to plant fruit trees and grow high-nutrition crops.[15] The addition of fruits and vegetables to the diet has impacted positively on their health (al-Taher 1965: 53). In the course of educating nomadic Bedouin in agricultural techniques, the Bedouin were also taught medicinal, religious, personal, and professional hygiene and educated about diseases, pests, and climatic factors that impact on their crops and flocks of livestock and cattle (al-Hunaydi 1965: 72–96). It is worth noting that among the Bedouin in the northeast desert (*badia*) of Jordan, the first clinic was established in 1981, although most were introduced in the early 1990s; the government policy of introducing clinics and sedentarizing the pastoral nomadic Bedouin has significantly improved healthcare accessibility. Since the 1990s, the use of preventive medicine has become widespread, particularly ante- and postnatal maternal and child health services and children's vaccinations (Spicer 2005: 2165–76). Mothers working in pastoral production had limited time for childcare; conversely, sedentarized mothers currently have more time to monitor their children's health and hygiene, and employ health and illness practices expediently. In the past, measles and smallpox were widespread. Frequently, herbal medicine was employed concurrently in the treatment of illnesses among children and adults, including intestinal pains, diarrhea, influenza, and fevers. Traditional medicines were also employed for some 85 percent of childhood illnesses. The importance of removing venom from snake and spider bites and scorpion stings from the victim's blood was recognized (Abu-Rabia 1999a: 75–78; Spicer 2005: 2165–76). Jordanian nomadic pastoralists in the northeastern desert view government services, especially schools and health clinics, and employment opportunities in the state sector as incentives to settling down (Dutton, Clark, and Battikhi 1998). While livestock, milk, and milk products continue to be the main sources of income, today a significant proportion of Bedouin families include members employed by governmental entities, including military forces and police services (Abu-Rabia 2001: 31–92; Spicer 2005: 2165–76).

Sudan

In Sudan the tsetse fly was a major health problem in the first half of the twentieth century. Prior to the building of the Aswan Dam, flooding of the Nile River left pockets of water that served as breeding grounds for mosquitoes, flies, and other insects that served as disease-carrying vectors detrimental to both humans and livestock. Other prevalent, harmful flies were Tabanidae[16] that live in pools of water or grazing land and affect both humans and livestock (Saber 1965: 244–48). Under British colonialism in the 1930s and 1940s, the delivery of Western health services was seen as part of a larger effort to administer and control indigenous populations (Baer, Singer, and Susser 1997: 16), yet despite colonialism's negative aspects, the British administration had a positive impact on care of livestock, and the establishment of veterinary clinics by colonial public health authorities led to the development of animal husbandry as an economic sector (Saber 1965: 271). Indeed, Bedouin were as concerned for the health of their flocks as they were for their own health (Saber 1965: 271–89). Veterinary services were generally provided by the government gratis.

According to Saber (1965: 298–301), there are certain advantages and disadvantages to pastoral nomadic life in arid and semiarid regions. On the positive side, the climate does not encourage the incubation of endemic and epidemic diseases, and the low population density retards the spread of disease. On the other hand, desert Bedouin life is characterized by negative environmental and social factors that make nomadic populations more susceptible to disease, including malnutrition, low awareness of health issues, and a shortage of water in general and of fresh, uncontaminated water sources in particular. Consequently, medical care, both preventive and curative, is very important. Once a contagious disease strikes, it is likely to spread very rapidly within an encampment due to the absence of means to treat it, the Bedouin's immune systems being weakened by malnutrition, and inadequate shelter that leaves inhabitants exposed to the vicissitudes of the elements, including sharp changes in temperature between day and tonight. While the Bedouin diet is rich in protein from milk products and meat, adequate quantities of fruits and vegetables are often lacking, both due to ingrained dietary customs and to shortages of such produce locally and their high price, which is often beyond the means of many Bedouin. As a result of an unbalanced diet, Bedouin are prone to certain diseases: anemia, a frail composition, and particularly pellagra,[17] diarrhea, inflamed mucous membranes, and mental confusion and delusions. Weakened immune systems and malnutrition also leave Bedouin vulnerable to tuberculosis. Their health is further jeopardized by periods when families and livestock suffer from a shortage of food due to drought. While the Bedouin, who are not large-scale growers, are not affected directly, drought conditions cause shortages that drive up prices of staples such as wheat and barley. Among the contagious diseases that Sudanese Bedouin are exposed to due to seasonal changes and geography are cerebrospinal meningitis, relapsing fever, smallpox, malaria, and venereal disease. Bilharzia is another health problem in Sudan and Egypt, where the disease is spread by a water snail that serves as the host; the snails attach themselves to the hooves of cattle, and the migrating herd infects grazing land and humans far from the original disease source.

The spread of bilharziasis (schistosomiasis) as the consequence of irrigation methods (i.e., flooding fields via open irrigation channels) is illustrative of the kinds of epidemiological problems anthropologists have encountered in developing countries (Foster and Anderson 1978: 22). For example, in Sudan mosquitoes in stagnant water pools are the primary source of malaria. The Bedouin would flee a watering spot immediately after malaria was discovered in their encampment, but malarial mosquitoes were entrapped among their belongings when they rolled up their tents, leading to the spread of malaria to other sites by a rather unconventional "carrier." Thus, water sources and inhabitants far from the original malarial pool were subsequently infected.[18] In other words, the Bedouin themselves served as vectors or carriers of diseases as a result of their nomadic lifestyle. The same is true of their flocks: as Bedouin moved from place to place, their goats, sheep, cows, horses, camels, and dogs served as carriers of diseases that affect both livestock and humans far afield—spreading brucellosis, anthrax, and rabies. According to Musil (1928: 424), when cholera ravaged the country in 1898, the Bedouin fled to the desert to escape the contagion; ever since, they have called that year *sanat abu faksa/ fagsa*—the cholera year.

Nomadic tribal society holds beliefs tied to health and disease that reflect nomadic culture. Disease is viewed as a matter of fate or the will of Allah. Consequently, treatment has a large faith-based component founded not only on traditional medicine such as burning (for cauterization) and use of local medicinal herbs, but also magic, spells, incantation, charms, and amulets (Saber 1965: 301–2). Distance and accessibility—or lack of accessibility as the case may be—are also factors that affect Bedouin health. While the Bedouin's mobility plays a role in the spread of disease despite low population density, the location of regular hospitals and clinics in permanent points of settlement, from hamlets to towns, render such facilities largely inaccessible to Bedouin. To counter this barrier, governments in Arab countries of the Middle East and North Africa have established mobile clinics that, instead of bringing the Bedouin to hospitals, bring modern medical care to Bedouin centers via four-wheel drive vehicles and the training of local Bedouin as medics, male nurses, and female midwives capable of meeting contingencies typical in their communities (Abu-Rabia 2001: 52; 2005: 421–29). Educational campaigns targeting Bedouin stress the nature, benefits, and location of medical care; preventive medicine efforts are designed to nurture awareness of nutritional and hygiene issues. Nevertheless, because folk medicine is so deeply entrenched in traditional patterns of life, fundamental change can take place only when traditional social structures are replaced by new social structures—that is, when Bedouin cease to be nomads and opt for permanent settlement (Saber 1965: 302–3).

It is important to keep in mind that medical services for people cannot be effective without parallel veterinary services for livestock; people and animals in Bedouin society constitute one health framework where many diseases are passed back and forth between humans and domesticated animals. When governments provide veterinary services and preventive measures for livestock, the impact is registered in the health status, nutritional status, and economic status of the Bedouin. Some of these services are provided to villages, individual tribes, and nomad centers through mobile clinics, while others are carried out by Bedouin veterinary medics and assistants within the tribe who have been trained by the government. Such care includes treatment for regular diseases and outbreaks of epidemics, vaccinations, and educating shepherds about the importance of preventive medicine for family members and livestock alike. Bedouin generally cooperate with veterinary teams due to the core role livestock play in Bedouin life as a source of nutrition and economic wealth, social stature, and influence. Thus, nomads have a vested interest in maximizing the well-being of their animals. Nomads, their flocks, and the environment are intermeshed in a reciprocal, mutually dependent relationship with its own unique lifecycle and seasonal patterns. Consequently, nomads provide food and water (at existing watering spots or by digging wells) for their livestock, which in turn provide food, transportation, and shelter. The survival of all three hinges on balancing pasturing and fodder for flocks with sustainable land use, choosing the most suitable animals and crops, following good grazing practices, and keeping herd size in balance with nature's regenerative properties (Abu-Rabia 1994a: 50–54; Draz 1969; Saber 1965: 303–6). According to one of the sheiks of the Baggara tribe,[19] flies in Sudan were their tribe's primary foe, and also the primary menace of humans and livestock among pastoral tribes along the Nile. In the 1920s, a program of fly eradication was launched in order to settle some of the nomadic tribes in these areas. Livestock were vaccinated, and animals, both domestic and wild, were sprayed at monthly intervals against certain flies, such as the tsetse (*dhubab nawwami*)[20] that cause diseases such as sleeping sickness (*mard al-naum*) (Saber 1965: 306–26).

In settling nomads, authorities need to take into account the cultural lag between old cultural values and new realities. Settlement planners and coordinators need to mitigate psychosocial conflicts and pressures that such nomads face (Saber 1965: 345–46; Sadalla and Stea 1982: 3–14). The process of the Bedouin's transition from one way of life to another was marked by a tragic waste of human life (Kay 1978: 145). The Zande tribe[21] in Southern Sudan is a case in point.

At the outset of the twentieth century, the Zande tribe underwent what was championed as health settlement. The objective was to enhance the tribe's health status and level of environmental hygiene by eradicating the tsetse flies through transferring the tribe out of the forests and settling them closer to roads so authorities could provide them with access to preventive and curative medical services (Saber 1965: 356). According to Muhammad al-Sayyad (1965: 421–24), however, the settlement process brought new health problems and led to poverty, unemployment, and delinquent behavior. In the area of al-Jazirah in Sudan, the settlement process led to smaller flocks of sheep, bringing about a shortage of milk and milk products and a drop in the amount of meat Bedouin consumed. Ironically, although their economic status improved, sedentary Bedouin were found to have higher levels of malnutrition than nomadic Bedouin. A rise in the incidence of disease among sedentary Bedouin was also registered: the settlement process led Bedouin to engage in agriculture, but puddles from irrigation pipes served as breeding grounds for disease, particularly malaria, bilharzia, hookworm, dysentery, and other ailments. Crowded dwellings, close proximity between families, and poor sanitation fueled the rapid spread of tuberculosis. Moreover, newly settled Bedouin were far more susceptible to disease than urban populations, who over generations had built up some natural immunity to microbes found in urban environments (al-Sayyad 1965: 421–24).

Saudi Arabia

In Saudi Arabia at the outset of the twentieth century, the situation of nomadic Bedouin was marked by a very high level of illiteracy, constant movement, and poor health due to the absence of modern preventive and curative medical services (al-'Abd 1965: 378–89). There was a great deal of sickness and disease among the Bedouin throughout Arabia in the early twentieth century, mostly traceable to lack of nourishment and to poor water; life was very hard for men as well as women (Dickson 1951: 505). Many nomadic Bedouin suffered from malnutrition, serious kidney problems, hepatitis. Leeches in water sources such as wells were another problem.

The settling of Saudi nomads resulted from the concerted effort of a host of Saudi ministries—Health, Welfare, Finance, Housing, Transportation, Agriculture, and Labor. The regional health centers that were established in settlement areas operated in the following domains: the provision of preventive and curative medical services to the settled Bedouin; public health education; supply of clean, running drinking water; eradication of flies and other insects; education regarding proper nutrition; and veterinary services.

Salah al-'Abd (1965: 457–60) found that Saudi Bedouin tribes were the nomads most in need of preventive and curative medical services. Thus, these services, provided by the government free of charge, were wide ranging, both stationary and mobile, and offered offering a broad array of services, including stationary clinics and first-aid stations that provided both preventive and curative care though clinics and hospitals in the northern and the southern deserts. Health centers for Bedouin were established and located in areas where they congregated, such as water sources, wells, and pools, in good grazing areas and near grazing preserves where herds were pastured regularly or were open to Bedouin tribes during certain seasons of the year. In addition a number of countrywide projects in Saudi Arabia have contributed to Bedouin health. In Saudi Arabia's "War on Tuberculosis," the Bedouin were the primary population infected. Consequently, hospitals, clinics, health centers, and sanatoriums to treat patients and sources of infection were established throughout the kingdom. Another campaign, conducted in collaboration with the WHO, focused on the eradication of malaria and smallpox, and was successful countrywide, but particularly among the Bedouin. The government also established special services for Bedouin, including the Clinical Cancer Unit for Bedouin, and a Unit for the Paralyzed and Physically Disabled that treated patients and fitted prostheses and artificial limbs for those in need. Preventive measures included periodic testing and quality analysis of water sources to ensure drinkable water, locate and treat pollutants, and so forth. In addition to stationary health services, the Saudi government also established and operated mobile medical services, mobilizing forms of transportation as varied as cars and helicopters (al-'Abd 1965: 461–71) to bring medical services to nomads wherever they were, rather than expecting them to travel to sources of medical care. Car-based mobile medical units equipped with medical equipment and devices and medication follow the Bedouin's movements in search of pasture and water, setting up camp where the Bedouin camp. In spring and summer when nomads are known to gather in specific areas, the units can preplan to locate preventive and curative medical services at these sites, based on predictable, entrenched movement patterns. Four marine medical units are operated by the Saudi Navy—three on the Red Sea and the fourth on the Arabian Sea, providing medical services to coastal communities. In addition, helicopters serve as flying ambulances, outfitted with sophisticated equipment to conduct emergency field operations, thus providing first aid, emergency medical care in remote areas, and evacuations of those in need to hospitals in the city. There is a mobile hospital for the Bedouin in the southern desert (*Badiyat al-Janub*) 'Asir region and a second mobile hospital that serves Bedouin in the Hijaz region (*Badiyat al-Hijaz*). Other mobile hospitals are situated in Jeddah, Medina, and Riyadh. In Saudi

Arabia it is customary for a patient's mother and siblings to accompany them to the hospital and stay at their bedside, adding to the patient's sense of well-being (Kay 1978: 30).

Mobile malaria eradication units operate in collaboration with the WHO in areas where Bedouin populations are concentrated and in regions frequented by Bedouin during their migrations. The Saudi Red Crescent provides mobile emergency medical services in time of disaster such as floods and severe drought, offering free medication, food, blankets, and economic assistance. The staff includes doctors, registered and practical nurses, paramedics, lab workers, veterinarians, and animal paramedics. The Red Crescent also provides health and hygiene education at schools through teachers, nurses, and physicians, and free medical care for students (al-'Abd 1965: 463–71). In the 1970s Bedouin families were progressively introduced to medical treatment, especially in American-run military hospitals where they enjoyed access to treatment as dependents of Bedouin service personnel (Kay 1978: 31). In Wadi Fatima, the social development center was charged with raising local cultural, agricultural, educational, and public health and hygiene standards (Katakura 1977: 62–65). Settled Bedouin in Saudi Arabia have much better nutrition than nomadic Bedouin—attributed to the intensive intervention of the government's steps to enhance their overall living conditions (Sibai and Reinke 1981). A case in point is the al-Murrah Bedouin tribe who reside in the Empty Quarter of Saudi Arabia. Bedouin of the Empty Quarter raise camels—livestock that carry diseases that can impact on the health of their owners (Philby 1933: 267–73, 328–46). Yet, the boom years of the late 1970s and early 1980s in Saudi Arabia—particularly manifested in large-scale infrastructure projects initiated by the government, sedentarization efforts, construction of hospitals and clinics, and better healthcare in general—have enhanced mother and child health and increased the size of nuclear families. The government has invested heavily in schooling and education—now more accessible and increasingly in demand. This includes a growing number of Bedouin students who gain higher education in Saudi Arabia and abroad (Cole 1975; 2006: 370–92). The sedentarization of the Shararat Bedouin in the northern region of Saudi Arabia also had a positive effect in the realms of education, health, and employment. The clinic that opened in 1956 was replaced by a modern hospital in 1985. Strict regulations that encouraged parents to vaccinate their children against polio, measles, and hepatitis were introduced. The benefits of modern healthcare are reflected in the rise in the percentage of Shararat Bedouin among the general population and the fall in numbers of victims of diseases such as tuberculosis that was common among the Shararat in the past (al-Radihan 2006: 840–64). In terms of diet, according to Doughty (1921: 132–33) the Bedouin of *Medain Salih*[22] in northern Arabia also hunt and eat porcupine and wild goats (*bedun*). They hunt ostriches, eat the eggs, and dry the breast meat. The bird's fat is considered precious and is believed to be endowed with medicinal powers; the Bedouin drink small coffee-cups full of ostrich fat, believing it is a remedy for heat and cold as well as a host of diseases.

Oman

The 1970s was a period of tremendous transformation for Oman as a whole. It was marked by the establishment of modern roads and communication with the rest of the world. Social welfare services, running water, electricity, schools, health clinics, and hospitals became widespread during this decade (Chatty 2006: 506).

A series of special wards designed for Bedouin were built in the hospital. They were not quite tents but were as out-of-doors as possible, with space provided for the family to camp nearby and cook for themselves and their sick relatives. In this way, the transition from the desert to the hospital was eased and the patient was not isolated from his agnatic family and friends (Kay 1978: 31).[23] The government also introduced a host of schemes designed for Bedouin in the fields of health, education, social services, housing, veterinary services, and supply of running water (Mohammed 1981: 336). Almost all studies that examine religion and social support find a significant correlation between the two. Religious people have large support networks, and the quality of that social network is higher and may be more durable than secular sources of support when chronic illness strikes (Koenig 2002: 10).

Yemen

Yemeni men make and solidify connections by participating in *qat*[24] parties, a local social institution, and this activity has a direct effect on their health and that of their families (Kennedy 1987; Weir 1985). Men and women traditionally chew *qat,* the leaf of a local shrub, for its mildly euphoric effect. They typically congregate in the afternoon to chew *qat* and to gossip and discuss business and politics. Expenditures on *qat* alone can take more than half a household's income. Thus, increasingly, the cost of getting ahead has undermined the traditional role of the Yemeni man as responsible for dependent women and children; for common problems such as diarrhea, mothers use home remedies first and only if they do not work do they go to the local doctor (Myntti 1993: 234–36).

Syria and Lebanon

In Syria, nomadic tribes were provided with preventive and curative medical services and veterinary care in areas with high concentrations of Bedouin. The Syrian Health Ministry operated a special health project among the tribes in conjunction with the WHO, including school curriculums that addressed health education—ranging from instruction on good health habits to medical services, occupational health services, and settlement services designed to enhance the health status of Bedouin (Syrian Delegation 1965: 479–83).

The Bedouin in Syria have been reported to use herbal medicine (Jabbur 1995: 64–81). Among the Bedouin of Syria and the Lebanese plains (*beqa'*), women contribute to the family's nutrition and health by tending to the livestock, producing milk, milk products, and meat—thus providing cash crops for their families from the sale of these products (Chatty 1978). In the Syrian steppe, the first cooperative for Bedouin was established in 1968 and supplied its members with essential services that included healthcare for themselves and veterinary surgeons for their herds (Bahhady 1981: 258–66). While the limited access to preventive and curative medicine and the absence of health and nutritional awareness could be factors in the poor growth profile of Bedouin children (Topp et al. 1970: 154–62), Bedouin children also suffered from stunting and underweight at least partly due to nutritional factors, including low intake of protein, fats, carbohydrates, minerals, and vitamins. Deficiencies did not exist among children of settled Bedouin who received rations subsidized by the government, and whose families were more prosperous, engaged in raising livestock, crop production, and off-farm income-generating activities (Baba et al. 1994: 247–59).

In Lebanon, among low-income households, it is believed that a woman's anger or fatigue makes her milk hot, which in turn might harm her infant; beliefs regarding the milk of a pregnant woman—that it is poisonous and unfit for children—have been found among pastoral tribes in Lebanon (Harfouche 1965: 59).

Egypt

If the country has adequate resources and can provide basic and advanced healthcare services, as some Middle Eastern countries do, there is no problem. However, in some countries in the region where resources are limited and basic health services are lacking, the implementation of advanced healthcare services—while it could benefit a certain sector of the population—could be unjust, because it deprives a major sector of the population of basic health services. In this context, there is a collision between the principles of justice and equity (Serour 1997: 188). It is well known that successful development often significantly increases the incidence of certain diseases, creating health problems formerly absent or relatively minor. Until recently, endemic malaria has left many fertile, tropical lowlands almost uninhabited, and sleeping sickness caused by the tsetse fly severely limited the exploitation of much of Africa (Foster and Anderson 1978: 26–27). The purpose of building the Aswan Dam and the reservoir (Lake Nasser-Nubia) it created on the Egypt-Sudan border was to check seasonal flooding of the Nile and to supply dependable irrigation water for agriculture, generate hydroelectric power, and promote the fishing industry. On one hand flood control carried a health dividend: prior to the building of the Aswan Dam,[25] flooding of the Nile River left pockets of water that served as breeding grounds for mosquitoes and increased the spread of malaria.[26] Yet, the mammoth project harbored an unplanned health hazard: In Africa and the Middle East, as well as South America, bilharziasis is caused by any one of several species of parasitic blood flukes of the genus *Schistosoma,* vectored by a water snail (Foster and Anderson 1978: 28). Among Egyptian peasants, bilharziasis and other parasitic infections that weaken people but do not cause overt pain are not attended to (Read 1966: 26). In Egypt, within three years of completion of the Nasser High Dam, brackish pools of water in drain-off areas and near the huge lake created by the dam became breeding grounds for bilharziasis, and infection rates rose among children from ages two to six from between 5 and 25 percent to from between 55 and 85 percent (Miller 1973: 15).[27]

From ancient times to the modern day, diseases among the Bedouin have been treated by traditional healers using herbal medicine, medicinal substances, animal species, and various kinds of minerals and substances of mixed origin (Hobbs 1989: 73–89; Shuqayr 1916: 87–92, 352–82). The Bedouin of Jabalia near St. Catherine's Monastery have developed a unique form of folk medicine designed to overcome the diseases and mishaps that typify their desert environment (Ben-David 1981: 107–28). Medicinal plants used by healers are readily available because they grow in the wild as part of the natural fauna (Bailey and Danin 1981: 145–62; Levi 1987: 251–308).

The establishment of clinics and schools and veterinary services in nomadic settlements by the Egyptian government has coaxed Bedouin to settle in traditional gathering places (Sabih 1965: 491–511). According to Qaramani (1965: 513–29 and 70–80), the economic status of the Bedouin has, in turn, been enhanced by employment opportunities in a host of occupations that are not part of traditional nomadic society. Bedouin have been regularly employed in places where there were industrial plants and mining, drilling, and quarrying operations in surface and pit mines for coal, phosphate, and magnesium; gas and oil fields; and quarries for building materials. Settlement of Bedouin near such plants has assisted government authorities (and sometimes enlightened employers, as well) in providing health and education and other services to Bedouin in the workplace and in the area. In the coastal region, fishing centers were established by the government and inhabitants were encouraged to engage in fishing for a livelihood, prompting Bedouin to settle down and relieving pressure on the government to provide services or occupational training (Mustafa 1965: 70–80). In turn, education, including education in the course of military service, has had an impact on the health status of the Bedouin.

The configuration of health services for Bedouin in Egypt is unique: mobile units for providing health and veterinary services and health education to Bedouin in the Sinai Desert were introduced by the Egyptian government parallel to welfare, religious, and sports services. The units, based on a caravan of vehicles and wagons, are staffed by doctors, nurses, paramedics, medical technicians, lab workers, pharmacists, and veterinarians. The caravans have equipment for lung x-rays and means to diagnose dermatological ailments. The health units are able to provide first aid and conduct simple operations, carry out doctor visits, and dispense medication—all provided free of charge by the government. There is also a veterinary medicine unit that includes nurses/paramedics and pharmaceuticals for Bedouin livestock (camels, sheep, horses, donkeys, cows, dogs, and poultry). Medical services for humans include both care for and vaccination against diphtheria and smallpox (Hasan 1965: 1–31). Welfare units distribute foodstuffs and clothing to destitute Bedouin in Sinai. As the Bedouin adopted a more sedentary lifestyle, they have planted barley and orchards in desert areas close to water sources for irrigation, growing food such as grapes, figs, almonds, peaches, carob, dates, and various vegetables and fruits, and engaged in tending herds, raising poultry, and fishing, in addition to quarrying. Because swampy areas, water pools, and irrigated areas under cultivation are breeding grounds for mosquitoes, government medical services treat such breeding grounds in order to fight malaria.

In Egypt, along the Mediterranean coast and in the Western Desert, the primary staple in the Bedouin diet has been barley, supplemented with milk products and meat from sheep, cattle, and camels, and occasionally chicken, as well as fruit such as dates, olives, and grapes (Cole and Altorki 1998; Ismail 1976). Egyptian Bedouin have traditionally suffered from malnutrition that has led to ailments such as hemorrhoids and susceptibility to tuberculosis. Low levels of personal, public, and environmental hygiene led to the prevalence and spread of eye diseases and dermatological diseases (Hasan 1965: 31; Shuqayr 1916: 87–92, 352–82).

In general, until the 1960s, only a small number of medical services were available to the Bedouin in Sinai. These included a hospital for infectious diseases at al-Tur, the Egyptian military infirmary at the nearby St. Catherine monastery, and the Italian Oil Company's camp near Abu-Rudeis, where a physician was available at all times (Romem et al. 2002: 306–38). From 1967 to 1982, Sinai was under Israel military occupation,[28] and Israel supplied health services to the Bedouin there. Existing permanent clinics were transformed by the Israelis into medical centers and served as bases from which satellite clinics were established to enhance access to medical services. The first permanent clinic was established at Abu-Rudeis and operated there until the 1974 Israeli withdrawal from this part of Sinai as part of the September 1975 Interim Agreement designed to separate Egyptian and Israeli forces following the October War of 1973. While under Israeli control, the staff (a physician, nurse, translator, and ambulance driver) visited satellite infirmaries on a fixed schedule. First aid training courses were also arranged for the Bedouin.

In 1978, the St. Catherine medical center was transformed into a community hospital to serve the Bedouin, Israeli military staff, and tourists. The health services, which included preventive as well as curative medicine, were free of charge. New wells were dug and the water supply was chlorinated at regular intervals; malaria, which had been endemic, was largely eliminated by eradication of *Anopheles* mosquitoes. Rabies, which had been very prevalent and led to considerable morbidity, was also addressed (Romem et al. 2002: 306–8). In 1982 Egypt resumed control of Sinai.

The diet of the Bedouin in Northern Sinai in the 1980s consisted mainly of wheat bread, goat milk and cheese, desert herbs and plants, birds, bird eggs, fish, dates, figs, beans, some citrus fruits, occasional garden vegetables, and at rare intervals chicken and goat meat (McDermott 1984: 444). The Bedouin population suffered from malnutrition in general as well as specific maladies including night blindness due to vitamin A deficiency and osteomalacia (rickets) among women due to vitamin D deficiency. They also suffered from viruses such as influenza and hepatitis, infections such as otitis media (inflammation of the middle ear) and urinary tract infections; digestive tract problems such as diarrhea; respiratory ailments from pharyngitis and tonsillitis to bronchitis and tuberculosis; and valvular heart disease. In addition to dermatological ailments such as impetigo, sand flies caused cutaneuos leishmaniasis (face lesions). Cases of bilharzia and haematobium infections (parasitic worms), hypertension, obesity, and Type II diabetes were also reported (McDermott 1984: 442–45).

After Israel's withdrew from Sinai, Egyptian authorities limited medical services in Sinai to the large coastal towns in the south of the peninsula. Bedouin living far away from the coastal margins do not utilize these facilities, and thus have little or no access to Western medical care (Coatesworth et al. 2002: 83). Environmental conditions such as extreme temperatures and zero humidity as well as chronically low water intake take their toll on the health of Bedouin in the form of a host of ear, nose, and throat ailments. The main healthcare requirements of the Bedouin population today are tied to problems of water quality and nutrition (Coatesworth et al. 2002: 85–86).

Iraq

Both sedentary and nomadic Bedouin in Iraq have suffered in the past from dermatological diseases—including syphilis (*bajal*)[29] and eye inflammations and diseases such as trachoma ('Arim 1965: 120). The Iraqi Bedouin diet was based on their herds and camels—both for food and for barter—exchanging milk products, curdled milk (*rayb*), processed butter (*samnih*), fish, meat, wool, as well as rice and dates with villagers and city-dwellers in return for foodstuffs needed during the Bedouin's migrations through desert areas ('Arim 1965: 12; Salim 1970: 3–37, 376–87).

In Iraq as in other places in the Middle East, settlement of the Bedouin enabled the government to provide education and health services, as well as employment ('Arim 1965: 85–154). One of the primary factors in encouraging settlement was the drilling of artesian wells in the desert for the Bedouin ('Arim 1965: 128). Some of the Bedouin in the village of Echibayish engaged in reed gathering, breeding buffalo, and raising cows and other livestock (Salim 1970: 3–37, 376–87). Efforts by the authorities to settle the Bedouin include not only allocation of land and water quotas but also building schools, medical clinics, and hospitals. Needless to say, with or without the benefits of modern medicine, traditional medicine is still used by Iraqi Bedouin, including herbal medicine (Hooper 1937; Townsend and Guest 1980: 100, 122, 183, 224–37, 259–72).

Kuwait

In 1951, Bedouin in Kuwait were reported to suffer from head lice and scabies, stomach aches and other intestinal disorders such as worms, whooping cough (*abu-hamaiyir*), smallpox (*jidri*), measles (*hasbah*), chicken pox (*shanaitir*), consumption/phthisis, syphilis, and eye problems from cataracts to trachoma and conjunctivitis (Dickson 1951: 505–14). According to al-Rajib (1965: 165–66) there were no medical services in Kuwait and tribes relied solely on traditional Bedouin healers until 1913, when the first medical clinic was established, staffed by one doctor who cared for the ill and dispensed free medication. In 1936, a general health authority was established that created the first government-run clinic, staffed by a doctor, a physician's assistant, a paramedic, and a pharmacist. Only in 1949 was the first hospital established, with a staff of four doctors. By 1964 there were 12 hospitals, with a total staff of 380 doctors, and 38 area clinics throughout the country. It should be noted that all medical services in Kuwait are free of charge (al-Rajib 1965: 175–76). The government also launched orientation, guidance, and instruction campaigns on personal and environmental hygiene. Yet, when health services were unavailable or inaccessible due to distance or urgency, and in cases of certain diseases, the Bedouin still turned to their traditional medicine.

Initially, in the middle of the twentieth century, a portion of the Kuwait Bedouin moved into unhealthy "permanent housing" in earthen dugouts, tin and wooden shanties, and adobe houses. As a result, they became susceptible to a host of health problems and the rapid spread of diseases such as tuberculosis (al-Rajib 1965: 157–61). From the perspective of medical anthropology this is a common phenomenon. It is well known that

> the migration of village peoples to crowded urban slums causes a variety of health problems. In the shanty towns surrounding the core cities in almost all Third World countries living conditions are crowded, dirty, and unsanitary. Frequently there is no potable water system, and water-borne diseases, particularly dysentery, are endemic. The nutritionally wise allocation of food money is not something that is easily learned; consequently, new urban dwellers often suffer significant nutritional deficiencies. (Foster and Anderson 1978: 30)

Following the discovery of oil, some of the oil companies employed Bedouin, built housing for them, and provided schools and clinics and other services—benefits that encouraged other Bedouin to settle nearby. Some Bedouin were also employed by the government, the army, and the police force. Assistance in education and occupational training by the government increased the pace of permanent settlement. The spread of literacy—and the reading of newspapers, as well as exposure to radio and television—has broadened the horizons of Bedouin, over time, changing their perspectives, behavior, desires, and expectations. Most Bedouin obtain spouses in endogamous marriage, a practice that cause a high incidence of congenital defects. A study that investigated major congenital abnormalities in babies born in Al-Jahra Hospital in Kuwait from January 2000 to December 2001 showed a high incidence of congenital defects as well as a high rate of consanguinity, which can lead to the risk of these conditions. Of 7,739 live and still births that took place during this period, 97 babies had major congenital malformations (12.5/1,000 births): 49 (50.6 percent) babies had multiple-system malformations, while 48 (49.4 percent) had single-system anomalies. Of the 49 babies with multiple malformations, 21 (42.8 percent) had recognized syndromes, most of which were autosomal recessive, while 17 had chromosomal aberrations. Isolated system anomalies included the central nervous system (12 cases), the cardiovascular system (9 cases), the skeletal system (7 cases), and the gastrointestinal system (6 cases). Of the parents, 68 percent were consanguineous. Genetic factors were implicated in 79 percent of cases. Genetic counseling services need to be provided as an effective means of preventing these disorders (Madi et al. 2005: 1–8).

Libya

Cyrenaica, the eastern coastal region of Libya where most Bedouin reside, was an Italian colony from 1911 to 1940 after being taken over from the Turks. Previously, Turkey had controlled Libya for centuries. For the first two decades under European colonial rule, the Bedouin conducted a guerilla war against Italian control that was only subdued in September 1931, when their venerated leader 'Umar al-Mukhtar was captured and hanged (Peters 1990: 49, 282). After crushing the resistance, the Italians pursued a policy of pacification. Although during the preceding two decades thousands of Bedouin had died in battle and in concentration camps, in air raids on their camps, or due to poverty (Peters 1990: 95), other men in their twenties and thirties, together with women and younger children, took refuge in Egypt. Those that survived returned to Libya after the World War II, where only two were reported to be too old for working the land or herd husbandry, and even they were sufficiently robust to participate as leaders in political disputes (Peters 1990: 49, 282).

The Italians were expelled from Cyrenaica in 1943 by joint British and Sanusi (Libyan religious revivalists) forces. Henceforth, most of Libya, including Cyrenaica, was governed by the British—first under a military government (Peters 1990: 112). From early 1948, civil administration was established under a UN trusteeship for all three Libyan provinces (Cyrenaica, Tripolitania, and Fezzan). Libya received independence in December 1951.

Beyond elevated casualties in wartime, the vagaries of Cyrenaica's climate took a toll. In any given year, one area might be drenched with rain, providing excellent pasture for animals and good crops, while a nearby territorial strip might suffer partial drought resulting in insufficient pasture and poor crops. These climatic conditions determine whether in a given year a particular tribe would enjoy higher or lower milk yield from livestock and better or worse living conditions for human beings. Over a period of years, such factors led to uneven population distribution. Whatever the cause, genealogies show that the population of numerous tertiary sections is unequal. Some are so weak numerically that they have to join a collateral section. Others are so strong numerically that the natural resources at their disposal are insufficient to meet the needs of all inhabitants (Peters 1990: 93–94).

The discovery of oil in Libya in 1959, nearly a decade after independence, contributed greatly to the settlement of Libyan Bedouin and improved their access to educational and medical services. According to Sharaf (1965: 177–247) Libya initiated projects designed to enhance the educational and economic status of Bedouin society and to settle the population. This included drilling wells, establishing agricultural settlements, educating Bedouin in farming, establishing clinics for Bedouin, and operating schools, including occupational training.

Contact with non-Bedouin society has improved the Bedouin's economic status and changed behavioral patterns of housing, diet, dress, and more. Fruits and vegetables not in the traditional diet that were either unavailable or beyond their means in a traditional Bedouin economy were added. Modern communications, including radio, television, and newspapers, raised consciousness. At the same time, access to veterinary services for livestock and camels operating out of mobile units prevented diseases and lowered losses among livestock. These changes have been paralleled by improvements in human health as the result of the opening of medical clinics in Bedouin areas providing medical care and medications, and the combined efforts of doctors, teachers, instructors, and technicians have raised awareness of health issues and hygiene among Bedouin (Sharaf 1965: 247). More recently, significant improvements in the nutritional status of Libyan preschoolers have been attributed to socioeconomic factors, including longer breastfeeding, supplementing breastfeeding with semi-solid or solid foods, greater availability of high energy foods, and heavy governmental subsidization of basic foodstuffs (Hameida and Billot 2002: 1–11).

Among the nomadic Bedouin of the Cyrenaica province (Peters 1990: 197), when the first child is born an animal is presented by the relatives, and if the child is a male, the gift may be several sheep or even a few camels if the father-in-law is very wealthy. Needless to say, during his life cycle a baby is fed milk, milk products, and the meat of these animals. All cooking is done by the Bedouin women. Most meals consist of cereal dishes of various sorts, so grinding grain with heavy millstones must be an ongoing activity in order to meet demands for large quantities of flour. Millstones are bought in nearby villages (Peters 1990: 203). Surplus grain

FIGURE 1.1 In the nomadic seasons—spring, summer, and fall—Bedouin move with their animals for pasture and water.

reaped in years of abundance is stored above ground in the desert and semiarid areas for as long as five years. Tribesmen's diets hinge on milk, milk products, and meat of their animals, grains, and dates. While meat is more abundant in the sheikh's tent, whenever he or a lesser tribesman slaughters an animal, all members of the camp partake of the meat (Peters 1990: 120). The sharing of a slaughtered animal not only provides food but also establishes a special bond between members of the tribe, although various cereal dishes that constitute their regular meals are said to play a similar role (Peters 1990: 190). Groups decamp every ten days or so in the rainy season (Peters 1990: 116); this contributes to hygiene and sanitation, preventing the spread of disease, since garbage and human and animal wastes are left behind every time the tribe pulls up stakes.

Tunisia

There has been almost no detailed information on the status of Tunisian pastoral tribes for more than four decades. In 1965 it was reported that the government had established free schools, clinics, and outpatient clinics for the Bedouin in the southern desert. In addition, running water, electricity, and education have been offered within the framework of agricultural projects and settlements in small villages, in an effort to integrate the Bedouin into Tunisian civil society (al-Fīlali 1965: 139–99). In addition to using modern medicine services, they continued to employ their own traditional folk medicine practices.

Morocco

The Bedouin in Morocco were accustomed to using stagnant water, exposing communities to a host of health problems. Watering their sheep with pond water also led to disease and loss of livestock. Veterinary medicine was almost nonexistent, and the inhabitants used traditional Bedouin healing methods based on the medicinal properties of *Artemisia herba-alba* (*shih*) and other medicinal plants (Boulos 1983; Westermarck 1926). The use of seasonal grazing regimes (*hema*) contributed greatly to the health of flocks and the ability of Bedouin to keep seasonal diseases under control (al-Nasiri 1965: 249–78). The *hema* system is well known and practiced throughout the Middle East (Draz 1969). Information about the status of Moroccan pastoral tribes is very scanty, however, and the most recent information is more than two decades old. Particularly notable is the lack of input on the Sahrawi tribes in the disputed territory of Western Sahara.

Algeria

Sedentarization and changing patterns of social organization among the Tuareg of Algeria have their effects on the health of Algeria's nomadic populations, specifically the prevalence of sexuality transmitted diseases (STDs), the poor state of women's health, and the high incidence of infant mortality. A survey among the Dag Rali since the beginning of the 1990s reveals that 17 percent of babies died at birth or in infancy (Keenan 2006: 932–33). Using traditional medicine and belief, Algerian mothers in the early twentieth century, both in the desert and hill regions, would wear the right forefoot of a porcupine to prevent or cure sore breasts (Hilton-Simpson 1922: 42).

Palestine and Israel

During four centuries of Ottoman rule in Palestine (1516–1917), the Bedouin relied mainly on traditional medicine, including herbal remedies, cauterization, bloodletting, leeching, and cupping by traditional folk healers, augmented by amulet writers, midwives, religious healers, bonesetters, and visits to holy grave sites.

Conditions during World War I exacerbated health conditions in Palestine among all populations. The population of Palestine—Jews and Arabs—was exhausted and depleted by famine, disease, and displacement (Reiss 1991: 15–16)—including scarcity of water (Avitur 1976: 43; Pink 1991: 38–44). Among the Bedouin, the problematic state of healthcare was predominantly the result of water scarcity and water source contamination. The British Mandate in Palestine (1918–1948) led to the establishment of basic Western public health services that focused on the eradication of contagious diseases, enforcement of quarantine regulations, construction of sewage and drainage systems, draining swampland, hygiene education, supervision/licensing of food and drugs, provision of hospital equipment and investments in the healthcare system, and other related health issues such as nutrition and infant mortality (al-Labbadi 1986; Karakrah 1992: 55). Although the healthcare system focused initially on preventative measures, it soon included clinical treatment as well.

Malaria, tuberculosis, and trachoma were widespread in Palestine during the British Mandate (Sufian 2002: 29). According to Spoer (1927: 116), the local Arab Palestinian population that suffered from malaria[30] was not found in mountainous regions or in the desert, but rather primarily in the towns and villages where cisterns served as breeding grounds for mosquitoes. Special hospitals for contagious diseases and epidemic stations were established.[31] Mobile hospitals mounted on camel-back[32] were organized in emergency situations—each capable of treating 40 patients. Mandatory health authorities began training local personnel, including inspectors, nurses, orderlies, and obstetricians (Assaf 1970: 290; Civil Administration of Palestine 1922: 35–36). Dietary habits and the composition of nutritional components impacted on the health of Arab Palestinian populations, including the Bedouin tribes (Kligler et al. 1931: 72–92); malnutrition seems to have been due to lack of essential elements.

No one knows the actual number of Bedouin currently living in the Gaza Strip, but by late 1948 and early 1949 some 32,000 Bedouin had arrived there from Beer-Sheba and the Negev Desert as refugees. An approximate 3,000 had also arrived from the Ramla and Jaffa areas. The current population could be as high as 60,000. They tend to live on the edges of populated areas, away from clinics, offices, schools, and so on, and have little interaction with other members of the population. Many, however, live in makeshift shelters that are inadequate for winter cold and storms. Whereas they live away from populated areas, they tend to have settled near groves and orchards and often maintain small gardens so that some fruit and vegetables are available. There are no statistics relating to the health of the Bedouin living in the Gaza Strip, but because of their isolation, wariness of strangers, and lack of money, adequate medical assistance is difficult for them to obtain. The nearest medical clinic is frequently several kilometers away and the nearest hospital much farther. They are basically a healthy group of people, but the treatment of health problems would greatly improve the quality of life of many families.

There are no up-to-date statistics relating to Bedouin refugees living on the western and eastern banks of the Jordan River. In Jordan most Palestinian refugees, including Bedouin, were granted citizenship (Brynen 1990). People may retain their refugee status long after they have adapted to a new environment. But by then the meanings of being refugees may have changed. During the earlier phase, refugee status may have referred to their dependence, while later it may mean that the refugees organize in order to better negotiate with the state (Marx 1990). Refugees around the world suffer from pressing problems that require solutions. One of these refugee groups consists of the Negev Bedouin refugees. There is a need to examine the exact nature, numbers, and conditions of the Bedouin refugees in the Gaza Strip, the West Bank, and Jordan, and to determine the impact of the 1980 "Requisition of Land in Negev Law (Peace Treaty with Egypt)" on the Bedouin lands of the Negev.

Negev-Bedouin Health Services

In 1900, the Ottoman Turks established Beersheba as the capital of the fifth subdivision (*Qada*) of the Jerusalem *mutasarriflik* (al-'Aref 1934: 192, 244; Marx 1967: 31–32). They built the *Saraya* (government house) (1900–1903), city hall (1904–1906), and a school for Bedouin children. The government encouraged Bedouins to settle in the new city with land grants of one *dunam* (a quarter of an acre). The authorities appointed a pharmacist, who had been living in the city. Bedouin were employed in road and railway construction for the Ottoman army, and the enormous demand for beasts of burden and mutton during the World War I fueled economic prosperity among the Bedouin. This, in turn, had an impact on Bedouin lifestyle in terms of food and health.

After the outbreak of World War I in 1914, Beersheba served as a key Ottoman Turkish command and control center. The school was converted into a Red Crescent hospital. In the winter of 1916, epidemics of cholera and typhus devastated the Turkish ranks. To ease pressures on the military facility that was operating beyond capacity, a field hospital was established in tents behind the mosque, serving mainly German and Austrian patients (Gal-Pe'er 1991: 89–92). General Allenby conquered Beersheba on October 31, 1917 (al-'Aref 1934: 245–48; Luke and Keith-Roach 1930: 27).

When the British began to administer Palestine following the defeat of the Turks, governance was subsequently institutionalized as a League of Nations mandate, and British authorities employed Bedouins in the construction of roads and military bases and bought Bedouin lands for military use. The rise in Bedouin standards of living impacted on a number of social and economic spheres and health conditions and status (al-'Aref 1934: 254–78; Bresslavsky 1946: 253–56; Gal-Pe'er 1979: 283–84). When British forces entered Beersheba in 1917, there was a single military hospital situated in a school building serving the entire Beersheba region. After the World War I, it again became an educational institution and a state hospital was built. In 1918, British authorities began establishing public health services, including several epidemic stations, hospitals, and mobile hospitals on camel-back mainly for the Bedouin in Palestine and Trans-Jordan (Abu-Taha 1984; Abu-Rabia 2000; Assaf 1970: 290). Under the British Mandate for Palestine,[33] Beersheba also became a center for medical and veterinary services. Some Negev Bedouin suffered from disease, isolation and ignorance, while stressors linked to economic conditions played a key role in high mortality rates. Most illnesses stemmed from exposure to mosquitoes and inadequate shelter (cold and dampness in winter, at times extreme). Many infants died at birth, and mothers died in childbirth. Shepherds, often inadequately clothed and exposed to the elements, contracted pneumonia, developed rheumatism, and were vulnerable to tuberculosis; those encamped near swamps contracted malaria (*wakham*) (al-'Aref 1944: 154–60). Arab physicians served as state physicians and also managed the hospital in Beersheba.[34] Since they were the only doctors in the entire district, Bedouins had to bring even the seriously ill to Beersheba; thus Beersheba became identified in the Bedouin's mind as a medical center. The city's eight-bed hospital employed a physician, a pharmacist, three nurses, and several other health personnel, including several male nurses. The hospital and its outpatient clinic treated some 200 patients a day, and served as a medical center for outlying clinics,[35] which the hospital's physicians periodically visited. During al-'Aref's tenure as *Qaimaqam* (governor) between 1929 and 1939, a district health officer with offices in Beersheba was appointed and among his duties visited encampments in outlying areas and dispensed medical aid and advice. One of the health officers (in 1933) was Ibrahim effendi Abu-Ghazaleh. Al-'Aref notes that tribes in the northern and western Negev that were situated closer to urban centers tended to be more trustful of Western medicine and physicians than those living in the eastern and southern sectors. This phenomenon became more pronounced in the 1930s, after the Bedouin faith in modern medicine matured, leading to frequent visits to hospitals and groups of Bedouin in need awaiting visits by doctors to their encampments (Abu-Taha 1984; al-'Aref 1934: 269–83; Gal-Pe'er 1979: 93, 281–82).

The Negev Bedouin were also treated by Jewish physicians who lived in Beersheba.[36] Relations between Palestinians and Jews in the healthcare domain during the British Mandate were informal, with collaboration based on private (e.g., nongovernmental) initiatives, and witnessed ups and downs. Jewish physicians treated Arabs in towns and villages. In addition, the hospitals and clinics of Jewish healthcare organizations Hadassah[37] and Kupat Holim,[38] Dr. Ticho's Ophthalmic Hospital in Jerusalem, and gynecologist Dr. Alexandra Belkin's women's clinic in Jaffa[39] treated Arabs (Karakrah 1992: 27; Reiss 1991: 12; Shvarts 1987: 158; Levy 1998: 142–46).

The British Mandate over Palestine terminated in May 1948. A United Nations Resolution (November 29, 1947) to partition Palestine between Jews and Palestinians sparked the outbreak of war between Arabs and Jews throughout Palestine. The British withdrew from Beersheba on May 14, 1948, in an impressive ceremony attended by Bedouin sheikhs and notables, senior government officials, and Muhammad 'Abd al-Hady, the last *Qaimaqam* in Beersheba during the British period. The Union Jack was lowered, and the Palestinian flag was flown over the *Saraya* House by the mayor of Beersheba, Shafiq Mushtaha. Arab rule over Beersheba lasted only a few months, until the city was conquered by the Israel Defense Forces, on October 21, 1948, and its Arab citizens were expelled. Needless to say, no Palestinians stayed in Beersheba at the close of the war (Abu-Khusa 1994: 274–86; al-Dabbagh 1991: 360). The sudden forced expulsion of most Palestinians from their homes caused an increase of contagious diseases, severe poverty, and increased mortality among Palestinian refugees due to poor hygiene and sanitary conditions and the vacuum created by the withdrawal of British medical services, and widened the almost unbridgeable gap between Jews and Palestinians (Abu-Khusa 1994: 274–86; Abu-Rabia 2001: 58; al-Dabbagh 1991: 350–60).

The Negev Bedouin in Israel

Estimates of the Bedouin population in the Negev at the close of the British Mandate vary from 65,000 to 103,000 (Shimoni 1947: 3–46; Israeli Defense Forces 1954: 1–22; Marx 1967: 2–34; Abu-Khusa 1979: 7–75; Muhsam 1966). When the Israel Defense Forces conquered the Negev in 1948, the majority of Bedouin tribes were expelled to Jordan, the Gaza Strip, and Sinai (Diqs 1984: 5–63; Higgins 1969: 147–49; Marx and Sela 1980). Other Bedouin who had participated in the war against Israel left the Negev out of fear of Israeli authorities (Abu-Khusa 1994: 7–75; Abu-Rabia 1994b: 7–9). The situation remained unstable until 1953, when only about 11,000 Bedouin were allowed to stay in the Negev (Abu-Rabia 1994b: 8; Marx 1967: 12). Most Bedouin who remained were remnants of tribes or belonged to small tribal branches; they banded together around nineteen tribal heads recognized by the Israeli authorities as sheikhs. These groupings were concentrated under military rule in the northeastern Negev, in a closed area. Special permits from the military authorities were required to enter or leave the area, and at times even movement between one tribe and another required a permit. Sheikhs and notables were given special permits, which allowed them freedom of movement out of the closed area, on condition that they returned to their tribe by evening. The rule of the military government was repealed in 1966 (Abu-Rabia 2001: 93–94).

In the 1950s and early 1960s, the health of the Negev Bedouin was negatively affected by the harsh conditions of desert life in a host of realms—inadequacies in housing and clothing, water resources, nutrition, transportation, and work (Ben-Assa 1969: 13–18). Inadequate and unbalanced diet weakened the Bedouin's constitution, making them vulnerable to disease and shortening their life expectancy. The mobility of tent life largely eliminated health problems linked to poor sanitation, but did not prevent other problems tied to nomadic life—for example, the prevalence of leeches in well water, cisterns, and water containers; animal and insect bites; and household disasters such as fire. On the other hand, certain aspects of desert life are beneficial. Walking long distances develops muscles and proper breathing (Ben-Assa 1969: 13–18).

Dietary habits and customs among the Bedouin are a very important health issue. In the 1960s a study of Negev Bedouin health and nutrition status found that 75 percent of their caloric intake was derived from carbohydrates, about 13 percent from fat and only approximately 12 percent from protein. In the 1950s and 1960s, the Bedouin diet (mainly because of its high content of high-extraction flour and small quantity of meat and dairy products) was characterized by a very high percentage of carbohydrate calories, a low percentage of fat calories, and an adequate amount of linolenic and linoleic acids. Due to the high protein and vitamin B content of whole-wheat flour, intake of protein, thiamin, riboflavin, and niacin intake was adequate and therefore diseases such as famine edema or vitamin B deficiency were nonexistent. Wheat flour, however, is low in vitamin A and vitamin D. Most Bedouin got vitamin A from eggs and from mallow plants (Groen et al. 1964: 37–46). Mallow (*malva = khubiza, khubaizih*), is plentiful during winter and spring, and is dried for both food consumption and medicinal purposes during the summer and fall (Abu-Rabia 2005f: 404–7). Vegetables were another source, if they were available.

Some Negev Bedouin have become commercial growers of agricultural products, cultivating barley, wheat, sorghum, lentils, broad beans, citrus, grapes, apples, apricots, almonds, figs, olives, pomegranates, tomatoes, onions, pumpkins, summer squash,[40] and watermelon (Abu-Rabia 1994a: 7–9; 2001: 15–16).

Most of the Negev Bedouin continued to maintain their traditional way of life and habits, including traditional food, until the mid-1960s, when Israeli authorities allowed them to integrate into the modern Israeli labor market (Marx 1967). In the mid-1960s, plans were drawn up to settle the Negev Bedouin, and implementation progressed significantly in the 1970s (Lithwick 2000). The transition from a pastoral nomadic life pattern to town life caused changes in lifestyle—including eating habits and health status. The urbanization process brought with it better access to health services, but entailed a significant drop in physical activity among the Bedouin, although some youth have gone to work in rural Jewish *kibbutz* and *moshav*[41] settlements, in factories, and in construction. Urban Bedouin women's traditional roles involving physical work were sharply curtailed, but due to sociological factors and traditional values, they did not seek work outside the home, resulting in a loss of status and leading to a passive and idle lifestyle (Tal 1995). Changed eating habits, particularly the consumption of foods rich in cholesterol, and changes in the rhythm of their lives as Bedouin as they integrate into the fast-tempo, high-pressure environment of the Israeli workplace have led to a high incidence of obesity, diabetes, and cardiovascular disease, all of which were almost nonexistent three decades earlier (Abu-Saad et al. 2001: 14). While the incidence of traditional diseases has declined, in addition to the above, Bedouin have begun to suffer from asthma, ulcers, and shortness of breath (dyspnea—*dhig nafas*). Throughout the 1950s and 1960s there was little evidence among the Negev Bedouin of ischemic heart disease (Ben-Assa 1961: 211–13, 1964: 450–53; Weiss 1961) but since the early 1970s there have been indications that it is on the increase (Kain 1985). Accumulated data and other evidence suggests that cardiovascular disease in general (which was very rare among Negev Bedouin until the 1970s) has been on the increase since the 1990s as a result of the settlement process of nomadic Bedouin in towns and changing habits and lifestyle (Fraser et al. 1990: 273–78). Likewise, previous studies show a low prevalence of diabetes among Negev Bedouin, but new evidence suggests that since 2000 diabetes has become highly prevalent. It is possible that diabetes and obesity are indicators of an epidemiologic transition from a traditional to modern lifestyle (Abou-Rbiah and Weitzman 2002: 687–89).

When traditional medicine fails to satisfy the Bedouin's needs or expectations, they turn to doctors trained in modern medicine. Yet, it is not

uncommon for Bedouin—including modern Bedouin who are conscious of personal health matters and avail themselves of Western health services—to go concurrently to both a traditional healer and a modern doctor for relief (Ben-Assa 1974: 73–76).

It is well known that people who undergo rapid urbanization, such as the members of nomadic and seminomadic tribes in the Middle East and Africa, face psychosocial conflicts and pressures (Sabir 1965: 345–46; Sadalla and Stea 1982: 3–14; Tal 1995). In cultures as varied as the Zulu (Scotch 1963: 1205–13) and rural residents of western North Carolina (Tryoler and Cassel 1964: 167–77), such change has been found to be associated with increased hypertension and/or coronary diseases. The epidemiology of psychological disorders in situations of rapid change also merits discussion. A good deal of evidence indicates that an increase in such disorders is the consequence of stressful living conditions (Hughes and Hunter 1970: 474–79). Among settled Bedouin in Northern Jordan (Jaddou et al. 2003: 472–76), 11 percent were found to suffer from hypertension, although this was significantly lower than the 16 percent reported in other modernized Jordanian communities.

Until the 1980s, transportation constraints and distances still had a considerable adverse impact on the spatial accessibility of Negev Bedouin to health services. A significant improvement in the availability of and accessibility to special health services has taken place since the mid-1980s. Nevertheless, the health-related well-being of the Negev Bedouin is still highly constrained (Meir 1997: 179–80); the high prevalence of infectious and respiratory diseases among the Bedouin population in the past has been replaced by a growing predominance of degenerative diseases (Meir 1987).

As of 2015, some 60 percent of the 230,000 Bedouin in the Negev live in seven towns[42] established by Israeli authorities, with standard single-dwelling houses. Most of the remaining 40 percent live in tribal settlements, various sized clusters of tents, wooden or corrugated iron shanties, or cement block or stone houses considered "unauthorized/unrecognized settlements" by Israeli authorities (Abu-Rabia 2006: 865–82; 2015 [Source: "Statistical Yearbook," Central Bureau of Statistics, Jerusalem 2015]). Scattered across the landscape, these settlements lack basic municipal services and public utilities such as running water, connection to the electricity and sewage grids, garbage collection, and social and health services. Consequently, such communities have the highest rate of infant mortality in Israel and a high incidence of respiratory diseases; a large percentage of Bedouin children are hospitalized each year in Soroka Medical Center in Beersheba (Dloomy, Almi, and Sawalha 2006: 33; Almi 2003).

Some mothers work outside of their homes, leaving their infants with grandmothers and other women for bottle-feeding. Sometimes mothers seem to be the "victims" of advertisements for baby formula. Many perceive it as the "modern and progressive" and are unduly swayed by marketing claims that commercial formulas are nutritionally superior to mother's milk. Illiterate mothers who adopt bottle-feeding use too much or too little formula, or use contaminated water that subsequently leads to diarrhea and in some cases dehydration that requires that babies be hospitalized.

Despite the constant decline in infant mortality rates in Israel throughout the years (1980–2004), since 1997 the direction is far less clear vis-à-vis infant mortality rate among the Negev Bedouin. Data from 2003 shows 13.3 per 1,000 live births, which in 2004 rose to 15.8—while the general rate declined to 4.73 (Amitai 2005; Almi 2003).[43] The high level of infant mortality among the Negev Bedouin is the product of a lower living standard than other areas, less modern dwellings, and low access among some of the Bedouin population to health services and basic services such as running water and electricity. Substandard living conditions and the physical distance between Bedouin communities and medical facilities are the primary reasons for poor hygiene that lead to poor public health standards. These factors intermix with a Bedouin-type living style that leads to a higher level of infant mortality than the Arab population in Israel as a whole (Huleihel 2005: 162).[44] According to Meir and Ben-David (1991: 139–46), governments should deliver extra health care to the Bedouin who are in the process of sedentarization, until full adaptation to the new sociocultural and biomedical environment is attained. In conclusion, it seems that the causes of poor health among the Bedouin, in Israel as well

Infant Mortality Rate	Gross Death Rate	Gross Fertility Rate	Gross Birth Rate	Infant Deaths	Deaths	Live Births	Year
Muslims in the Beer Sheva Sub-District							
13.9	3.4	9.15	56.6	97	397	6.675	2001
15.1	3.0	9.01	55.7	110	373	6.951	2002
14.6	2.8	9.00	55.4	95	368	7.295	2003
14.6	2.6	8.35	51.5	104	363	7.159	2004
14.2	2.5	7.61	46.9	101	369	6.844	2005
13.7	2.3	7.26	44.6	79	357	6.805	2006
12.5	2.2	7.14	44.1	76	350	7.021	2007
7.2	4.7	3.68	25.9	104	2.712	15.060	Total - Be'er Sheva Sub-District
10.6	2.2	6.91	43.3	65	365	7.198	Muslims in Be'er Sheva Sub-District
3.9	5.4	2.96	21.5	594	39.255	156.923	Total - Israel
7.1	2.5	3.84	28.5	237	3.096	34.860	Muslims in Israel

FIGURE 1.2 Live births and deaths, infant mortality, gross birth rate, gross fertility rate, gross mortality rate, and infant mortality rate among Muslims in the Be'er Sheva subdistrict, 2001–2007. Source: "Statistical Yearbook," Central Bureau of Statistics, Jerusalem, 2009.

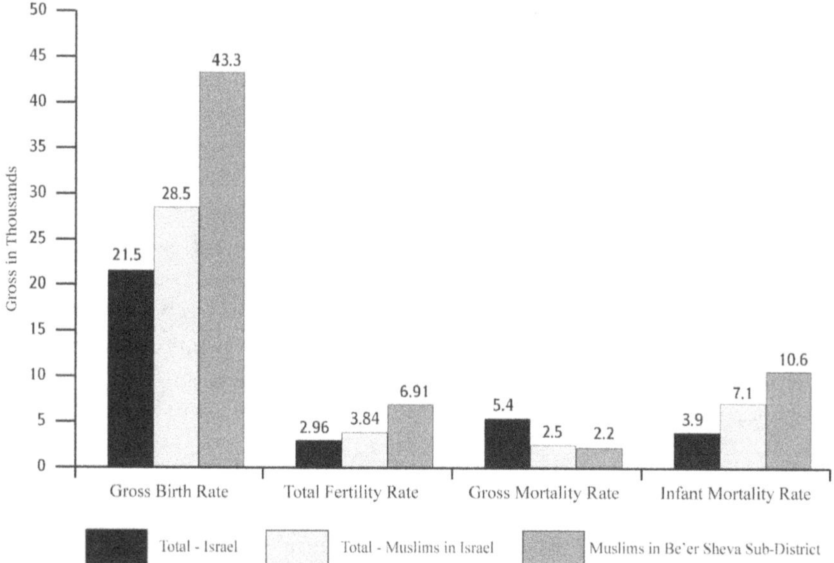

FIGURE 1.3 Birth and death rates among the general population in Israel, Muslims in Israel, and Muslims in the Be'er Sheva subdistrict, 2008. Source: "Statistical Yearbook," Central Bureau of Statistics, Jerusalem, 2009.

as in Arab countries, require socioeconomic, educational, and political solutions.

In 2004, the infant mortality rate among the Bedouin was 16.9 per 1,000 live births. In 2005 this rate dropped to 15, while in 2006 the Bedouin infant mortality rate was 11.9 per 1,000 live births compared to 8 in the general Muslim population in Israel and 4.3 in the overall population. In 2006, the infant mortality rate among the Bedouin population was 1.5 times higher compared to all the Muslim population in Israel and 2.8 times higher than in the general population in Israel. In 2007, the infant mortality rate fell slightly among the Bedouin population to 11.5 per 1,000 live births (Ministry of Health Report 2008) .

Summary

This chapter describes changes that occurred in the Bedouin lifestyle in the realm of socioeconomic and health services during the twentieth century. The primary moving force behind change in healthcare methods was the establishment of new towns in the last decade of Ottoman rule. Parallel to the construction of new towns, Bedouin were exposed to and gradually given access to Western health services. This process of Westernization of health services in certain towns intensified during British and French Mandates in the Middle East.

Middle Eastern countries have historically been a crossroads between Asia, Africa, and Europe, and served as a cultural, economic, political, medical, and military meeting point. Many factors affected Bedouin health during the periods of Ottoman rule and the British Mandate. Some of the diseases, mainly eye diseases and inflammations, were contracted due to poor nutrition and/or poor hygiene and sanitation practices linked to the scarcity of water. This was compounded by harsh environmental and geographic conditions—a hot, dry climate that also includes periods of cold, humidity, and dust paralleled by inadequate shelter that contributed to poor personal hygiene, further exacerbated by socioeconomic factors such as overcrowding, proximity of livestock, and a low level of education and low health awareness.

Due to an absence or lack of access to modern health services mainly among isolated villages and Bedouin encampments, traditional healers continue to treat patients, and patients continue to appeal to their traditional healers. From the viewpoint of the healers, modern medicine does not endanger their position, but is useful for solving some of the more complicated cases; healers consider modern medicine complementary to their healing methods, not opposed to them. The benefits of early systematic treatment and preventive medicine coupled with education on the elementary principles of hygiene need to be brought to the Bedouin's doors, at schools, tribal meeting areas, community centers, and local councils. For the Bedouin, achieving the right to health in practice involves four core elements: availability, accessibility, acceptability, and quality. This should be a primary national priority for all countries in the Middle East. Currently, the socioeconomic status, education level, health status, and political and religious environment of Bedouin is at different stages and levels of sedentarization and urbanization across the Middle East, but all Bedouin face tremendous challenges in the twenty-first century.

Notes

1. The Rwala tribe camps in northern Arabia between latitudes 28° and 34° north and longitude 36° and 42° east (Musil 1928: 676).
2. *Semum* or *samum/simoom* are pestilential hot winds that cause disease.
3. There are ditties sung by defenders of the camp that speak of the good fortune blowing on the wind, spelling success or the fortunes of war: *Habbi lana hbub ar-rih habbi lana* (Blow luck to us, O wave of the wind! Blow, until our riders are assembled) (Musil 1928: 542).

4. Ague (*hemma*) is a fever that marked by paroxysms of chills, fever, shivering, and sweating that recur at regular intervals. Hence, *ague* can refer to both chills and fevers.
5. *Thamila* are small, hidden pools of water that lie under the surface of a dry, sandy watercourse that do not percolate down and disappear completely because they are trapped by a layer of impervious subsurface rock or clay (Dickson 1951: 61).
6. Compare that to John the Baptist when he wandered about in raiment of camel's hair, in Judea, and "his meat was locusts and wild honey" (Matthew 3:4).
7. The lambs eat the dry stubble that falls from the *arfaj* bushes (Dickson 1956: 403); according to Mandaville (1990: 294–95) *'arfaj* is *Rhanterium epapposium,* a plant of great economic importance, being the dominant constituent of valuable rangelands. It is itself grazed by livestock.
8. Most of the Mano of Liberia are extremely clean in their personal habits; they take a hot bath every evening at sunset, and defecation takes place in the bush instead of in towns, which are remarkably free of vermin (Harley 1941: 73–74). The earliest expression of such practices was cited the 1890s in the refusal of the Tswana in South Africa to comply with sanitary prescriptions, particularly use of the "privy." Black African youth deplored this practice and considered it "defecation in the house" (Comaroff 1993: 324). "In societies in which belief in witchcraft is strong, people are careful to conceal their excreta and other bodily wastes so that evil-doers cannot find materials on which they can work contagious magic. To such people, the thought of advertising the presence of excreta in a sanitary latrine, advocated by public health workers, is the height of folly. In a pilot project in social medicine among the Zulu of Durban in South Africa, projects such as home gardening and compost pits were modestly successful, but pit latrine programs less so. Adults and children are found to micturate in the immediate vicinity of their huts, but defecation, except in the case of infants and young children, always took place some distance from the homestead. Bushes were preferred, but as long as a place was found that offered protection from the public gaze it was considered satisfactory. Modesty, and perhaps even more important, the desire to conceal the identity of the persons defecating, demanded this protection" (Kark 1962: 26).
9. During Musil's visit to Aqaba in 1910, he found the Ottoman soldiers were lying ill, suffering from fever and malaria. The soldiers' post had not been supplied with money, food, medicine, or doctors (Musil 1926: 84).
10. Dr. Shelly Avery Jones (b. 1911) served as medical officer in charge of the mobile medical unit for Trans-Jordan, Department of Health, Palestine Governmen, 1936–1945; seconded to Trans-Jordan Government (Aurel and Cornfeld 1945: 87; Cornfeld 1947: 133).
11. *Shenan, shinan, ishnan, ushnan* (*Seidlitzia rosmarinus*); for the use of plants as soap or for producing soap, see Abu-Rabia 2001: 47–48; Burckhard (1822: 354–55), Cohen (1989: 81–85), Doumani (1995: 122, 187) and al-Nimr (1961: 288–89).

12. The pastoral nomadic Bedouin could receive vitamin C from wild plants such as *Apium* (*karafs*), *Anthriscus cerefolium* (*baqdunas barri*), *Crithmum maritimum* (*qarn al- ayal, shamrah bahriyah*), *Malva* (*khubiza, khubayzih*), *Matricaria camomille* (*babunaj, rabil*), *Petroselinum sativum* (*baqdunis*), and *Rumex acetoe* (*hummad saghir*) (Abu-Rabia 2005a: 295–300, 2005d: 1–15, 2005f: 404–407). Mineral content has been determined in several edible marine sea vegetables. Seaweeds contain a high proportion of sulphate, and contain large amounts of both macro-minerals (Na, K, Ca, Mg) and trace elements (Fe, Zn, Mn, Cu). Seaweeds also contain high concentrations of carbohydrates, protein, and minerals and are employed both as a food and for pharmaceutical uses (Ruperez 2002: 23–26; Campanella, Crescentini, and Avino 1999: 533–40).
13. For instance, the project of Mithgal al-Fayz, chief sheikh of Bani Sakhr (*sheikh mashaykh* Bani Sakhr), who planted fruit trees (grapevine, olive, apple, and fig) in Um el-'Amad (about 17 km from Amman) in 1958 encouraged other villages and tribes to follow suit and to put their land to work (al-Taher 1965: 45–47).
14. al-Qatranah, al-Jafr, Bayir, al-Hisa, al-Rājif, and al-Mudawwara.
15. Potatoes (*batata*), broad beans (*foul, ful*), lentils (*'adas*), carrots (*jazar*), beets (*shamandar, salq, banjar*), cabbage (*malfuf*), and cauliflower (*qarnabitt, garnabitt*).
16. Tabanidea/taḅanid: a family of bloodsucking flies that includes the genera Tabanus (horsefly) and chrysops (deerfly and mango fly), which are involved in the transmission of several blood-borne parasites. Tabanus: gadflies and horseflies; a genus of biting flies, some species of which transmit *surra*, infectious equine anemia, anthrax, and other diseases (Stedman 2000: 1781).
17. A disease caused by deficiency of the B-complex vitamin niacin that causes scaly skin sores.
18. This phenomenon can be compared to the spread of measles among the South American Indians—the Yanomamo of Venezuela and Brazil in 1960s (McElroy and Townsend 1996: 7–20).
19. For more details about the nomadic Baggara tribe, see Cunnison 1966.
20. Glossina: a genus of bloodsucking Diptera (tsetse flies) that serve as vectors of the pathogenic trypanosomes that cause African sleeping sickness in humans and in domestic and wild animals (Stedman 2000: 753). Trypanosome: common name for any member of the genus Trypanosoma or of the family Trypanosomatide. Trypanosomiasis; any disease caused by a Trypanosome (Stedman 2000: 1883).
21. For more details about the Zande tribe, see Evans-Pritchard 1937.
22. *Medain Salih*/Madain Salih is located at al-Hijr. Al-Hijr is an ancient oasis in northwest Saudi Arabia, and lies between the cities of Medina and Tabuk, 22 km north of the city of al-'Ula.
23. Indeed, "in Uganda, the hospitalized children whose mothers took the greatest interest in them and who stayed with them recovered faster and more completely than those whose mothers were indifferent" (Geber and Dean 1956: 3–14).
24. *Catha edulis Forsskal*

25. The digging started in 1960, and the first part of the project was completed in 1964. The whole project was completed in 1970, and in 1976 Lake Nasser reached its full capacity.
26. This is in contrast with the case of the Panama Canal when yellow fever defeated the French engineer De Lessup's first attempt to dig a canal; only after the mosquito vector was eliminated was it possible to complete the canal (Foster and Anderson 1978: 26). But unwittingly creating conditions for spread of disease due to poorly conceived "bio-aquatics" is not unique to the Nile project: In the Caribbean littoral or coastal zone, systematized agriculture provided conditions for an increase in *Anopheles* mosquitoes and malaria. In Malaya rubber plantations were established in malaria-free areas. However, after clearance of natural forest, ideal conditions were created for *Anopheles* mosquitoes to breed, introducing malaria. The same process of introducing malaria occurred in southern India (Miller 1973).
27. A similar phenomenon was registered after the construction of the Volta Dam in Ghana. The construction site of the Volta Dam in Ghana contained host snails for the *Schistosoma* parasite; the ecological balance was upset so rapidly by this dam that by 1972 more than 70 percent of a sample of 1,000 children in a lakeside study area within 10 miles of the dam were infected (Scudder 1973: 50).
28. The occupation was the result of the Six-Day War in 1967 between Israel, Egypt, Jordan, and Syria. As a result of the Camp David Accords that led to the 1979 Egyptian-Israeli Treaty, Israel returned Sinai to Egypt in exchange for peace and normalization of relations, and withdrew from Sinai in April 1982.
29. *Bajal* is a non-venereal endemic syphilis (*bejel, bajlah, zahri ghayr tanasuli*) (Benenson 1975: 624; Hitti 1984: 84).
30. Spoer (1927: 115–42) mentions the following diseases among Palestinians in the 1920s: fever, eye inflammations and styes, measles, smallpox, jaundice, back pain, ear inflammations, asthma, scorpion stings and snakebites, skin diseases, paralysis.
31. Nazareth, Safad, Tiberias, Migdal, Bisan, and Jenin (four to eight beds in each).
32. From the view point of history, 'Ubaydulla ibn al-Muzaffar al-Bahili (Hispano-Arab physician) a poet as well as physician, entered in 1127 the service of the Saljuq Mahmud ibn Malikshah in Baghdad and provided him with a field hospital, transported on forty camels (Hitti 1951: 578).
33. The British civil administration in Palestine was established in 1920.
34. Dr. Muhammad Ali Shukair (August 1923 through April 1925). Dr. Khalil Abu Ghazaleh served as a medical officer in Beersheba during the period 1921–1923, and 1924–1929 (from 1923 to 1924 he served in Haifa); Dr. Sami Shihab (June 1929 through August 1931); Dr. Sulayman Selim al-Sama'yn, who was manager of the hospital (December 1936 through April 1937, but continued to work in Beersheba through the forties); Dr. Hamad (unknown when arrived, through 1948). In addition, the private physician Dr. Abd al-Razzaq Qlibu [Kleibo], who also served as a *Qaimaqam* in 1926–1927, practiced in the city, as well as a Greek physician named Dr. Alexander Dimitriadis who lived in the

town during the 1940s (al-'Aref 1934: 55, 269–283; Aurel and Cornfeld 1945: 10; Aurel and Peretz 1945: 10; Cornfeld 1947: 56; Levy 1998: 470).

35. These were at 'Auja al-Hafir, al-'Imara, and al-Jammama.
36. During the years 1917–1936: Dr. Aharon Binyamini, Dr. Me'ir Berkovich, Dr. Levi [a veterinarian who treated humans when there was no Jewish physician in Beersheba], Dr. Rabinowich [dentist], Dr. Re'uven Richard Meir and his wife, and Dr. Shlomo Kar (Gal-Pe'er 1979: 93; Levy 1998: 469–70).
37. An American Jewish women's organization that supported health and welfare in Mandate Palestine, including Hadassah Hospital and mother and child clinics.
38. The General Federation of Labor's General Sick Fund, established by the Jewish Community of Palestine (the *Yishuv*) in 1911.
39. Between 1906–1914 her clinic treated a thousand patients, half of them Muslim, the rest Jews and Christians.
40. Often called *zucchini* or *courgette* (al-Khatib 1982: 689, 816).
41. Agricultural villages.
42. Rahat, Tel-Sheba [Tel al-Saba'], Kuseife [Ksifa], 'Aro'er ['Ar'ara], Segev Shalom [Shgib al-Salam], Hura, and Laqiya.
43. In comparison, nonwhite infant mortality in the United States hovered, for most of the twentieth century, at around three times the white rate (Sider 2008: 279).
44. It is insightful to compare the Bedouin's status with the findings of Baer, Singer, and Susser (1997: 175): "Class disparities in mortality rates are not limited to infancy, as substantial differences have also been found among older children. For example, children from inner-city poor families are more likely to die from respiratory diseases or in fires than children from wealthier suburban families. Inadequately heated and ventilated apartments also contribute to death at an early age for poor urban children, as well as hunger and poor nutrition in additional factors."

Chapter 2

The Treatment of Human Ailments

Illnesses suffered by the Bedouin from ancient times until the present day have been treated by traditional healers using herbs, animal substances, various minerals, and materials of mixed origin (Abu-Rabia 2005a: 404–7, 2005f: 295–300; Bailey and Danin 1981: 145–62; Hobbs 1989: 73–89; Levi 1987: 251–308; Shuqayr 1916: 87–92, 352–82). Analysis of the findings shows that many medicinal substances originated in Middle Eastern countries. For example, most of the plants used in traditional medicine were native to the Middle East, growing wild as part of the natural fauna. Minerals that were locally processed and used in traditional medicine included asphalt, various salts, sulfur, copper, and iron. Local spring water was also used. Some of these materials were exported to neighboring lands or to European countries.

The rich variety of approaches employed by Bedouin healers to treat illnesses attests to the depth and breadth of the indigenous medicine practiced in the region. Similarities exist regarding conceptions of health, disease, and treatment among Bedouin tribes in different locations, but different tribes use unique treatment techniques for certain illnesses. During my field work, which extended over more than thirty years, I collected and described these treatments.

Most of my work focuses on the Negev, the West Bank, the Gaza Strip, the Sinai Peninsula, and Trans-Jordan. I do not claim that all the treatment methods presented in this study exist today among Bedouin throughout the Middle East, or among all generations (adults and educated young people), particularly since modern medicine has penetrated Bedouin tribes in the course of their rapid urbanization and education. At the same time, I am convinced that many of these treatment methods still exist to varying degrees. When serious illness strikes—particularly incurable diseases—even educated people turn to traditional medicine for a remedy. I encountered cases of this kind three decades ago, and still encounter them today in 2014.

Abdominal Sprain (*mamsi, mamsy*)

An old woman relates a story about a Bedouin with an eight-month-old baby who had suffered an abdominal sprain after his sister lifted him up too quickly when his stomach was full of food. The baby lay on his belly, was very weak, and would not eat. The father took the baby to a Bedouin female healer who prescribed the following: "Take goat rennet (*masah*) and brush away the particles of dirt but do not wash it in water. Lay the inner side of the rennet[1] on the baby's belly and tie it with a scarf for two to three hours." This procedure was repeated the next day, and the child was completely healed. Rest was prescribed for one week.

Other treatments include light massage with lukewarm olive oil and the application of a poultice (*lazgih*) compounded of pure soap (*sabun bikr*) mixed with egg yolk or crushed wheat seeds (*jirishih*) and water to the sprain. In cases where the pain continues, burns are made on the sprain with a small needle. The Bedouin of the Negev (Shinnawi 1982) crush seeds of *hilbih* mixed with olive oil wrapped in a rag and applied to the sprain as a bandage (*lazgih*).

Abortion (*tanziyl*)

Various methods of abortion are in use. A woman who wants to terminate a pregnancy takes flowers of *Nerium oleander* (*difla*), grinds them and mixes them with mercury. She dips cotton wool into the concoction and places the wad in her vagina, causing an abortion. Alternatively, the leaves and bulbs of *Eminium spiculatum* (*irqita*) are eaten. The seeds of *Peganum* may be crushed in water and drunk. Powdered alum may be added to tar (*gitran*) extracted from juniper and placed in the vagina with cotton wool.

Dafni and Dafni (1975: 233) found that the Bedouin women of the Negev use the fruit of *Citrullus colocynthis* (*handhal*) as a method of inducing abortion. Levi (1978: 25–26) reports that the Bedouin women in Southern

Sinai boiled leaves of *Juncus litoralis* (*samar*) mixed with red spines of palm leaves in water and drink the mixture.[2]

Affliction by Jinn (*mahfuf*)

According to Bedouin belief, jinn are creatures with superhuman powers; they can traverse tremendous distances in no time and without effort, and then cause harm with only a light touch. Jinn are generally invisible, but can change at will into animals, birds, and even people. They live underground, although they can also be found above ground—in water, including springs, in fire and in the air, and in caves and rock crevices. At night, under cover of darkness, jinn go forth to do harm to human beings, inflicting physical and mental harm and mental illness (*mahfuf*). They attack either from the outside or by entering a person's body and taking control of it.

Anyone who suspects he has been affected (*mahfouf*) by a jinni or spirits is treated in a special ceremony. The healer, in this case a man, holds in his hands a mixture (*rshush*) of aniseed seeds, barley, cumin, cloves, incense, garden cress, lentils, rice, wheat, and verdigris (*junzarah*) and gives it to the victim while he reads verses from the Quran, the two *sura*s of the Daybreak and the Mankind: (113:1–5, 114:1–6). The victim is instructed to make four small mounds of earth around his bed in the directions of north, south, east, and west, and to place some of the compound on each mound and burn them. The patient performs this ceremony and reads the Opening Sura of the Quran every night before going to sleep for five to seven nights. Jinn can be also expelled by burning incense (*ktur*) and *rshush*/*rishush*[3] and inhaling it.

Another option is to visit a holy tomb or the sea. The patient travels with his family to the nearest seashore, prays there, and bathes. Livestock is slaughtered, cooked, and eaten there. During this ritual on the sea shore, the carcass of the livestock is placed inside its hide and thrown into the sea (Bailey 1982: 77–78; Bar-Zvi, Abu-Rabia, and Kressel 1998: 21–23; Levi 1987: 388; Murray 1935: 156–57; Shuqayr 1916: 354). Sometimes the Bedouin daubs (*bihanni*) the patient with the blood of the slaughtered animal (Bailey 1982: 74) before him in the sea. The slaughtered animal symbolizes the patient, while its blood symbolizes the patient's blood and the sea symbolizes health and recovery.[4] Interestingly, the sea denotes the spiritual experiences through which the mystic passes in his journey to God (Nicholson 1975: 74). It seems that this type of treatment has been inspired by the following verses: "He will turn again, he will have compassion upon us; he will subdue our iniquities; and thou wilt cast all their sins into the depths of the sea" (Micah 7:19).

Al-Damya

The symptom of this disorder is a change in body color, mainly the face, to black (*mkhanfis* [looks like a black beetle]). The Bedouin of Galilee (Hilf 1985) treat this illness by making an incision in the vein with a razor blade or knife and letting out the blood until it returns to its original color. (The healer would typically cause a patient to bleed through the laceration of a vein and allow it to bleed until he deemed the patient "healed.") Among the peasants (*fellahin*) in the southern Hebron Mountains, the author found that blood is let from the forehead, behind the ears, or the nape of the neck (*'ar'ur*).

Al-Farha

The symptoms of this disorder include unsteady movements, walking as if intoxicated (in babies), and foaming at the mouth. Treatments include burning incense for the baby to inhale, writing amulets, hanging them on the baby, and placing them under his/her pillow. Among the Bedouin of Galilee (Hilf 1985), a women healer whom the baby has not met before dresses in a robe (*thawb/zyj*), places the baby in the opening of her clothing near her breast, and takes it out through the lower part of her robe. The idea behind this procedure is to place the baby in a dark, mysterious place (inside the robe) in order to frighten him/her. It is thought that this procedure aids recovery.

Amputated Hand

In Sinai and the Negev, when a hand is amputed, the limb is immediately plunged into hot oil in order to facilitate its healing without further pain and to prevent infection.

Appendicitis (*Abu al-hgay, masir zayd, warwar*)

Treatments for appendicitis include burning certain areas of the body with a red hot iron or with ignited dried leaves of *Phagnalon rupestre* (*gadih*), as follows: one burn each on the right and left shoulder; two burns in the form of a cross over both kidneys, and two burns in the form of a cross in the vicinity of the genitals, and then drinking a glass of water in which a dried piece of dog excrement has been dissolved. In this context, it is interesting to note that according to Westermarck (1926: 103), in Morocco some degree of *baraka is* attributed to the dung of cattle, which is used for pacification or medicinal purposes. In a tribal village of India, dog excrement is used as a remedy for cholera. They believe dogs never get cholera, so the simple logic is that its intestines must contain some anti-cholera substance. A "microphage" is something more powerful than penicillin; it is found in the intestines of animals and can dissolve bacteria, not merely kill them (Pisharoty 1993: 12, 17).

Asthma (*azmih, dhig nafas*)

To treat asthma, a handful seeds of *Lepidium sativum* (*hab al-rashad*) are ground, mixed with a soft egg yolk, and consumed early in the morning for a month. Another remedy consists of mixing a small amount of resin of myrrh (*Commiphora myrrha* [*mur batarikh*]) with tobacco, rolling it into a cigarette, and inhaling the smoke. Alternatively, the bulbs of *Urginea maritima* (*hallouf*) may be burned in the hearth, and the smoke inhaled. The following are mixed together and a spoonful of the mixture is taken every night for three to four weeks: *Boswellia carterii* (*hasa al-ban*), *Glycyrrhiza glabra* (*'irq al-sus*), *Lepidium sativum* (*hab al-rashad*), rose water, and *Terminalia chebula* (*sha'ir hindi*). During this time, the patient eats wheat bread (*khubz gamh*) with bran (*nkhalah*), drinks tea prepared from *Foeniculum vulgare* (*shawmar*), hyssop, and black cumin. Crushed alum may be mixed with Bedouin butter and eaten daily in the morning for forty days. An interesting remedy consists of eating boiled porcupine meat. The rationale behind this custom is that the Bedouin know the porcupine lives and burrows its holes underground, and has a limited oxygen supply, so it has adapted itself to this circumstance. Therefore, they believe, its flesh is remedy for shortness of breath such as that experienced in asthma. The Bedouin of Galilee (Hilf 1985) treat asthma by burns on the chest and on the spinal vertebrae, numbers three or four. The Bedouin of the Negev (Dafni and Dafni 1975: 235–39) treat asthma by drinking tea of *Matricaria aurea* (*rabil*) or *Foeniculum vulgare* (*shawmar*). Among the Rwala (Musil 1928: 130–31), tumbac (*Nicotiana persica*) is smoked in a water pipe (*nargilih*) by certain chiefs only. The common Rwala think that tumbac is injurious to the health and also hinders the powers of observation. Fahad Ibn Hadhdhal, the chief of the 'Amarat who camped on both sides of the middle Euphrates, like many other chiefs, carried his water pipe on his camel, even when migrating or on long marches. During the short halts, he would pour water into the pipe from a small pouch, put some moistened and crushed tumbac in the bowl, lay a red coal on top of it, and smoke. Such smokers usually have the tumbac tied in the lappets of their long shirt sleeves. An inveterate smoker of tumbac is generally punished with asthma (Musil 1928: 131).

Baby Care

Among the Bedouin in the Negev (Abu-Rabia 2010: 454) it is customary for the midwife to hide the umbilical cord under the supporting pole of the tent (*wasit al-bayt*)[5] or in the tent lining (*btanit al-bayt*) to symbolize the baby's continuing loyalty to his family. One old woman, Um Mahmud, related to the author that she hung her son's cord on the neck of a she-camel (*naqa*) to symbolize his connection to camels; indeed, when he grew up he loved tending camels and was even nicknamed "father of the camels" (*abu al-niaq*).[6] After tying and severing the umbilical cord, the Bedouin midwife washes and removes the birth stains from the baby with a clean white cloth or sponge soaked in lukewarm water and soap. Some midwives smear olive oil (*Olea europaea L.* [*zayt zaytun*]) and a little salt over the baby's body[7] to strengthen his bones and muscles and to prevent diaper rash (*nasaf*) and frostbite (*garsih, sagi'*).

Newborn infants are cleaned in various ways. For seven days after birth, the Rwala (Musil 1928: 243) bathed the child in camel's urine and massaged it with salt. Among the Bedouin Jabalia tribe near St. Catherine's Monastery in Sinai (Levi 1978: 29), the midwife (*daya*) washes the new baby with lukewarm water mixed with salt. Some women refrain from cleaning their baby for the first three days, believing that the material on the body vaccinates him against illness. On the fourth day, they wash the baby with salt and water. Among the Tarabin tribe in Sinai, women washed newborns with the urine of black goats or donkeys to vaccinate them against disease. In Arabia (Dickson 1949: 175) at the birth of a baby, the mother put a piece of steel in the cot or attached one to his clothes (see above) and the infant was bathed in urine of a female camel (Dickson 1949: 179).

During the first week, the mother exposes her baby to many smells. She does this to prevent him from developing allergies, nausea, vomiting, vertigo, and dizziness from the odors he will encounter as he grows up. The Bedouin believe a person can die from strong smells to which he has not been exposed as a baby and therefore, during these first days of life, he is introduced to a resin from assafoetida (*Ferula assafoetida* or *Ferula narthex* [*haltit* or *jiddih,* "the baby's grandmother"]) with very pungent scents.[8]

The Rwala (Musil 1928: 179) hated all strong odors and believed some of these gave rise to diseases, or at least irritated old wounds; for this

reason they stop the nostrils of sick people. It is considered a matter of individual taste which odor is harmful and which helpful. He who cannot tell an injurious odor from one that is beneficial looks with disfavor on the person or the object from which the odor is disseminated.

Backache (*waja' dhahar*)

Treatments for backache include burning the spinal column between the vertebrae in several places with smoldering *Phagnalon rupestre* (*gadih*); rubbing the back with saltwater or hot desert sand; massaging the back with lukewarm olive oil; eating grilled spleen (*thal/itthal*); removing the thorns from the pads or shoots (*luh*) of *Opuntia ficus-indica* (*sabr, sabir*), heating them on a fire, wrapping them in white cloth, and placing them on the back where the pain is once a week during the night, in order to make the body sweat (it should not be exposed to wind); or rubbing the back with a tincture produced from the roots of *Asphodelus microcarpus* (*swai*).

Spinal pain combined with headache and strong fever is treated by complete rest and cauterizing the head and temples with a red-hot iron. The Bedouin of Galilee (Nejidat 1984: 30) also use burns to treat backache. In Palestine (Hareuveni 1930: 118), backache was treated by rinsing the back with asphodel sap. The Bedouin of the Negev (Shinnawi 1982) make burns on the back and the left hip and massage the back with hot table salt. The Bedouin of Galilee (Hilf 1985) treat "back fever" (*hamm fi al-dhahar*), which causes back pain and instability in walking, by cupping (*kasat hawa*). The healer uses three cups, burning a piece of paper inside each cup and placing it on the affected area of the back for two to four minutes. Some healers make a slight incision with a razor blade at the spot after the cupping in order to let out the "tainted" blood.

Among the Rwala (Musil 1928: 666) to treat *khubta,* pain in the spine and the head, combined with a strong fever, the patient lies only on the flat of his back and is burnt with a red-hot iron around the head and temples. This occurs most frequently in winter. The Rwala Bedouin (Musil 1928: 667) treat pains in the small of the back that cause the afflicted person to walk with a stoop by burning the afflicted spot.

Bleeding after Delivery (*nazif damm*)

Treatments for bleeding after childbirth include the following: drinking water in which the leaves of *Juncus litoralis* (*samar*) and the fruit of Jericho rose have been boiled; boiling the flowers of arabic rose with flowers of the *Scirpus litoralis* (*diys, dis*) in water and drinking; drinking a mixture of the crushed leaves of *Salvia hierosolymitana* (*marmarya, miramya*) and *Hammada salicornica* (*rimth*) mixed with cold water twice daily; eating a mixture of seeds of *Nasturtium officinale* (*jarjir*), black cumin, and olive oil.

Bleeding from the Womb (*nazif damm min al-rihm*)

Bleading from the womb can occur at any time. Treatments for it vary. Levi (1978: 28, 1987: 264) found that Bedouin women of southern Sinai boiled the flowers of *Juncus litoralis* (*samar*) and drank the liquid. They also boiled the flowers of rose, *Scirpus litoralis* (*diys*), and *Juncus* in *samnih* and drank the resulting brew. Bailey and Danin (1981: 152) note that the Bedouin of the Negev and Sinai soaked crushed leaves of *Hammada salicornica* (*rimth*) in cold water and drank the tea twice or three times. Hilf (1985) found that among the Bedouin of Galilee, bleeding women after delivery were treated with a mixture of the crushed seeds of black cumin with olive oil, which was inhaled through the nose. Pinczuk (1994) found that the Bedouin of the Negev drink tea with *Hammada salicornica* (*rimth*) or wash the womb with lukewarm water and crystalline plant sugar (*sukkar fadhdhi*).

Blood in the Urine (*damm fi al-boul*)

Blood in the urine is treated with an infusion of the leaves of the following plants: *Pituranthos tortuosus* (*zaqquh, zagguh*), *Mentha longifolia* (*na'na' barri, habaq*), and *Artemisia judaica* (*ba'aythran, bu'aythiran*). The leaves of these plants are steeped in boiling water and the liquid is drunk. In addition, a long needle (*makhatt*), the spout of an earthen jar (*ba'abuz ibrig*), and a "retention" bead (*kharazat al-hasir*) that are reputed to cure retention of urine are hung around the patient's neck. The urine is released a few hours later. A piece of dried livestock bile (*mararah*) is cut up and put in a glass of water and the water is drunk. The urine is released immediately. Dried donkey or ass droppings from the previous spring (*saun himiyr*) are placed in water and drunk. This is also a remedy for kidney stones. The healing properties of the droppings come from the spring pasture vegetation, especially the flowers.[9] The Bedouin of Galilee (Hilf 1985) treat retention/obstruction of urine (*hasir boul*) by boiling the leaves of *Petroselinum sativum* (*bagdunas*) in water and drinking it. They also treat stones in the urinary system, or blood in the urine, by boiling the leaves of *Teucrium* (*ja'adih, ja'adit al-sibyan*) in water; or drinking the liquid drained through the process of producing goats's yogurt (*mayss*).

Blue Baby (*walid azrag*)

When a baby is born with slightly blue skin, his mother or the midwife give him *Pituranthos tortuosus* (*zagguh*) to smell, cloves, *Ferula assafoetida*, or *Ferula narthex* (*jiddih, haltit*) with very pungent scents, which cause him to sneeze very hard. The Bedouin women of the Negev (Shinnawi 1982) give him onion to smell, in order to make him sneeze, to ease his condition.

Bowel Pain (*maghs masarin*)

To treat bowel pain, the Bedouin of the Negev and Sinai (Bailey and Danin 1981: 151) drink tea made with *Achillea fragrantissima* (*gisum*), *Teucrium leucocladum* and *Teucrium polium* (*ja'adih*), *Cynomorium coccineum* (*turthuth, tarthuth*), *Artemisia herba-alba* (*shih*), *Artemisia judaica* (*ba'aythran*), or *Thymus decussates* (*za'tar barry, zu'taran*). The Bedouin of Galilee (Hilf 1985) drink tea made from the *Salvia fruticosa/triloba* (*marmarya*) or *Coridothymus capitatus* (*zahayfy*).

Breast/Nipple Infection: Breast Bead (*kharazat al-diud*)

Bedouin use beads to treat various illnesses and diseases: the breast bead (*kharazat al-did, diud, dioud*) is hung on the woman's cleavage, or worn as a necklace (*gladih*). It is used as a remedy for a woman with swollen or inflamed breasts, or with insufficient milk for nursing. It is also a cure for a nursing mother's inflamed nipple or breast and for a baby's belches, burps, or hiccups during nursing. Another treatment consists of smearing lukewarm olive oil on the nipple, twice to three times a day. Ben-Assa (1964: 452) comments that in the early 1960s, mastoiditis was very rare among the Bedouin of the Negev. Bedouin women sprinkled ground coral on their breasts to ensure sufficient milk supply and cure any swellings or infection. The coral is white and perforated, as are her nipples (Bailey 1982: 82). Such practices are based on a belief in the reciprocal action of like on like. The color of the bead is white like milk, and the bead originates in the sea—signifying fluids, so the wish is that the breast will supply plenty of milk.

Broken Bones/Limbs (*kasir 'idham*): bone-setting (*tajbir, mujabbir*)

For broken bones/limbs/hands, splints (*tab*) and bindings are used. When a hand bone breaks, the flesh is washed with hot water and smeared with an egg yolk and flour in the form of a poultice. The edges of the broken bone then drawn together and the limb bound tightly with a rag (Haj Hammad Salem Abu-Rabia, personal communication, 17 June 2000).

The Bedouin of the Negev (al-'Aref 1933: 243) treat a broken arm by washing the hand in lukewarm water, followed by massage and bandaging. The Bedouin of the Negev also use splints and bindings for a broken nose (Shinnawi 1982).

Among the Rwala (Musil: 1928), fractures were healed by setting the broken bone, laying the limb between narrow boards, and then packing it around with a dough made of barley flour, salt, eggs, and *Trigonella foenum-graecum* (*hilbih*). This mixture hardens like rock. After twenty-five days the bandage was loosened, but was removed only after forty days. During this time, the patient was forbidden to eat anything sweet and was fed on meat only, or, if meat was unavailable, on milk. Similarly, in Arabia (Dickson 1949: 511), simple fractures were treated with splints, a concoction of barley flour, salt, and eggs, and bandaged for twenty-five days. Lawrence (1979: 225) related the following:

> He crashed off and broke an arm. Mohammed coolly tied him up with rags and camel-girths, and left him at ease under a tree to rest a little before riding back to Ugila for the night. The Arabs were casual about broken bones. In a tent at Wadi Ais I had seen a youth whose forearm had set crookedly; realizing this, he had dug into himself with a dagger till he had bared the bone, re-broken it, and set it straight; and there he lay, philosophically enduring the flies, with his left forearm huge under healing mosses and clay, waiting for it to be well.

Burns (*harg nar*)

Burns caused by fire or boiled water, oil, or hot materials may be treated by applying a mixture of egg yolk and flour, the ashes of the burnt leaves and roots of *Lycium shawi* (*'awsaj*), olive oil, or *nilih* to the burn. Blisters (*habat*) that occur as a result of a burn are treated by applying goat, sheep, or camel milk to the affected area several times a day or boiling leaves of *Matricaria aurea* (*rabil*) and *Anthemis pseudocotula* (*rbayan*) and rinsing the burn.

Shinnawi (1982) found that the Bedouin of the Negev treated burns with donkey blood, *Indigofera articulata* (*nilih*) powder, or coffee powder. Levi (1978: 74) found that the Bedouin of Southern Sinai used a tincture of *Globularia arabica* (*handagug*) or *Lycium shawi* (*'awsaj*) on the burn. Dafni and Dafni (1975: 238) found that the Bedouin of the Negev crushed roots of asphodel in a handkerchief and rubbed the burn.

Cauterization (*kay, kaiy, kawi, makwa*)

In the Middle East, cauterization involves placing a heated metal object, usually a nail or a small rod much like a branding iron, on the patient's skin. The procedure is painful, burning the skin and leaving a permanent scar. Cautery may be used directly on the site of a patient's bodily complaint (e.g., lower back, arm or leg joints), or it may be used on other sites of the body to "tighten" relaxed nerves and muscles, and for infertility (Inhorn 2005: 3834–39).

Bedouin often resort to cauterization as a medical treatment. One method is to place a tiny ember on the affected spot. *Ephedra* (*'alanda*) is a species of large bush, and nails and other iron fragments may be used as cauterization instruments (Bailey 1991: 177, 320).

Chest Pains (*waja' sadir*)

To treat chest pains the leaves and branches of *Pituranthus tortuous* (*zagguh*) are boiled in water and the brew is drunk on an empty stomach early in the morning for a week. The chest may be massaged with lukewarm olive oil in the evening before sleep. It is also recommended to eat a soft-boiled egg early in the morning. Water in which fenugreek seeds have been soaked may be drunk three times a day for a week. An additional treatment involves drinking a teaspoon of olive oil every morning for a week.

Chicken Pox/Varicella (*abu-hmar*)

Coridothymus capitatus (*zahayfy, za'tar farisy*), hyssop, or *Achillea fragrantissima* (*gaysum, qisum*) is boiled in water. The patient drinks one cup of this liquid a day, and washes his body with it once a day for one to two weeks. The Bedouin of the Negev (Shinnawi 1982) inhale a tincture produced from the following plants: *Anchusa strigosa* (*ihmim, lisan al-thur, hemhem*), *Eryngium creticum* (*kursannih*), *Polygonum equisetiforme* (*qudhdhab, godtabb*), *Pituranthos tortuosus* (*zaqquh, zagguh*), *Noaea mucronata* (*sirr*), *Solanum dulcamara* (*hulwa murra, sabra murra,'inab al-dib*), and crystalline sugar (*sukkar fadi*).

Circumcision (*tuhur, tuhr*)

The word commonly used to denote circumcision is *tuhur*, which means purification of the body. Circumcision, cutting the foreskin (*ghulfe*),[10] usually takes place under the age of two years and is carried out by a special circumciser (*mtahir, mutahir, shalaby*)[11] or even by a physician or nurse.[12] In Palestine (Granqvist 1947: 196), when the circumciser cuts off the foreskin, it is put into a little bag and buried, or it is put in a little box and then wrapped in a piece of cloth and buried lest the dogs eat it. If they eat it, harm will come. The circumciser changes the pad on the penis the day following the circumcision, rubbing it with olive oil.

If there is swelling, infection, or bleeding, the circumciser smears the penis with a special medicinal herbal powder (*rshush, rishush,*[13] *dhrur*[14]). This medicine is assigned magic, symbolic, and healing qualities. It is bought in the market at a perfume vendor (*'attarin*) and is composed of the following plants: *Artemisia judaica* (*b'aythiran*), *Artemisia herba-alba*[15] (*shih*), *Achillea fragrantissima* (*gisum*), *Retama raetam* (*ratam*), *Coridothymus capitatus* (*zahayfy*), cinnamon (*girfih*), *Cleome droserifolia* (*samwih*), and *Ballota undulata* (*ghassih*). A week is usually required to recover from circumcision. Infections are treated with a powder made from the dried powder/leaves of *Artemisia judaica* (*b'aythiran*), which is also placed on the penis at the time of circumcision to reduce bleeding, heal the cut, and reduce the danger of infection. Levi (1978: 36) found that the Bedouin of Southern Sinai rub the infection with a tincture produced from *Achillea fragrantissima* (*gisum*), or *Artemisia herba-alba* (*shih*). In Arabia (Dickson 1949: 507) circumcision sores are sometimes very grave, and are caused by dirt and flies.

In Palestine (Granqvist 1947: 194–95), when boys are circumcised, no unclean woman may be present. It would be a sin for women to be present, since the boys are regarded as being ill. Circumcision is carried out at seven years old in the month of July (Granqvist 1947: 175–77). The boy is encouraged to bathe in the sea, since the salty water acts as an antiseptic.

Among the Jews in Israel, in order to prevent complications from mishaps, one must begin the healing process of the circumcision wound immediately. A compress and cumin are applied. The cumin seeds are ground and put on the wound to stop the flow of blood. The compress is dipped in a mixture of olive oil and wine and the bandage is wrapped on the wound with a piece of yarn or flax. Some used wax or tree sap (Rubin 1995: 103). The foreskin is part of the human body that is severed, and as such perhaps it is viewed in a manner similar to an amputated appendage. In any case, it must be hidden or buried. And perhaps it is supposed to be preserved and related to with affection, since it is living proof that the commandment has been performed. The attitude towards to foreskin is transformational: as long as it is connected to the body, it is viewed as repugnant, but once it has been cut off, it is—at least—not something that is viewed as unhealthy (Rubin 1995: 105).[16]

Common Colds (*bard*)

Remedies for the common cold include drinking tea brewed from the following plants with a teaspoon of sugar: leaves of chamomile, hyssop (*za`tar*), *Artemisia herba-alba* (*shih*), or *Eucalyptus bicolor* (*keina*). Colds are also treated by inhaling the steam from a pot of water boiled with chamomile leaves.

Congenital Malformations (*mshawwahin*)

The Bedouin believe children are born with malformations for the following reasons: as punishment for an evil deed committed by the parent against God or people; it is God's will that the child be a cripple so others will see and fear; it is God's desire to test the patience and faith of the parents, to put them through an ordeal; jinn and devils have affected the fetus or the infant at birth; a woman cast an evil eye on the mother during pregnancy or birth out of jealousy of the infant's beauty or the number of his male brothers; a curse was put on one or both parents out of hatred or jealousy; the woman or her children were afflicted during pregnancy or after the birth by a female demon (*qarina*) or evil spirit. Another explanation is that the baby inherited the defect from a relative who carries the malformation.[17]

It is believed that vaccinations carried out during pregnancy or immediately after birth cause malformations. Moreover, it is believed that any of the following during pregnancy can cause congenital malformations: injections or pills; carrying a heavy burden; falling; sleeping or lying on the stomach; general discomfort when lying down; eating *Eminium spiculatum* (*rgita*) (this is allowed after birth); seeing a deformed child; talking about deformed children; talking about diseases, misfortunes, devils; sudden fear or shock; nervousness, morning depression; contracting a disease like measles, scarlet fever, or smallpox; visiting a woman who has had an unexplained miscarriage.

There is a claim that the practice of consanguineous marriage, which can increase the rate of congenital malformations, has probably survived in the Middle East to varying degree because of specific political, economic, and social advantages that it offers.[18]

Constipation (*msak*)

Treatments for constipation include drinking 1–2 tablespoons of olive oil, or one spoonful of castor oil (*khirwi'*) early in the morning; drinking water in which carob pods (*kharrub*) has been soaked, or eating carob; eating watermelon several times a day; drinking a half-liter of camel's milk in the early morning; drinking tea with boiled leaves of *Coridothymus capitatus* (*zahayfy*) several times a day; or, in the case of a baby, inserting a small suppository of soap in the baby's anus. The Bedouin of the Negev (Dafni and Dafni 1975: 233) squeeze the juice of *Citrullus colocynthis* (*handhal*), in water and drink it. In Palestine (Hareuveni 1930: 119), the Bedouin used *Euphorbia* spp. (*lbina, hullyba*), *Tulipa* spp. (*thraya*); or castor oil (*zayt khirwia'*). The Bedouin of the Negev (Shinnawi 1982) seat the patient over steam from boiling water. The Bedouin of Sinai (Cohen 1936: 246) squeeze the fruit of *Citrullus colocynthis* (*handhal*) in a cup of water and drink it. The Bedouin of Southern Sinai (Levi 1978: 55–56, 1987: 2986) use the following plants, as tea: *Citrullus colocynthis* (*handhal*), *Cassia* (*kasiah, sinamakky*), *Tephrosia apollinea* (*sana*), *Convoluvulus hystrix* (*middaidy*), *Artemisia judaica* (*b'aythiran*), and *Thymus decussates* (*za'tar barry*). The Bedouin of the Negev and Sinai (Bailey and Danin 1981: 145–62) use *Citrullus colocynthis* (*handhal*), *Euphorbia hierosolymitana* (*hulliba*), and *Convoluvulus hystrix* (*middaidy*), as tea. The Bedouin of the Negev (Abu-Khusa 1979: 106–11) drink camel's milk early in the morning on an empty stomach. Other treatments include drinking turmeric (*kurkum*) with water or castor oil (*khirwi'*). The Bedouin of Galilee (Hilf 1985) take one spoon of honey with one glass of milk, three times a day. In Arabia (Dickson 1949: 511) the Bedouin treated constipation with purgative medicine.

Contraception (*man' haml*)

There are various methods of contraception. For example, a piece of cotton wool is dipped in indigo dye (*nilih*) or alum powder and placed in the vagina before sexual intercourse.[19] During and after menstruation, the woman drinks tea prepared from anise, or *Coriandrum sativum* (*kuzbarah*). The Bedouin of Southern Sinai (Levi 1987: 262) eat broad beans (*Vicia faba L./Faba vulgaris* [*foul*]); or drink tea with cloves for forty days; or drink tea boiled with steel (*hadid*). Pinczuk (1994) found that Bedouin woman in the Negev eat or swallow several roasted coffee beans or seeds of *Ricinus communis* (*khirwia'*) after delivery, or after menstruation. They put cotton wool in indigo dye powder (*nilih*) and insert it in the vagina before sexual intercourse; taking it out just before sexual intercourse; or drink tea with anise or with *Coriandrum sativum* (*kuzbarah*). In Egypt (Pillsbury 1978: 44–45) *afass,* Indian barley (*hindy shi'riy*), *novalgi,* and honey are inserted as vaginal suppositories prior to sexual intercourse or taken orally as a contraceptive.

In early Islamic medicine, ointments for men and oily suppositories for women were prescribed to encourage the semen to drip out of the vagina and not travel up through the cervical canal to the uterus (Omran 1992: 156).

Cough (*sa'alih, gahah*)/Coughed-Up Blood (*gati' damm*)

Coughs are treated by inserting one quarter-spoonful of powdered of resin of myrrh (*Commiphora myrrha* [*mur batarikh*]) in a slightly opened egg, then placing the egg near a fire or in hot ashes and consuming its contents. This treatment is repeated early in the morning for a fortnight. Other treatments include boiling the leaves of *Artemisia herba-alba* (*shih*), *Teucrium* (*ja'adih*), and hyssop in a glass of water and drinking the brew early in the morning.

When blood is coughed up (*gati' damm*), the Bedouin drink one of the following: olive oil, oil of black cumin, egg yolk with myrrh, hyssop, thyme, or *Varthemia iphionoides* (*slimaniya*), early in the morning on an empty stomach. Other treatments include mixing pure honey with oil of black cumin and drinking it in the early morning, boiling the leaves of *Rosmarinus officinalis* (*iklil al-jabal*) in a glass of water and drinking the brew once a day, and drinking tea made with *Varthemia iphionoides* (*slimaniya*).

For chronic cough or cough with sputum (*nkhamah*), egg yolk is mixed with the resin of *Boswellia carterii* (*hasa al-ban*) and the concoction is drunk in the early morning. The leaves of *Eucalyptus globules* (*kina*) are boiled in a glass of water and drunk twice a day. In Palestine (Hareuveni 1930: 122) in the mid-twentieth century, they drink tea made with *Matricaria chamomilla* (*rabil*), and *Ruta chalepensis* (*fayjan*). The Bedouin of the Negev (Shinnawi 1982) treat cough and bloody sputum (*gati' damm*) with burns on the chest and on the back made with a small needle and massage the chest with olive oil. The Bedouin of Sinai (Levi 1978: 62) drink a tea prepared from the following: hyssop, *Rhus tripartite* (*'irn*), *Cleome droserifolia* (*samwih*), *Mentha,* and *Artemisia herba-alba* (*shih*). The Bedouin of the Negev and Sinai (Bailey and Danin 1981: 145–62) drink tea made with *Artemisia herba-alba* (*shih*), *Haplophyllum tuberculatum* (*imjenina*), hyssop, *Origanum* (*mardagush*), or *Hyoscyamus* (*sakaran*). The Bedouin of Galilee (Hilf 1985) treat cough by making burns on the neck (*jura*). The Bedouin of the Negev (Dafni and Dafni 1975: 236) treat cough and cold by drinking *Artemisia herba-alba* (*shih*) with sugar or milk. They also treat harsh and chronic cough and pains in chest with honey and yolk egg taken in the early morning (Abu-Khusa 1979: 106–11). Among the Rwala Bedouin (Musil 1928: 667) a severe cough with vomiting is treated by drinking asses' milk.

Cracked Heel/Ankle Pain (*ka'ab mitshagig*)

Samnih, a kind of processed butter or olive oil, is boiled and the ankle/heel is washed with this liquid twice a day for one to two weeks. The Bedouin of Galilee (Hilf 1985) rub the ankle/heel with a tincture produced from henna and *Opuntia ficus-indica* (*sabr*). Animal fat or olive oil is rubbed around the ankle/heel.

Cramp (*fathat al-'asab*)

Cramp is treated with complete rest for one to two weeks. Another treatment consists of massaging the affected body part with lukewarm olive oil mixed with table salt and wrapping it in a rag. The patient is forbidden to engage in any sexual activity. The Bedouin of Galilee (Hilf 1985) wash the affected body part in hot water, massage it, and tie it with *al-mashad/mishad.* If the pain persists, burns are made on the painful spot with small needle.

Crying Baby (*siah*)

A baby who cries during the night or day is treated by allowing him to smell incense or by putting a Quran under his pillow during the night. In cases of persistent crying, the baby is taken to visit a dervish, who reads holy phrases over his head, and smears his saliva on the baby's forehead (Sheikh Mahmud Muhamad Abu-Badr, personal communication, 1975).

FIGURE 2.1 Abu-Bader, left, a famous dervish in the Negev with the author. Abu-Bader was the author's mentor for more than fifteen years.

The Bedouin believe that each baby has his or her star in the sky, which exercises a mysterious influence upon his life, either propitious or not. If he has a strong health and personality, his star is strong—if he is ill or his personality is weak, his star is weak (*najmih khafif*) and sways from side to side. The newborn baby is regarded as vulnerable (*hassas*) to the gaze of a stranger or a strange gaze by someone familiar to the family, so he may be affected by the evil eye (Abu-Rabia 2005: 248). The Bedouin of

the Negev (Shinnawi 1982) treat the baby by reading phrases from the Quran and hanging a special amulet on his body.

Cutting the Umbilical Cord

The cutting of the umbilical cord (*sirr, habil al-surra*) is delayed so that mother and child can rest and the weak and tired newborn can "drink strength" from the placenta, which is also referred to as a comrade or a sister. "From the morning till the noon the afterbirth remains in the basket beside the child so that it draws strength from it." Thus, the placenta remains with the child from the morning until the afternoon or from the evening until the morning. "It helps the child who drinks of its blood." This custom applies to both male and female children. According to Canaan (1927a: 165), in the 1920s this was not done before the seventh day. If a child was born in the evening, the placenta was left till the next day. In the evening nothing was cut, also because the afterbirth was not traditionally buried at night.

Delivery Bead/Induced Delivery/Birth Bead (*kharazat al-nfas, infas*)

A woman about to give birth wears a special bead around her neck whose name is the same as that of her birth-giving state (*nfas*). It promises her a complication-free delivery. The Bedouin believe that carrying this bead induces birth.[20] Alternatively, the bead may be steeped in a cup of water, which the woman then drinks.

In the 1950s, when Bedouin women in the Negev were first introduced to Western medical services, which included maternal and child care, vaccination, and delivery in the hospitals, they were at first hestitant, but gradually got used to them. Today, most of the Bedouin women in Israel deliver their babies in the hospitals, even in the face of possible violations of Bedouin traditional birth customs and taboos. The newly educated mothers consider delivery in the hospital healthy and safe for their babies and themselves.

The medical treatments and beliefs surrounding childbirth are diverse. Levi (1978: 28) found that among the Bedouin of Southern Sinai, pregnant woman took sitz-baths or saunas with leaves of *Mentha* and *Pyrethrum* (*ghirdib*). Pinczuk (1994) found that the Bedouin of the Negev drink tea made from *Asteriscus graveolens* (*njud*). Krispil (1986: 110) found that they boiled leaves of *Asteriscus graveolens* (*njud*) in water and drank the infusion to treat venereal diseases and nausea, and to stimulate childbirth.

In Palestine (Canaan 1927a: 160), it is believed that the running string of the trousers (*dakkit al-serwal*) of a pure and honest man hastens a difficult labour if it is carried around the abdomen of the suffering woman. In Arabia (Dickson 1949: 173) a woman after delivery becomes unclean (*najsih*) and the husband cannot go near her for forty days. At the birth of the baby, the mother places a piece of steel in the cot or attaches it to the baby's clothes (Dickson 1949: 175).

In the early twentieth century, when a pregnant woman could not be delivered of her child the Berber of Aglu (Westermarck 1926: 69) would scratch some grit from a rock at the tomb of Lalla Ta'bullat, a holy spinster, mix it with hot water, and give the mixture to the woman to drink. If the child was born alive, five tufts of hair were left on its head, and later, when the child had grown bigger, these were shaved off at Lalla Tab'ullat's grave and left there.

Diabetes (*sukkari*)

There are many treatments for diabetes. A brew may be made by boiling one of the following plants in water and drunk: leaves of *Paronychia argentea* (*rijl al-hamam*), *Achillea fragrantissima* (*gisum*), roots of *Sarcopoterium spinosum* (*billan*), or seeds of fenugreek (*hilbih*). The leaves of *Atriplex halimus* (*gataf*) may be eaten several times a day. Pieces of twig from the *Salvadora persica* (*arak, siwak*[21]) may be chewed several times a day. The leaves of *Artemisia herba-alba* (*shih*) may be eaten several times a day or, alternatively, boiled in water and drunk. The ground roots of *Lycium shawi* (*'awsaj*) may be boiled in a liter of water for at least two hours on a low fire and strained into a bottle, and half a cup of the liquid is drunk every morning. The fruit and roots of *Prosopis farcta* (*yanbout*) are boiled in water and the juice strained and drunk. Tomato (*bandurah*) or pomegranate (*rumman*) juice may be drunk several times a day. Onions may be squeezed into a tablespoon and drunk on an empty stomach early in the morning. *Brassica oleracea* (*malfuf*) may be boiled in water with onion added in order to absorb the bitter taste. This water is replaced with fresh water, which is boiled again and then drunk and the stew is eaten five times a day. Olive oil or cotton oil may be drunk. The Bedouin of the Negev (Shinnawi 1982; Shani et al. 1970: 344–49) boil the roots of *Sarcopoterium spinosum* (*billan, natsh*) and drink the infusion, while the Bedouin of Sinai (Ben-David 1981: 124–25) treat diabetes with a medicine composed of forty plants mixed with cotton oil and crystalline plant sugar. The Bedouin of Sinai (Levi 1978: 69–70, 1987: 274, 302) treat the disease by boiling leaves of each of the following plants in water and drinking the brew: *Convolvulus hystrix*

Vahl (*lublab*), *Lupinus albus* (*turmus*), *Cleome droserifolia* (*samwih*), *Achillea fragrantissima* (*gisum*), *Artemisia herba-alba* (*shih*), and *Trigonella arabica* (*handaquq*). Levi (1987: 274) found that the Bedouin healer Salih Mbarak treated diabetes by making incisions on the head and shoulders of the patient and spreading powder made from *Peganum* (*harjal*), crystalline plant sugar (*sukkar fadhdhi*), and alum powder (*shabbih*). The Bedouin of the Negev and Sinai (Bailey and Danin 1981: 145–62) treat diabetes by boiling leaves of *Cleome droserifolia* (*samwih*) in water and drinking the infusion. The Bedouin of the Negev (Abu-Khusa 1976: 70; 1979: 106–11) boil *Achillea fragrantissima* (*gisum*) in water, pouring it into an earthenware container (*ibrig fukhkhar*) and drinking four cups a day; or boiling the pads/cladode/shoots (*luh sabir*) of *Opuntia ficus-indica* in water, soaking *Lupinus albus* (*turmus*) in water, eating bitter food or bitter plants, boiling the roots of *Sarcopoterium spinosum* (*billan*) in water, or drinking pure honey early in the morning each day.

The prevalence of diabetes among the Bedouin of the Negev during the last twenty to thirty years is a result of displacement, forced settlement, urbanization and the concomitant change of eating habits and lifestyle, the Israeli-Western bureaucracy, hardships, and other reasons (Abu-Rabia 2002: 202–11; Abu-Saad et al. 2001: 1–14; Fraser et al. 1990: 273–78; Almi 2005; Tamir et al. 2007: 652–55; Weitzman, Lehmann, and Abu-Rabiah 1974: 391).

Diarrhea (*hrar, ihrar*)/Diarrhea with Bloody Stool (*hrar dam*)

Diarrhea is treated by boiling the leaves of one of the following plants and drinking the brew: *Teucrium* (*ja'adih*), *Salvia triloba* (*marmariyih*), *Artemisia judaica* (*b'aythiran*), *Eucalyptus bicolor* (*kina*), *Achillea fragrantissima* (*gisum*), *Artemisia herba-alba* (*shih*). The body may be massaged with lukewarm olive oil once a day for two days. A poultice (*lazgih*) prepared with a cloth soaked in powdered fenugreek mixed with lukewarm water may be placed on a child's abdomen, once a day for three consecutive days. The bulbs of *Cyperus rotundus* (*si'd, su'd*) may be boiled in water to be drunk once a day. The mother may wash a baby's body with this water, and sometimes she gives the child bulbs of nut grass to eat as a medicine and to strengthen him. The leaves and roots of *Lycium shawi* (*'awsaj*) may be crushed and mixed with garlic, flour, and warm olive oil, to be eaten for three consecutive days. One tablespoon of pure honey may be taken three times a day for a week. Tea with lemon may be drunk three times a day for three consecutive days. Tea made with *Varthemia iphionoides* (*slimaniya*) may be drunk. Wheat bread may be eaten, or wheat grains soaked in water and the mixture drunk. In addition, pepper and spicy foods should be avoided.

The Bedouin of Southern Sinai (Levi 1978: 54) drink tea made from one of the following plants: *Varthemia montana* (*ihnaydih*), *Reaumuria negevensis* (*millih*), and the fruit of carob, *Ceratonia siliqua* (*kharrub*). They also consume onion soup, rinds of pomegranate, and up to forty other plants. The Bedouin of the Negev and Sinai (Bailey and Danin 1981: 145–62) drink tea made from *Frankenia* (*millihy*). The Bedouin of the Negev (Dafni and Dafni 1975: 236) drink *Artemisia herba-alba* (*shih*), eat the fruit of *Punica granatum* (*rumman*) early in the morning on an empty stomach, or drink tea prepared from the leaves of *Rhus coriaria* (*summag*). Ben-Assa (1974: 73–76) reports that the Bedouin women in the Negev believe that the milk of a nursing mother who is pregnant is harmful and causes diarrhea in her baby.

Almi (2003: 27) reports that the Bedouin in the Negev who live in tribal villages "un-recognized" by the Israeli authorities and are not connected to running water bring water to their settlements in containers/mobile tankers, which are stored in the yards outside the homes. Algae grow in the plastic containers, and rust develops in the metal ones. In both cases, this provides an ideal environment for the growth of fungi and bacteria, as well as discoloration of the water and alteration of its taste (Almi 2003: 27), causing diarrhea, dehydration, and stomach infections. A variety of organisms can infect drinking water, including parasites such as amoebae, bacteria such as salmonella or shigella, and viruses such as rota. Peripheral measures can be effective only for a short period, during a crisis in the water supply, and not on a long-term basis.[22] Figures for the hospitalization of children at Soroka Medical Center confirm that these dangers are not abstract. In August each year, the hottest of the summer months, when the "diarrhea plague" erupts, some 16,000 Bedouin children are hospitalized, compared to 5,000 Jewish children.[23] Thus, some 80 percent of children hospitalized with diarrhea and intestinal infections are Bedouin, although the Bedouins constitute just 25 percent of the total population of the region (Almi 2003: 28). The relatively high rates of intestinal infections among children in the Bedouin population are a direct result of their living conditions—their harsh ways of life, close proximity to animals, crowded quarters, the use of water from unclean water sources, and improper nutrition (Israel State Comptroller 2001: Paragraph 421).

Dislocated Hip (*fakkit al-wirk*)

Hip dislocation is treated by placing the patient on the back of a donkey, which must be sated with barley seeds but very thirsty. A trough of water is placed in front for it to drink. The belly of the donkey slowly fills with water and enlarges the distance between the patient's legs, until a sound like something broken is heard, which means that the dislocated hip has returned to its original place. The patient should dismount from the donkey and walk carefully. According to Shinnawi (1982) the Bedouin of the Negev make burns around the hip using a needle or *Phagnalon rupestre* (*gadih*) to treat hip dislocation.

Disinfection (*ta'gim*)

The Bedouin in the Negev and Jordan use vinegar (*khall*) as a disinfectant for wounds. They also put tablespoon of vinegar in a cup of water and drink it to treat bowels after diarrhea, stomach disorders, or flatulence.

Dizziness (*dukha, dawkha, pl. dwakh*)

Treatments for dizziness include smelling hyssop or *Pituranthos tortuosus* (*zagguh*), *Foeniculum vulgare* (*shawmar*), or the seeds of black cumin; breathing fresh air and pouring cold water on the head; and drinking tea with lemon or mint. The Bedouin of Southern Sinai (Levi 1978: 60) cut onions and allow the patient to smell them. The Bedouin of Galilee (Hilf 1985) eat crushed seeds of *Coriandrum sativum* (*kusbara*) mixed with honey before breakfast.

Dysentery (*maghabut*)

Treatments for dysentery include drinking a glass of water in which the leaves of the *Eucalyptus globulus* (*kina, keinia*) have been boiled or in which the leaves of the *mudar* plant (Calotropis procera [*'ushur*]) have been soaked three times a day for a week, drinking a glass of water in which the bulbs of *Cyperus rotundus* (*si'd, su'd*) have been boiled three times a day for a week, drinking water in which the leaves of *Achillea santolina* have been boiled, drinking sour milk in which a small quantity of catechu bark (*Acacia catechu* [*kad hindi*]) has been ground and mixed early in the morning for three days, administering a spoonful of bitter coffee mixed with one quarter-spoonful of white lead (*isbidajih*) (not toxic in small quantities) to children as an early morning drink for three days, or drinking a glass of water mixed with a half-spoonful of chebulic myrobalan (*Terminalia chebula* [*sha'ir hindi*]). The Bedouin of Galilee (Hilf 1985) boil the dried leaves (*karmish, girmish*) and gum/resin (*'ilk*) of *Pistacia lentiscus* (*butum*) with seeds of *Mentha,* and drink before meals every day for one week. Other treatments include cauterization with a long red-hot needle around the navel and cauterization in the shape of an X on the lowest vertebra. Interestingly, the Rwala (Musil 1928: 478) believed that melted butter was liked by everyone, but should not be the exclusive food, as it would cause death from dysentery.

Ear Infection/Earache (*waja' adhan*)

Treatments for ear infections include ear drops prepared from onion squeezed in a glass of olive oil and administered twice a day for one week. Fresh breast milk is used as a disinfectant for ear infections in babies; water is mixed with table salt, onion, and mother's milk and used as ear drops. Ear-shaped seashells called *idhynih* are hung on the child's cap. Ear drops are prepared from leaves of *Artemisia judaica* (*b'aythiran*) and *Achillea fragrantissima* (*gisum*) or by heating the leaves and fruit (*nabag*) of Christ's thorn (*Ziziphus spina christi* [*sidrih*]) in a glass of olive oil. Ben-Assa (1964: 452) reported that in the early 1960s the Negev Bedouin often suffered from inner ear infections. Shinnawi (1982) noted that Negev Bedouin used onion boiled with olive oil as ear drops. Levi (1978: 67, 1987: 301) reported that the Bedouin of Southern Sinai used ear drops made from salty water, onion, and mother's milk (see above) or hung a special bead on the patient's neck/chest. The Bedouin of Galilee (Hilf 1985) treated ear infections or pain by dropping a tincture produced by boiling radish seeds in water with liquids taken from the fresh kidneys of domestic animals.

Edema (*zalal*)

Edema, a swelling that results from the accumulation of an excessive amount of fluid in cells or intercellular tissues, is treated by boiling crushed roots of *Anchusa strigosa* (*ihmim*) in water, soaking a handkerchief with the tincture and wrapping the affected area once a day for one week. The area may also be rubbed with oil of black cumin. Another treatment consists of soaking leaves of *Ruta chalepensis* (*fayjan*) in lukewarm water, drinking the infusion, and washing the body with it.

According to Shinnawi (1982), the Negev Bedouin drink and wash the body or create a sauna using *Peganum* (*harjal*), *Achillea fragrantissima* (*gisum*), and *Matricaria aurea* (*babunaj, rabil*) boiled in water. The Bedouin of Galilee (Hilf 1985) boil *Coridothymus capitatus* (*zahayfy*) in water and wash the body with it and avoid eating salted food.

Epilepsy (*ṣara', sara', shawka*)

The Bedouin believe that a spirit or a jinni that has entered the body causes epilepsy. The Rwala (Musil 1928: 634) call the moaning and cries of an epileptic or a demented person *tefu'i*. Islamic law has its own perspective on epileptic people (Rispler-Chaim 1996: 90–106; al-Jawziyya 1998: 46–50). Treatments include making a burn on the patient's forehead, the center of the head, and the nape of the neck (*'ar'ur*), hanging an amulet on the patient's body, preventing the patient from carrying out hard work or any work that creates tension, and boiling the leaves of *Paeonia* (*'ud al-salib*) and Jericho rose (*kaf maryam/kaf al-rahaman*) in water for the patient to drink.

Evil Eye (*nafs*)

To protect against the evil eye,[24] an "evil eye bead" (*kharazat nafs*) is hung on the baby, child, or adult. It is customary to hang blue beads (*kushshash*) above the head of a child, attached to the child's headdress or as part of a necklace. Usually it is the mother or the grandmother of the child who prepares these beads and hangs them while reciting verses from the Quran and other blessings. Some women put alum (*shabbih*) in the beads, so that if the evil eye does appear, it will attack the *shabbih* and grind it to a powder instead of harming the infant. The blue beads with alum inside are called *kushshash* due to the shape of the beads which are tied with thread that resembles the legs of an infant and which are said to hit or kick the evil eye.

When someone has been afflicted by the evil eye, the ceremony of freeing that person from the spell (*tkhiffif*) is usually performed by a grandmother or a woman healer, although any suitable (righteous) man or woman can inherit or be taught the healing profession. There are many variations of this ceremony, but I will describe the most common one. The healer (in this ceremony, usually a woman) takes three pieces of alum, symbolizing man, woman, and the jinni in her right hand, and swings them around the head of the affected person (*manfous,'ardhan*) several times. She beseeches Allah and the prophets to heal the victim, condemning the evil eye and ordering it in the name of Allah and His prophets to leave the person's body without harming it. She reads verses from the Quran (2:255; 113:1–5; 114:1–6) and again entreats the evil eye in the name of Allah and His prophets to leave. The healer places the pieces of alum in the embers of the fire burning in the tent, where they crackle and change shape. This change of form is believed to have magical meaning, and the healer removes the pieces of alum from the embers and examines their shape to determine whether the evil eye comes from a man, a woman, or a jinni. A skilled healer can tell the victim the precise source of the evil eye. The healer then grinds the three pieces of alum in her hand and smears the powder on the patient's forehead (*saddanih*), right elbow (*marfag, kou'*), left ankle (*rummanih*), left elbow, and right ankle, in that order. She mixes the remaining powder with salt, flour, and water to form a paste (*'ajinih*), which she throws behind the tent saying, "O, evil eye, go away" (*u'gub ya sharr*). The healer ties a scarf around the patient's forehead, gives him a glass of hot tea to drink, and makes him lie down until he recovers.

The healer may experience some of the symptoms felt by the patient, such as yawning, tearing eyes, choking, and hoarseness. These are signs that the evil eye is responding to the healer's entreaties and threats and is leaving the patient's body through the healer. She is protected from harm by her holiness and by the angels and saints who guard her during the ceremony, as she utters the names of Allah and His prophets and saints and verses from the Quran.

According to the Prophet Medicine, 'Aisha said regarding *ruqya*: "The Prophet ordered me or someone else to do *ruqya,* if there was danger, from an evil eye." Another saying, related by Um Salama, was that the Prophet saw in her house a girl whose face had a black spot. He said: "She is under the influence of an evil eye, so treat her with a *ruqya*" (al-Bukhari 1974: 426).

If the source of the evil eye has been identified as human, another ceremony called "healing by smoke" (*ktur*) is performed in addition to or instead of the above ceremony. A small piece of material (*'alag*) or a thread[25] is taken/stolen from the suspected person's clothing without his knowledge and burned. The smoke is allowed to enter the nostrils and eyes of the afflicted person.

Beads, stones, and bones may also be used to thwart the evil eye. The evil eye may be driven from a child, especially a boy, by attaching special beads to his bonnet (*augayih*), including blue beads containing alum (*shabbih*) that signify the removal of the evil eye. One of these beads, called (*nafs*), guards against the evil eye. Other measures used against the evil eye include hanging a small flint-stone or the tooth of a hyena around the neck or on the head of the victim. The Bedouin say: "Use flintstone against the [evil] eyes of women" (*as-sowwan fi 'uyun an-niswa*) (Bailey 2004: 96).

In Palestine (Hareuveni 1930: 122) *Ruta chalepensis* (*ruta, fayjan, sadhab*) was used to prevent the evil eye. The Bedouin of Southern Sinai (Levi 1978: 52) hang branches of *Eucalyptus bicolor* (*keina, kina*) on their tents or place leads with water in cups; the Bedouin of Galilee (Hilf 1985) read phrases from the Quran or hang alum or blue beads on the patient's body.

The Bedouin of the Negev (al-'Aref 1933: 247) borrow salt and flour from a pious widow, spread it on the fire or the hearth, and let the patient inhale this smoke. Alternatively, a healer/dervish from the Hasanat bin Sabbah tribe (of the Jbarat/Jubarat clan) or from al-'Aayaidih (of the al-Sawarkih clan) spits in the face of the one who is afflicted with the evil eye. It should be noted that the saliva of a man treats men, the saliva of a woman treats women, boys treat boys, and girls treat girls. Alternatively, as mentioned above, healing by smoke (*ktur*) is performed or lead in hot water is used. The Negev Bedouin also use *ktur,* read phrases from the Quran, smear black soot (*sawad saj*) from the bottom of the the metal plate used to bake bread on the victim's forehead, or hang blue beads or a gold coin in the case of babies (Abu-Khusa (1979: 106–11). Pinczuk (1994) reported that Negev Bedouin women treated babies with *ktur* as mentioned above, or with incense (*bakhkhur*) on Mondays and Thursdays, and allowed children who were thought to be afflicted with the evil eye to inhale the smoke. Among the Rwala (Musil 1928: 409), small sea shells with red, white, and green spots, called *kharazat al-nafs,* or a pair of marbles are recommended for protection against the evil eye.

Some of the Bedouin of Northern Sinai and the Negev, as well as those of the Gaza Strip, accompany the exorcism of the evil eye with drumming on special drums throughout the night while reciting Quran verses and other sayings. The person affected by the jinni sits near a fire, which emits a scent of incense. The drum used by the exorcist is called a *tar.*[26] This ceremony is practiced by special healers on certain days of the week (Sheikh 'Aid ['Ayd] al-'Aamreh al-'Hamadat, personal communication, 1976). The drum must not be touched during the day, when the jinn surround it, and may be played only at night. Only those affected by the evil eye are allowed to participate in this ceremony. Men are treated separately from women, and male and female healers can treat patients of either gender. In pre-Islamic Central Asian Turkey, lead was used to draw out evil spirits from patients (Bayat 2002: 55).

Facial Paralysis[27] (*abu al-wjouh,* face: *wijih*)

The following case study illustrates the treatment of this condition. A sixty-year-old man, married and father of six children, felt pains in his head and ears, especially the left ear and the left side of the head. After two days of severe pain and liquid draining from the ear, he was admitted to Soroka Medical Center in Beer-Sheba for ten days. During this time, a facial nerve paralysis developed and the patient was discharged. Three days later, he visited a friend in Hebron, a healer, who gave him a facial massage and wrapped a scarf around his head and under his chin. The man returned home and went back for repeated treatments, three times a day. The folk healer claimed to have found a "hard" nerve under the chin, which softened completely during the massage. The head pains and earaches vanished, but the facial expression did not return to normal. The patient then visited another friend in Hebron, who took him to a dervish (*darwish*). Every day for a week the dervish came to the friend's house to treat the patient. He claimed the man was afflicted because of nervous strain, and had undergone crises that had brought on the facial paralysis; he could not exclude the possible influence of the devil. The patient's family confirmed the nervous strain and crises. The dervish brought a porcelain dish, wrote secret verses inside it with red ink and filled it with hot water. He dipped his hands in this water and massaged the patient's face, taking one of the man's shoes[28] and lightly stroking his face with it; he then spat on the patient's face, read verses from the Quran and other verses, the meaning of which only he knew. Then he took the dish with the remaining water, held it near the patient's eyes and told him to stare into it for half an hour without moving his eyes or head. This treatment was repeated twice a day for a week, in the morning before eating or drinking and at dusk, in a relatively warm, dark room. The patient was instructed to dress warmly to make him perspire, and sometimes a charcoal brazier was placed in the room. The patient was forbidden to talk or receive guests, with the exception of one of his sons. At the end of the week, his facial expression had improved markedly, but was not yet completely normal. He was sent home to rest with an amulet to hang on his neck, and told that the paralysis would disappear in three months. While under the dervish's treatment, the patient also sought the help of other folk healers. The last one ordered him to do the following: "Go home and go into seclusion (*hijbih*) in a small room for forty days, and receive no guests except someone from your family." His wife was to bring him food and he was not to leave the warm room except at night to go to the bathroom. He was to avoid looking at dogs or cats. The healer read the patient several verses from the Quran and other sources and sent him home. The patient recovered towards the end of the period of seclusion and the facial paralysis practically disappeared.

Among the Rwala Bedouin (Musil 1928: 667) *aba wagh,* which is stiffness of some part of the face, is treated by burning the corners of the mouth and inserting three lead balls under the skin of the part of the face affected, which is then covered with a red cloth. Sometimes, the healer beats a little drum to treat paralyzed women (Musil 1928: 403). The Lebanese used seeds of anise (*Pimpinella anisum*/*Anisum vulgare* [*yansun*]) to treat spasms (Philips 1958: 8).

Fainting Baby (*fahham, ghimi, ghamyan*)

A child who faints or nearly loses consciousness from laughing or crying is given milk mixed with *Paeonia coriacea* (*'ud al-salib*) once a day for a week. A baby who is born blue is given onions to smell, *Pituranthos tortuosus* (*zaqquh, zagguh*), *Foeniculum vulgare* (*shawmar*), or *Coridothymus capitatus* (*zahayfy*).

Fertility/Infertility (*haml/'agir*)/Impotence

Reproduction, particularly of male offspring, is important in all Middle Eastern societies. A common Bedouin saying (Bailey 2004: 414) claims: "The man with male children is not dead". (*Illi 'aggab ma mat—ghayr illi 'igbih banat*). Similarly, in Palestine, according to Granqvist (1947: 29) he who has sons born to him does not die. According to Islam, fertility, infertility, and the delivery of a boy or a girl are in the hands of Allah (Quran 42: 49–50).

Infertility is a global health issue that affects approximately 80 million of people, more than half whom are Muslims, worldwide (Serour 1992). Despite the high prevalence of male infertility, infertility is usually considered to be a female problem (Van Balen and Inhorn 2001: 3–32). Thus, the role of male infertility is vastly underappreciated and even hidden in many societies (Inhorn 2003: 6). Childlessness in Middle Eastern society may not be politely concealed and it is often a source of pain and gossip. Female infertility may lead to divorce, polygamous marriage, social isolation, loneliness, and despair (Inhorn 1996). During the last ten years, Inhorn (2012) found through ethnographic research that, contrary to popular belief, infertility is more commonly found in men than women among couples in childless Middle Eastern marriages. Inhorn documents the marital, moral, and material commitments of couples undergoing assisted reproduction, revealing how new technologies are transforming their lives and religious sensibilities. Moreover, she looks at the changing manhood of husbands who undertake transnational "egg quests"—set against the backdrop of war and economic uncertainty—out of devotion to the infertile wives they love.

Customs and cures surrounding infertility vary from place to place in the Middle East. Among the Rwala (Musil 1928: 231), the man must not touch the woman for from three to five days during her monthly period and not for forty days after the birth of a child. If a man wants to beget a boy, he must have intercourse with his wife on Thursday or Friday nights. In Palestine, the pool of Siloan and the bath of *Sitti Mariam* (Virgin Mary) are renowned for their help in cases of infertility in women (Canaan 1920–1921: 166). In Arabia (Dickson 1949: 162), both men and women are required to bathe after sexual intercourse. During her monthly period, a woman is forbidden to have intercourse with her husband for a full seven days. In Arabia (Dickson 1949: 191) the Birzan tribe, "having been blessed by the Prophet Muhammad himself for their kindness and hospitality, [was] rewarded by being told that even their blood was blessed—hence it is believed that to drink a Birzani's blood will cure a man of impotence, cause an infertile woman to conceive, and counter the poison of a mad dog."[29]

In Bedouin society, an infertile woman was traditionally considered a source of harm for the children of others due to the possibity of her casting an evil eye because of envy, and was thus she avoided by fertile women, who feared for the own children (Abu-Rabia 2005e: 241–54). Infertile women face a sad life, certain that their husbands will, at the very least, take second wives (Abu-Lughod 1988: 125–26). In Bedouin society, as in other Middle Eastern societies, infertility in a woman can lead to polygamy or even divorce (Abu-Rabia 2005e: 241–54).[30]

Fever (*hamm, skhounih*)

Treatments include, especially in the case of a baby, washing the patient in two liters of water boiled with half a kilogram of barley; mixing the gall of a hyena with water and drinking once a day; mixing tamarind (*Tamarindus indica* [*tamr hindi*]) in a glass of water with a tablespoon of crystalline sugar and drinking it; and boiling the bulbs of *Cyperus rotundus* (*su'd, si'd, habb al-zulum*) in water and drinking the mixture. The body is washed with the rest of the liquid. Eating the bulbs is a good treatment for fever. Alternatively, the body is washed in *Achillea fragrantissima* (*gisum*); *Artemisia judaica* (*ba'aythran*), *Achillea fragrantissima* (*gisum*) and *Coridothymus capitatus* (*zahayfy*) are boiled in water and the body is washed with this liquid twice a day. The Bedouin of Southern Sinai (Levi 1978: 53–54) use crushed wheat seeds (*jirishih*), leaves of *Artemisia herba-alba* (*shih*), and leaves of *Eucalyptus bicolor* (*keina, kina*). Alternatively, they drink a soup made from rock rabbit (*Procavia capensis hyrax* [*wabr*]),[31] smell smoke from the burnt flesh of bat (*khaffash, watwat*), or make burns on both sides of the temples (*sudgh*).The Bedouin of the Negev and Sinai (Bailey and Danin 1981: 150–158) use *Achillea fragrantissima* (*gisum*), *Varthemia iphionoides* (*slimaniya, ktilih*), and *Haplophyllum tuberculatum* (*imjenina*). Negev Bedouin (Dafni and Dafni 1975: 234) also wash the body with water in which leaves of *Achillea fragrantissima* (*gisum*) have been boiled. The Bedouin of the Syrian Desert dissolve a hyena's bile/gall bladder in water to drink as a treatment for fever. They also use the hyena's teeth as a necklace to protect their children from certain illnesses (Jabbur 1995: 89). According to the Prophet Medicine, fever is from the heat of Hell, so it is cooled with water (al-

Bukhari 1974: 416). Indeed, medication works through its opposite (*dawa' al-shay' bi-didihi*).

Flatulence (*nfakh, infakh*)

Treatments for flatulence include tea made with *Mentha longifolia* (*na'na'*), *Salvia fruticosa/triloba* (*marmarya*), *Coridothymus capitatus* (*zahayfy*), or *Teucrium polium* (*ja'adih*). *Ammi visnage* (*khall, khillih*) is drunk early in the morning and before bed. Broad beans (*Vicia faba L./Faba vulgaris* [*ful mdammis/foul, fool*]), chickpeas (Cicer arietinum [*hummus*]), and *falafil* made from chickpeas, normally a staple, are avoided for one week.

Foot/Knee Sprain (*fakkit rukba rijil*)

A one-and-a-half year old girl began to limp after falling. She was taken to her paternal grandmother, who assumed it was a sprained knee and massaged it. There was no improvement, and a week later she was taken to a physician in Beer-Sheva who examined her, x-rayed the knee, and referred her to an orthopedic clinic. She was examined again a week later, found to have no pathological signs, and sent home without treatment. The girl continued to limp and her mother and grandmother began to worry. The grandmother examined her again, washed her leg in lukewarm soapy water and massaged the entire leg. She then placed an egg yolk in a piece of cloth and bandaged the girl's knee with it. The child rested the leg for two days, and after a week the limp disappeared. Other treatments include making burns around the knee with a small needle and complete rest for one week.

The Bedouin of the Negev (Shinnawi 1982) mix egg yolk with small pieces of soap (*sabun Nabilsi*), wrap this paste in a rag and apply it as a poultice (*lazgih*). In cases of foot sprain, burns are made around the sprained area. The Bedouin in Southern Sinai (Levi 1978: 75, 1987: 305) use a tincture produced from *Retama raetam* (*ratam*), onion, and *Mentha.* The Bedouin of Galilee (Hilf 1985) recommend burns on the belly and complete rest.

Forty-Fold Medicine (*dawa'al-arba'yn*)

The medicine of "Forty" is composed of forty plants. It is well known and used by the Bedouin and *fallahin* populations. It used for most ailments: fear, dread, fertility problems, sexual loss and impotency, nocturnal enuresis, joint pains, rheumatism, intestinal diseases, bronchitis, heart diseases, influenza, colds, and more.

Frozen Shoulder/Shoulder Pain (*waja' kitif*)

In adults who suffer from shoulder pain and cannot work with their hands due to cold stroke, or adults with back and shoulder pains during work or when perspiring, the treatment consists of applying olive oil to the patient's shoulder and exposing it to the hot sun. Usually, small blisters appear on the shoulder and these are pierced with a needle heated over a flame. The shoulder is dried, kept warm, and the patient rests for two weeks. Shoulder pain that results from falling from a donkey, camel, or horse is treated by burns on the shoulder, light massage with lukewarm olive oil, and complete rest. According to Shinnawi (1982), the Bedouin of the Negev also treat this shoulder pain with burns on the affected shoulder.

Hair Loss/Dandruff/Balding (*tasagut sha'r, gishrih, sala'*)

The meat and fat of the lizard *Varanus griseus* (*waral*) is applied to the hair as a remedy for balding, hair loss, and dandruff (*gishrih*), and to make the hair shine. The hair may be washed with an infusion made by boiling *Matricaria aurea* (*rabil*) in water. In cases of balding (*sala'*), table salt is mixed with lemon and garlic and the head is rinsed with it. The hair may be washed with the urine of livestock or camels. Levi (1978: 65, 1987: 300) found that the Bedouin of Southern Sinai boil *Ochradenus baccatus* (*gurdhi*), *Alcea setosa* (*khutmiyya*), sap from fig leaves, and *Cleome chrysantha* (*samwih*) and massage the head with this concoction. Hilf (1985) found that the Bedouin of Galilee make small incisions in the scalp and rinse them with a tincture made of crushed garlic and table salt to encourage hair growth. Abu-Khusa (1979: 106–11) found that the Bedouin of the Negev treat boils or abscess (*habat*) on the head by washing the head with water in which leaves of *Malva sylvestris* (*khubbayzih*) have been boiled. To treat baldness, they rinse the head with a mixture of crushed garlic and lemon juice. In Arabia (Dickson 1949: 157) women use camel urine to wash their hair to kill head lice. They also use a mixture of herbs (*rshush*), the leaves of *Trigonella stellata* (*nafal*), or henna.

Hand-Wrist Pain (*waja' rusgh iyd*)

Treatments include massaging the affected area with lukewarm olive oil or mixing egg yolk with flour and wrapping it as a poultice around the wrist for two weeks. According to Shinnawi (1982), the Bedouin of the Negev make a burn with a small needle on the painful spot.

Headaches (*waja' ras*)

Treatments include drinking infusions of mint, sage, hyssop, *Pituranthos tortuosus* (*zagguh*), or *Achillea fragrantissima* (*gisum*). Two tablespoons of crushed *Anchusa strigosa* (*ihmim*) root are added to a glass of water, wrapped in a piece of cloth and bandaged on the forehead for half an hour. A poultice of soft eggs may be placed on the aching part of the head for a day or two. The treatment is repeated if the headache persists. Porridge is made from henna and a small amount of water and placed on the head in the evening as a poultice. (This red dye is extracted from the leaves and stems of the henna plant, *Lawsonia inermis*). Five-millimeter-thick rounds of peeled raw potato (*batata*) are placed on the forehead and secured with a scarf. The slices are changed every five to ten minutes, until the headache disappears. Tea with lemon is drunk three to five times a day. A piece of lead is melted in a receptacle, a container is held above the patient's head, and the liquid lead is poured into it. The resulting crackling noise drives out the headache, especially if it is believed to have been caused by the evil eye or evil spirits. Incense is burned at four points around the patient during the night. An amulet of verses from the Quran is tied around the patient's head.

In Palestine (Hareuveni 1930: 118) they would crush the dried seeds of *Hyoscyamus* (*sakaran*), mix them with flour and water, put the paste in a kercheif (*mandil*) and wrap it round the head for one to two hours. Alternatively, the head could be wrapped in a kerchief with no medicine. The Bedouin of the Negev (Shinnawi 1982) make burns around the neck or on the temple. The Bedouin of Southern Sinai (Levi 1978: 54, 1987: 295) use an extract of *Haplophyllum tuberculatum* (*imjenina*) or *Citrullus colocynthis* (*handhal*) as nose drops to treat headache Sinai (Bailey and Danin 1981: 145–62). Other treatments consist of smelling and inhaling smoke from the smoldering leaves of *Cleome chrysantha* (*samwih*) or wrapping the head in a kerchief.

The Bedouin of the Negev (al-'Aref 1933: 243) treat headache by practicing blood-letting (*hijama*), making incisions on both temples (*sudgh*). They treat migraine by applying tattoo (*washm*) marks between the eyes and the ears and on the forehead. The tattoo is made of the pounded leaves and roots of *Lycium shawi* (*'awsaj*) and is inserted with a small needle. Sometimes an incision is made in the head or the skull[32] for bloodletting, or the head is cauterized.

Heartburn/Sourness (*humudha, hmudha, hazzaz*)

Treatments for heartburn include drinking livestock or camel's milk, eating watermelon seeds and drinking water, and drinking a tea prepared from sage and mint or hyssop. The Bedouin of Southern Sinai (Levi 1978: 58) soak the following plants and drink the infusion as a remedy for heartburn: the leaves of *Gymnocarpos decander* (*jarad*), the fruit of *Ceratonia siliqua* (*kharrub*), and corn kernels (Zea mays [*dhrah*]).

Heart Pain (*waja' galb*)

Treatments for heart pain include burning bulbs of *Urginea maritima* (*halluf, 'Unsol, bussayl*) or dried seeds of *Hyoscyamus aureus* (*sakaran*) on a hearth and inhaling the smoke twice a day for one to two weeks. It is also possible to drink an infusion of *Coridothymus capitatus* (*zahayfy*) leaves or to rub the chest with a tincture produced from the roots of asphodel, twice a week, cupping the chest once. The Bedouin of Southern Sinai (Levi 1978: 69) drink tea made from *Solenostemma argel* (*arghel*), *Rhus tripartita* (*'irn*), *Artemisia herba-alba* (*shih*), *Ziziphus spina-christi* (*sidrih*), or *Capparis cartilaginea* (*lassaf, lussayf*). Alternatively, they inhale the smoke of *Hyoscyamus boveanus* (*sakaran*) or make burns on the chest. The Bedouin of the Negev (Abu-Khusa 1979: 106–11) eat honey to strengthen the heart. Ben-Assa (1961: 211–12, 450–53) found few patients with hypertension or diabetes and none with ischemic heart disease among the Bedouin of the Negev. He (1974: 73–76) points out that in the early 1970s, Bedouins complained of shortness of breath (dyspnea [*dhig nafas*]) as a result of their participation in modern life and the need to complete certain work in limited time, which caused some of them to develop cases of myocardial infarction. A decade later, the incidence of coronary heart disease had begun to rise in the Negev Bedouin population (Kain 1985; Zamir 1972). Data from the years 1994–1998 show an increase in hospitalization rates due to myocardial infarction among Bedouins of the Negev, from 7.47 to 8.14 (per 1000 population). In the same period, the rates in the neighboring Jewish towns dropped from 7.4 to 5.6 (per 1000 population). The rate of hospitalization due to stroke among Bedouins increased from 5.34 to 5.90, and decreased from 4.31 to 2.75 in the Jewish towns (Weitzman and Rosen 2001). Tamir et al. note that

> considering the coronary heart disease 'epidemic' and the increasing stroke incidence among the Bedouin of the Negev in the last 30 years, as compared with a decrease in morbidity and mortality from those diseases in the Jewish population, there is an urgent need to redirect research resources in order to establish a culturally and economically sensitive program to improve primary prevention of cardiovascular diseases among the Bedouin in the Negev. (Tamir et al. 2007: 655)

Hemiplegia (*khram/khurm*)

The patient's body is massaged with a tincture prepared from crushed seeds of black cumin, crushed garlic, and olive oil. The patient is seated in a place protected from wind in the early morning, when the sun's rays come into contact with his body. After half an hour, pustules will appear on his upper body. These must be lanced and cleaned.

The body is washed in water from boiled leaves of *Achillea fragrantissima* (*gaysum, qisum*) and *Pituranthos tortuosus* (*zaqquh, zagguh*). The Bedouin of the Negev crush garlic with olive oil and massage the blisters (Shinnawi 1982). The Bedouin of Galilee rub the blisters with a mixture of garlic and salt and lance them with a needle (*khram, khurm al-ibrih*) (Hilf 1985).

Hernia (*fatig, maftug, ba'j, mab'uj*)

Burns are made around the hernia, followed by ten days of complete rest. Alternatively, burns are made round the spot using *Phagnalon rupestre* (*gadih*) (Shinnawi 1982). The Bedouin of Galilee (Hilf 1985) spread a mixture of egg yolk and soap on the hernia for three days or a week.

High Blood Pressure (*dhaght damm*)

High blood pressure is treated with complete rest for the patient. An infusion made from the boiled leaves of *Micromeria fruticosa* (*gurnia*), sage, and seeds of fenugreek (*hilbih*) is drunk. The patient's forehead may be rubbed each morning with oil of black cumin.

Impetigo (*gubah, garha*)

Treatments include rubbing the affected areas with olive oil mixed with table salt, cauterizing the area around the impetigo, rubbing the skin with boiled leaves of *Ballota undulata* (*ghassih*) mixed with olive oil twice a week, and rubbing the affected area with mother's milk or the milk of a black goat once a day. The Negev Bedouin (Dafni and Dafni 1975: 237) rub the face with the green leaves of *Thymelaea hirsuta* (*mitnan*). Shinnawi (1982) found that the Bedouin of the Negev treat impetigo with *Cleome droserifolia* (*samwih*) and olive oil.

The Bedouin of Galilee (Hilf 1985) roast wheat grains in a pan, pound them, and smear the face of the patient with the paste. In Palestine (Hareuveni 1930: 123), Arabs treated *gubah* by squeezing *Asphodelus microcarpus* (*swai*) on the face.

Impurity Bead (*kharazat al-kbass*)

This bead is used to counteract the tension and stress of a woman who is unable to conceive (*makbusih*) after having one or more children. It is also a preventive measure against a baby becoming frail (*makbus*) and developing reddish-yellow eyes and yellow skin. A baby can develop these symptoms if (1) the mother is visited during or immediately after giving birth by another new mother who delivered during the previous forty days and is therefore impure; (2) the mother of a newborn baby is visited by a menstruating woman; or (3) the new mother is visited by a woman who has had an abortion or miscarriage during the previous forty days. The mother puts the impurity bead in an earthen jar (*ibrig*) with water and washes with this water after bathing three times, on a Sunday, a Wednesday, and the following Sunday.

The impurity bead is hung on the baby as for curative and preventative medical purposes. According to Bailey (1991: 118), brides traditionally have their hands stained with henna as an antidote to *kabsa,* as this condition is thought to be caused by an encounter with a menstruating woman. A bride "immunizes" herself by staining parts of her body with henna, which resembles blood. This resemblance constitutes the antidote to the ill effect of menstrual blood. According to Bailey (1982: 80), if a woman is visited after childbirth by a menstruating woman, she may become barren (*makbusih kabsih*).[33] In order to cure *makbusih,* each of seven families slaughters an animal (livestock), mixes the blood of the seven sacrifices (*saba' al-dhahya*) with water, and bathes the afflicted woman (*makbusih*) with this liquid on seven consecutive mornings (Bailey 1982: 83).

Certain beads, coins, and shells such as cowries are assigned magic, symbolic, and healing qualities, according to Bedouin belief (Abu-Rabia 1999a; Goren 1994: 294–98; Levi 1987). Bedouin women adorn their hair with strings of cowrie (couri) shells called *wada'*. From the side, with its opening facing outwards, the cowrie resembles a woman's vagina, while the color of the cowrie is white, as is a man's sperm, symbolizing fertility. When a woman is seen wearing the cowrie string, it means she is at the peak of her fertility. If a Bedouin woman does not have access to such shells, she will collect the bulbs of the *Colchicum* (*wada'*) as she herds her livestock. The bulbs of the *wada',* incidentally, are used as a medicine to treat sexual diseases (for both men and women), mainly among the pastoral nomadic Bedouin in the Middle East. According to Shinar (1982: 29–42), the colors and shapes of cowrie and certain other seashells are claimed to have magic significance.

In this context it is worth noting that the Mediterranean goddess Venus, in one of her phases, in her personification as a pearl, is lifted from the sea seated on a seashell. The Romans and Greeks wore pearls to win the favor of this goddess. Ancient and medieval writers attributed sexual qualities to gems and precious stones; Theophrast (a Greek writer) claimed that certain gems had the capacity to produce offspring (Fielding 1945: 55–57). Frazer notes:

> While a general magical efficacy may be supposed to reside in all stones by reason of their common properties of weight and solidity, special magical virtues are attributed to particular stones, or kinds of stone, in accordance with their individual or specific qualities of shape and color. The stones destined to multiply cattle had the shape of sheep. The ancient set great store on the magical qualities of precious stones; indeed it has been maintained, with great show of reason that such stones were used as amulets long before they were worn as mere ornaments. (Frazer 1962: 258)

Inducing Lactation[34]/Breastfeeding[35] (*ziadit halib*)

Bedouin women in the Negev and Sinai customarily smear sugar on their nipples to encourage the baby to breastfeed. Drinking large amounts of animal milk and water are linked to milk production. Bedouin use herbs that catalyze milk production, boiling the plants and drinking the infusion as tea. The Bedouin eat plants and animals (and animal products) in order to acquire certain desirable qualities with which they believe them to be endowed. Plants or animal can infect the person, just as much as the person can infect the plant, according to the principle of homeopathic magic. To increase milk supply the following methods are used: crushing caraway seeds (*Carum carvi L.* [*Karawiya*]), boiling them in water, and drinking the infusion. (This is also considered a good medicine for colic); drinking a cup of water/milk into which a white sap resembling mother's milk is added. The sap is obtained by squeezing *Euphorbia* leaves (*lbina, ilbina, hulayba*);[36] eating the roots of the crowfoot (*Ranunculus asiaticus* [*shtur al-naqa*]), which resemble the nipples of the she-camel (Abu-Rabia 1983: 18) (the Bedouin believe it assists in conception and increases the amount of milk in the breast); eating bread or porridge made from oats (*Avena sterilis L.* [*khafour*]) (this is also purported to strengthen the bodies of nursing women after childbirth); soaking the leaves of *Matricaria chamomilla* (*rabil*) and mallow (*Malva sylvestris L.* [*khubbayzih*]), and the seeds of fenugreek in water and drinking the liquid; eating soup made with lentils (*'adas*) or carrots (*jazar*) in the evening; preparing a drink or soup from the following plants: *Ocimum basilicum* (*habaq*), *Urtica urens* (*qurrais*), wheat, barley, *Foeniculum vulgare* (*shawmar*), *Zizyphus spina-christi* (*sedrih*, or eating the fruit, *nabaq*), *Salvia fruticosa* (*marmariya*), *Trigonella foenum-graecum* (*hilbih*), or the fruits and leaves of *Ziziphus spina-christi* (*sidrih*). When the mother cannot breastfeed due to lack of milk, she gives her baby the milk of goats, sheep, she-camels, or mares mixed with water. Among the Bedouin of Southern Sinai (Levi 1997: 266) a woman who has just given birth but has no milk at the outset brings the baby to a wet-nurse for the first few days; afterwards, she nurses him herself; there are Bedouin women who breastfeed their baby boys up to three years. In case there is no milk, leaves of *Ziziphus spina-christi* (*sidrih*) are boiled in water and the infusion is drunk (Levi 1978: 3–29). The Bedouin women of the Negev (Abu-Khusa 1979: 106–11) hang a nursing-bead called *khrazat al-dirrih*[37] on their breasts in order to increase their milk supply. They also drink water with *Trigonella foenum-graecum* (*hilbih*).

Infected Hand or Finger (*tsammum iyd/ussba'*), Infected Hand Wound (*tasammum*)

An elderly woman told me that her hand swelled after she injured one of her fingers. A doctor prescribed an ointment that did not help. She heated a sewing needle in a fire, opened the wound, and soaked her hand in half a liter of warm water with a tablespoon of salt. She repeated this procedure several times until the pus drained out completely and the hand was free of infection.

In cases where the infection is in the whole body or a major part of the body, leaves of *Matricaria aurea* (*babunaj*) are soaked in lukewarm water and the infected areas are rinsed in this liquid. Leaves of *Artemisia herba-alba* (*shih*) are boiled in water and the infected area is rinsed with this liquid. The Bedouin of the Negev (Shinnawi 1982) boil *Cleome droserifolia* (*samwih*) in processed butter (*samnih*) or olive oil and rub the mixture onto the infected area. For chronic wounds, they crush the leaves of *Achillea fragrantissima* (*gisum*), *Artemisia herba-alba* (*shih*), or onion and spread them on the wound, or soak leaves of *Eucalyptus bicolor* (*keina, kina*) in water and wash the wound with the liquid. There are some methods to protect a baby from a wound, with a kind of vaccination. The mother incises the baby's arm and places seborrhea capitis/fetus sack/amnion there. This material is absorbed by the body and immunizes him from wounds and other infections. Alternatively, the mother puts some seborrhea capitis in a small leather bag and hangs it around her baby's neck. Among the Rwala (Musil 1928: 97), camel fat, known as *shaham,* is chopped and boiled into suet (found around the kidneys and used for cooking), called *makhlu'* or *widak.* In the kettle in which the fat is thus rendered, a sediment called *khali'* remains on the bottom. The *widak* is poured into a leather bag and kept for as long as three years. In the hot season, the Rwala prefer it to butter because it is cool. *Widak* is a good remedy for boils and suppurating wounds.

Infertility Treatments

If infertility is caused by a "closed womb" (*kabsih, makbusih*)[38] treatment is carried out by inserting a piece of cotton wool that has been dipped in a mixture of dried bile of rock rabbit (*Procavia capensis hyrax* [*wabr*])[39] and lukewarm olive oil into the womb. A "closed womb" may also be treated by boiling madder (*Rubia tinctorum* [*fuwwa*]), laurel (*Laurus nobilis* [*ghar*]), and aleppo rue (*Ruta chalepensis* [*fayjan*]) in a pot of water and allowing the steam to penetrate the female sexual organs. Another treatment consists of mixing a tablespoon of bicarbonate of soda (*karabunih*) in water and washing the genitals. This is good for infertility among women and for general hygiene.

For a woman whose genitals have been affected by "cold inflammation" (*iltihab bard, mariuha* [*rih*]) after giving birth, one spoonful of a mixture of *Alpinia officinarum* (*khoulunjan*), *Hibiscus cannabinus* (*juljul, tiyl*), *Terminalia chebula* (*ihlilag kabuli, sha'ir hindi*), aniseed (*Pimpinella anisum* [*yansoun*]), saffron (*Crocus sativus* [*za'fran*]), mastic/lentisk (*Pistacia lentiscus* [*mastika*]), and honey is administered early every morning for a week, immediately after menstruation.

Additional treatments for female infertility include drinking a spoonful of porcupine (*niyss*) blood or inhaling the vapors of boiled porcupine blood; bathing in a large bowl with mint and *Capparis cartilaginea* (*lassaf*) and allowing the steam to enter the vagina; bathing near a holy tomb or an ant[40] hole, a crossroads, or near the following holy trees: *Cupressus* (*sarrow*), *Cocculus pendulus* (*hamr al majnun*), or *Acacia negevensis* (*talh*). Alternatively, she may bathe in the blood of boy's circumcision, or in the blood of livestock slaughtered for a wedding.[41]

Other infertility treatments for women include inserting into the vagina a cloth containing crushed garlic mixed with *Myrtus communis* (*rihan*), taking it out before sexual intercourse; hanging an amulet on both the woman and the man; and rubbing the bodies of the couple with a mixture of water and henna. Another method involves the husband suddenly throwing a cat at his wife, in order to shock her and thus cure her infertility. The seeds of fenugreek may be soaked in the urine of both the man and the woman and planted in the soil. After a while, a healer looks at these seeds. The seeds that do not show signs of growing belong to the one who suffers from infertility. Female healers also carry out a special massage (*tamrij*) of the sexual organs of the infertile woman, using olive oil and table salt. The Bedouin of the Negev (Shinnawi 1982) treat infertility by smearing the woman's body with a tincture of *Cuminum cyminum* (*kamoun*).

The Bedouin of Southern Sinai (Levi 1978: 13–24) believe that if a Bedouin woman does not wash her body after intercourse (during the night or in the morning) she will become infertile (*makbusih*). Infertile women are treated with an infusion of the fruit of *Ziziphus spina-christi* (*sidrih*), *Artemisia judaica* (*b'aythiran*), the roots of *Trifolium arvense* (*nafal*), and *Pituranthos tortuosus* (*zagguh*) and are advised to wash in *Calotropis procera* (*'ushur*) (Levi 1978: 23). In North Africa, they treat infertility woman with seeds of *Peganum* (*harjal*) (Westermark 1926: 126).

The Bedouin of the Negev (Bailey and Danin 1981: 145–62) treat infertility with a sauna with *Capparis cartilaginea* (*lassaf*) and *Tamarix aphylla* (*tarfa*). According to Ben-Assa (1969: 13–18), Bedouin woman bathe in the sea[42] and sacrifice animals as a remedy for infertility. Women who suffer

FIGURE 2.2 The Jamayin Tomb, situated in Wadi Dahar close to 'Uja al-Hafir, is a place of pilgrimage. One of the founders of the Bedouin Dhullam Tribe is entombed here.

FIGURE 2.3 The author during a family pilgrimage (*zwara*) to al-Jamayin.

FIGURE 2.4 Animals are slaughtered during/or after the pilgrimage for the honor of the holy Jamayin Tomb. The animal's head is placed on the slaughter stone.

from *kabsih* (Ben-Assa 1974: 73–76) wash their bodies in water mixed with the blood of livestock that have been sacrificed for a feast.

Ben-Assa (1964: 452) mentions that in the early 1960s the Bedouin suffered almost no venereal diseases, but tuberculosis of the sexual organs caused infertility and approximately 3.4 percent of the Bedouin women patients were infertile.

Men suffering from impotence[43] are advised to eat the ripe fruit of mandrake (*Mandragora autumnalis* [*mjininih*]) or to drink tea prepared from *Nasturium officinale* (*jarjir*), Jericho rose, or sage. They may also make a pilgrimage to a holy tomb and sacrifice livestock, or rub the penis and testicles with a concoction of the following plants, which have aphrodisiac properties: *Costus* (*qust*), *Matthiola* (*manthur*), *Nardostachys* (*sunbul al-tib*), and *Nasturtium officinale* (*jarjir*). The Bedouin of Southern Sinai (Levi 1978: 22, 1987: 260) treat male infertility with onion soup. Abu-Khusa (1979: 106–11) recorded that the Bedouin of the Negev ate onions to strengthen potency. Three tablespoons of the crushed dried bulbs/roots of *Asparagus stipularis* (*tgaytgih*) may be taken daily with water. Additional treatments include a mixture of the male inflorescence of a date palm with *samnih*, spread in pita. Impotence is also treated by burns on the back, waist, or shoulders.

Impotence (*marbut*) is also treated with amulets and magic, according to the principle of opposite on opposite. Ben-Assa (1974: 73–76) mentions that a Bedouin of the Negev who suddenly came impotent attributed his condition to black magic (*marbut*), believing that a woman had made an evil amulet and hidden it in his tent.

In Egypt (Pillsbury 1978: 44–45) cures for infertility vary. Among them is a vaginal suppository of cotton wool (*sufa*) daubed with some supposedly fertility-inducing ingredient, such as sugar, fenugreek, or ichthyol solution. Also in Egypt, fright is believed to cause infertility in males (Morsy 1982: 153).

Supernatural events, from sorcery to the intrusion of spirits, are also identified as causes of male infertility. Among the Bedouin of southern Jordan, an infertile woman often borrows the robe (*thawb*) of a woman who has had many children, hoping to acquire the fruitfulness of its owner.

Inflammation/Discharge

Inflamed male and female sexual organs and discharge are treated with a mixture of tar extracted from the juniper bush (*Juniperus communis* [*'ar'ar*]), cumin powder (*kamun*), pomegranate bark, and caraway seeds (*Carum carvi* [*carawya*]), boiled together in water. A spoonful of this mixture is drunk in the morning and evening. Bedouin women believe that a woman whose hair whorl is like a whirlpool (*fatilat al-rass*) near her forehead cannot conceive. There is no known medicine for such a phenomenon.

Delayed or irregular menstruation is treated with a heated mixture of one teaspoon of olive oil, one half-teaspoon myrrh, and one half-teaspoon castor oil (*zayt khirwia'*) produced from *Ricinus communis* (*khirwia'*). A piece of cotton wool that has been dipped in this mixture is inserted into the womb of a reclining woman, kept there for one hour, and then removed. Another piece of cotton wool dipped in sesame oil (*Sesamum orientale* [*sirij*]) is placed in the womb for ten minutes. After it is removed the woman sits in a bowl of lukewarm water for half an hour. This treatment is repeated daily for a week after the menstrual period as a treatment for irregular menstruation.

Menstrual irregularity or absence of menses is treated with a piece of cotton wool dipped in a heated mixture of one teaspoon olive oil, one half-teaspoon of *Commiphora myrrha* (*mur batarikh*), and one half-teaspoon of castor oil (*khirwi'*). This is inserted into the womb of a reclining woman, left there for one hour, and removed. Another piece of cotton wool dipped in sesame oil is placed in the womb for ten minutes. After it is removed, the woman sits in a tub of lukewarm water for half an hour. This treatment is repeated daily for a week after the menstrual period.

Another treatment for irregular or delayed menstruation involves the woman washing her body in water mixed with the blood of livestock sacrificed for a male circumcision (*agirih*).[44] Alternatively, the woman may drink tea made from cinnamon, anise, *Matricaria chamomilla* (*rabil, babounaj*), *Artemisia herba-alba* (*shih*), sage, and/or Jericho rose (*kaf al-rahaman*).

Among the Rwala Bedouin (Musil 1928: 667), venereal diseases were treated by alum and herbal medicine and cured by inhaling the smoke of some drug strewn over hot coals. It is very rare among the Rwala.

Certain beads, coins, and shells are assigned magic, symbolic,[45] and healing qualities according to Bedouin belief (Abu-Rabia 1999a; Goren 1994: 294–98; Levi 1987).

Influenza (*dishbih*)

Treatments include drinking tea prepared from the following plants: lemon, hyssop, *Artemisia herba-alba* (*shih*), *Varthemia iphionoides* (*slimania*), *Mentha longifolia* (*na'na'*), *Coridothymus capitatus* (*zahayfy*), and *Achillea fragrantissima* (*gisum*). Eating garlic with food is highly recommended, as is wearing warm clothing. The Bedouin of Southern Sinai (Levi 1978: 61–62) use *Artemisia herba-alba* (*shih*), garlic, *Peganum* (*harjal*), sugar, *Capparis cartilaginea* (*lassaf*), *Pulicaria incisa* (*ra'ra'*), *Varthemia iphionoides* (*slimania*), *Salvia multicaulis* (*bardagush*),[46] hyssop, *Hyoscyamus boveanus* (*sakaran*), or *Polygonum equistiforme* (*gudhdhab*) to treat influenza. The Bedouin of the Negev and Sinai (Bailey and Danin 1981: 145–62) use *Teucrium polium* (*ja'adih*), *Pulicaria incisa* (*ra'ra'*), *Capparis cartilaginea* (*lassaf*), *Polygonum equistiforme* (*gudhdhab*), and *Eryngium creticum* (*kursannih*). The Bedouin of the Negev (Abu-Khusa 1979: 106–11) use lemon and a soup made of onions, and rub the chest of the influenza patient with lukewarm olive oil.

Intestinal Swelling (*nfakh, infakh*)

Treatments for this ailment include drinking a mixture of cumin (*kamun*), crushed fenugreek seeds, and sugar in a glass of water, once a day. If the patient is a baby, a small piece of soap (*saboun Nabilsi*) made in Nablus from pure olive oil may be inserted as a rectal suppository (*talbisih*). Cinnamon or ginger in a glass of water may be drunk twice a day. A teaspoon of honey may be taken several times a day.

Intestinal Worms (*dud fi al-batin, al-masarin*)

Treatments include drinking a tincture prepared from the fruit of *Citrullus colocynthis* (*handhal*), olives, black cumin, or olive oil or a cup of water mixed with one or two drops of kerosene (*kaz*). The Bedouin of Southern Sinai (Levi 1978: 58) drink tea made from *Artemisia judaica* (*b'aythiran*), *Cassia* (*kasiah, sinamakky*), or Arabic rose (*mayyit ward*), or eat *Chenopodium* (*Rejl al-waz*). The Bedouin of the Negev (Abu-Khusa 1979: 106–11) eat pumpkin seeds (*gara'*). In Arabia (Dickson 1949: 507), it is believed that worms are the result of drinking impure water and that they cause anemia and giddiness.

Janah/Majnuh (*janah, majnuh*)

The Bedouin derived the name of this disease, *janah,* from the appearance of a bird with a wounded, damaged, or broken wing (*majnuh*). *Janah* is an illness in both infants and adults. Its symptoms include fever, aches and pains in the back and the neck, chronic fatigue, pains in the joints and bones, rheumatic pains, sometimes yellow eyes, headaches, especially in the afternoon, respiratory problems, coughing and nose bleeds, and a burning sensation when urinating. Sometimes the patient shivers. Treatments include rest and sleep in the afternoon, and burning with a red hot iron or an Arabic coin (*riyal*) the following places: on the left wrist where a watch is usually worn, below the right knee, on the nape of the neck, and in the hollow of the elbow. Another treatment involves drinking water in which the bulbs of *Cyperus rotundus* (*si'd, su'd*) have been soaked. Infants are bathed in this water and sometimes babies are given one or two of the bulbs to eat for two or three days.

Jaundice/Yellow Fever (*safar, ghurnag*)

Treatments for jaundice and yellow fever include hanging a jaundice bead called *kharazat al-ghurnag* or an amber (*'anbar*) bead on the patient's neck. Alternatively, the bead may be placed in a cup of water for half an hour and the water drunk. The fruit of *Ecballium elaterium* (*faggous al-hamir*) may be squeezed into a liter of water or olive oil and this mixture sprinkled into the nose of the patient once a day for two to four weeks. A child suffering from jaundice should be kept away from the sun's rays or contact with other people, especially children, and should remain at home rest. The Bedouin of Galilee (Nejidat 1984: 29–30) also squeeze the fruit of *Ecballium elaterium* and sprinkle in the nose of the patient once a day for several days. Alternatively, a burn is made with a needle on the nape of the neck (*'ar'ur*). Hilf (1985) mentions burning with a needle on the nape of the neck or drinking a cup of water after soaking a bead *kharazat al-safar,* avoiding salty food or meat, or making a small incision under the tongue and letting the blood drain out—this blood is considered to be impure. The Bedouin of the Negev (Abu-Khusa 1979: 106–11) do the same, then place garlic under the tongue; or boil rhubarb (*Rheum* [*rawand hindi*]) in water and drink a tablespoon of the liquid in the morning and evening.

Jellyfish (Medusa) Sting (*gandil al-bahr*)

Treatments include moistening sugar and placing it on the sting, drinking olive oil and rinsing the sting with it, and soaking the leaves and flowers of *Heliotropium* (*dhanab al-'agrab*) in water and drinking the solution.

Kidney Pain[47] (*waja' kalawiy*)

Treatments for kidney pain include drinking a brew made by boiling leaves of *Paronychia argentea* (*rijil al-Hamamih*) in a cup of water every morning for a week. This breaks up kidney stones, and is effective against kidney diseases. Similarly, the leaves of *Artemisia judaica* (*b'aythiran*) or mustard (*Sinapis arvensis* [*khardal*]) may be boiled in water and several cups a day drunk for two to four weeks. The leaves of *Petroselinum sativum* (*baqdunis*) may be soaked or boiled in water. Several cups of this tea may be drunk daily for two to four weeks. The leaves and flowers or seeds of *Ammi visnage* (*khall*) and leaves of *Portulaca oleracea* (*farfahina*) may be boiled in water and two cups a day may be drunk, one in the morning and one in the evening. One cup of olive oil may be drunk in the early morning daily for one week. Alternatively, a piece of dried livestock bile is mixed in a glass of water and drunk daily early in the morning. The Bedouins of the Negev (Shinnawi 1982) treat kidney pains by making burns with a small needle around the kidneys or boiling leaves of *Ammi visnage* (*khall, khillih*) in water and drinking the brew. The Bedouin of the Negev (Abu-Khusa 1976: 71) mix the seeds of *Ammi visnage* (*khall*), radish (*fijil*), and *Portulaca oleracea* (*farfahina*), boil them in water, and drink a cup of the resulting brew morning and evening.

Kidney stones are treated by drinking a mixture of the crushed seeds of *Sinapis arvensis* (*khardal*) and honey with water or by drinking olive oil early morning. Ben-Assa (1964: 453) comments that cases of kidney stones were rare in the 1960s among the Bedouin of the Negev. The Bedouin of Sinai (Levi 1978: 68, 1987: 302) treat kidney diseases by eating the crushed seeds of *Lepidium sativum* (*hab al-rashad*) with egg yolk. In cases of blood in the urine, they drink tea prepared from one of the following plants: *Pituranthos tortuosus* (*zagguh*), *Rhus coriaria* (*summag*), *Zilla spinosa* (*sleis*), or *Mentha*.

Late Development of Walking (*ta'akhur mashiy*)

The Bedouin attribute this problem to several causes, including the evil eye or early eruption of teeth, which they believe occurs at the expense of learning to walk.

Treatment consists of binding the child's feet with a rope made of camel's wool (*wabar*) and burning the middle of the rope with fire while a healer shouts "fire, fire!" at the baby in a loud voice. The terrified baby tries to escape by starting to walk. This is a psychological-therapeutic approach to healing the baby while exorcising the evil eye from his body.[48] Other treatments include hanging an amulet on the child's body, visiting a holy tomb for prayer and making vows, binding the child's feet with a sheep's wool rope (*souf*), and placing the baby in the middle of large sieve (*ghirbal*) on the night of the full moon. The healer, the mother of the baby, and his relatives sit around him in a circle, praying and inhaling the scent of incense (*bakhkhur*).[49] Each of the participants must bring symbolic gift and place it inside the sieve. The healer then burns the rope as above.

Leeches (*'alaga, Pl. 'alag*)

Water sources, mainly cisterns and constructed wells, are often contaminated with leeches. Usually, the Bedouin put some lime inside the water to clean it; or pour one cup of kerosene (*kaz*) into the water to kill the leeches and other parasites. Sometimes they filter the water through a man's white headscarf after drawing it by bucket. Small stones of bituminous material (*hummara*) are also placed inside cisterns and constructed wells to purify them. Ben-Assa (1970: 218) related that some water sources among the Bedouin of the Negev contained leeches that stuck to the throat (*halg, zour*) through drinking, causing bleeding and even strangulation. Ben-Assa (1974: 73–76) also found that bleeding through the nose was caused by leeches in the throat. Treatment for leeches in the throat includes drinking olive oil or oil of black cumin to drive the leeches out, or removing them with the thorns of *Capparis cartilaginea* (*lassaf*).

Liver Pain (*waja' kibd*)

Treatments for liver pain include drinking camel's milk several times a day, drinking pure honey three times a day, or drinking water in which leaves of *Nigella sativa* (*habbit al-barakah*), *Rhus coriaria* (*summag*), *Cichorium pumilum* (*'ilk*), *Matricaria aurea* (*babunaj*), *Zygophyllum coccineum* (*rotrayt*), *Anthemis pseudocotula* (*rbayan*), or cloves (*grunful*) have been soaked several times a day.

Bailey (1991: 60) notes that the Bedouin believe that a man's strength comes from the liver, which digests food. A person's well-being, gauged by his appetite, is thought to be a function of the liver. The liver is also the source of anger (1991: 79). Accordingly, when the liver has "refused" to eat, one is sick (1991: 68): "The whole of last night I lay parched and pale, But my liver's revived and I no longer quail" (1991: 75).

Lungs (*ri'atyn, fash, shgira, shqira*)

Treatments include drinking one tablespoon of a mixture of ginger and black cumin seeds early in the morning before breakfast, drinking a solution made by boiling leaves of hyssop and *Coridothymus capitatus* (*zahayfy*) in water, and inhaling the smoke from bulbs of *Urginea maritima* (*halluf, 'unsol, bussayl*) that have been placed on the hearth. The Bedouin of Southern Sinai (Levi 1987: 299) boil the leaves and fruit of *Capparis cartilaginea* (*lassaf, lussayf*) in water and drink the liquid, place leaves of *Hyoscyamus* (*sakaran*) on the hearth and inhale the smoke, or make burns on the right and left sides of the chest. Ben-Assa (1964: 452) mentions that in the early 1960s many Negev Bedouin suffered from chronic lung infections and that 13.2 percent suffered from lung and other respiratory infections.

Madness/Insanity (*jin, jinn, junun, majnun*)

Various treatments for insanity are used in traditional Bedouin medicine. In the pre-Islamic period, the Arabs treated madness by hanging unclean objects, the ankle bone of a rabbit, or bones of a dead person taken from a cemetery around the patient's neck (al-Najjar 1994: 52–53). Cauterization of the head, neck, and back was a cure for madness in boys caused by jinn, according to Dickson (1949: 150).[50]

A dervish may prepare an amulet to be hung on the patient's neck or the patient may visit a holy tomb and sacrifice an animal. A medicine may be prepared from the following plants: *Matricaria aurea* (*babunaj, rabil*), Rose of Jericho (the fruit of *Anastatica hierochuntica*) (*Kaf al-Rahaman, Kaff Maryam*), ripe fruit of *Mandragora officinalis* (*Tuffah al-Majanin, imjinynih*), leaves of *Ruta chalepensis* (*Faijan, Shadhab, Ruta*), and the fruit and leaves of Christ's thorn, *Ziziphus spina-christi* (*Sedr, sidrih, sidr*). Incense, resin of *Boswellia carterii* (*luban, bakhkhur*), is burned on coals and inhaled before bedtime.

The Bedouin of the Negev (al-'Aref 1933: 245) treat madness by applying to the renowned dervishes Abu-Jrir and, in the Gaza Strip, al-'Aamarin. When the patient enters the house of the dervish, he blesses the patient, reads verses, and chants mystical passages, and the patient recovers. Sometimes the patient lives with the healer in his tent or house for several weeks in order to undergo treatment. The dervish's family cares for the patient. The healer is paid with a gift or symbolic money. When the patient recovers, he invites the dervish, his agnates, and friends to participate in sacrificial animal cermony.[51]

When a jinni has entered a person's body, that person is still able to communicate with a dervish or a religious healer[52] who reads verses from the Quran. During such healing rituals, the dervish drums on the *tar* and puts incense in the embers, since the spirits dislike this smell; the dervish is able to deal with the jinni, extracting a pledge that it will leave the per-

son's body and never return. Sometimes, the dervish beats the possessed patient with a stick, or whips his body or foot, from which the spirit is supposed to leave the body (Abu-Rabia 1983, 1999a). This practice and the dialogue with the spirits is comparable to the Western notion of spirit exorcism (Morsy 1978: 601[53]; Sharp 1994). When the jinni enters a human body violently, it causes the person to become insane, suffer epileptic attacks, or be too frightened to speak (al-Krenawi and Graham 1997; al-Krenawi 2000; Johnstone 1998: 46–50; Ibn 'Uthaymin 1991: 80–81). According to Boddy (1988: 11–12), the *zar* ritual puts the patient not just in a trance per se, but in a trance firmly situated in a meaningful cultural context—possession—that has medical, social, psychological, and often profound aesthetic implications.

Among the Bedouin of Cyrenaica (Peters 1990: 40–41, 64), dervishes (*morabtin bil baraka*) are accredited with *baraka* (divine goodness); they provide spirtual services to the Bedouin, comfort the sick, write amulets, circumcise the young boys, and are always present at peace meetings (*sulha*) to give them the weight of their *baraka*. When the dervish perspires copiously from beating his drum and pretending to pierce his body with a sword (his *baraka* protects him from harm)—his sweat is considered to bear a *baraka* and can be transmitted to others (Peters 1990: 279). Notably, "when the Kaaba covering at Mecca is taken down each year and renewed, the old cloth is cut up into small pieces and sold for charms for protection from evils and bad spirits" (Doumato 2000: 149) and madness.

Malaria (*malaria, wakham*)[54]

Mosquitoes are driven out of tents, houses, and caves by using smoke made by burning animal droppings (camels, donkeys, sheep, and goats).[55] Treatments vary. An infusion made by soaking the leaves and fruit of *Calotropis procera* (*'ushir*) in a cup of water may be drunk. The leaves of the following plants may be boiled in water and drunk twice daily: *Artemisia herba-alba* (*shih*), *Artemisia judaica* (*b'aythiran*), and *Artemesia arborescens* (*shiba*). Eating an onion several times a day is also recommended. High fever and malaria are treated by inhaling the smoke from the burning skin of a hedgehog (*gunfud*), including its spines. In Palestine (Hareuveni 1930: 113–17) in the early twentieth century, the Bedouin used *Varthemia iphionoides* (*slimania, ktilih*), *Marrubium vulgare* (*qriha*), *Teucrium polium* (*ja'adih*), *Achillea fragrantissima* (*gisum*), *Eucalyptus bicolor* (*keina*), *Matricaria aurea* (*rabil*), and *Opuntia ficus-indica* (*sabir*) to treat malaria. Alternatively, burns were made on the forehead. Patients were also encouraged to bathe in the *'iyn shdida/jdida* spring in Hebron. The Bedouin of the Negev and Sinai (Bailey and Danin 1981: 150–158) use *Eucalyptus bicolor* leaves (*keina*) or leaves of *Artemisia herba-alba* (*shih*) steeped in water as a drink (Abu-Khusa 1979: 106–11).

During the 1930s, an investigation in Palestine showed that Bedouin who camped near swamplands contracted malaria (al-'Aref 1944: 154–60). Quinine was the traditional treatment for malaria in Palestine in the first decades of twentieth century. The Arabs in Palestine extracted quinine syrup from Quina Laroche (*sharbit al-kina*). Taking quinine was so common that quinine sulphate (*sulphata*) was considered a household remedy.[56]

According to Sufian, among the different malarial fevers are found benign tertian malaria fever, quartan fever, and malignant tertian fever. In Palestine, benign tertian fever was said to be more common among the Jewish population, whereas malignant tertian fever was the most common form of malaria among the Arab population (Sufian 1999, 2002: 29). Paleopathologic research on skeletal materials going back to Bronze Age farmers in the eastern Mediterranean show that malaria was endemic in this area long before 2000 BC (Angel 1964: 369–71).

Measles (*hasbih*)

The Bedouin follow sanitary, hygienic rules and preventive measures against measles. The patient does not leave his house and avoids contact with other people. Only those who have been vaccinated or a few childless adult kin come to visit him, in order to prevent epidemics. His kin spread the news of the sicknes to prevent others from visiting. Among the Bedouin of the Negev (Shinnawi 1982), mothers protect the eyes of their babies by administering eye drops produced from *Solanum dulcamara* (*'inab al-dib*) mixed with the urine of an uncircumcised boy. They also dress the baby in red clothes, keep him out of draughts, and feed him sweet food for three consecutive days to drive the fever from his body (Abu-Khusa 1979: 106–11). Nose drops produced from *Solanum dulcamara* (*'inab al-dib*) are put in the patient's nostrils; and *kohl*[57] is placed in his eyes to protect them and to ease the fever. The patient is given lentils (*'adas*) with sugar to eat, because lentils resemble and signify measles spots on the skin.

The Rwala Bedouin (Musil 1928: 667) treated measles by feeding the patient warm dates mixed with pepper and butter. In Arabia (Dickson 1949: 507), when children had measles (*hasbah*), they were allowed to eat a limited amount of certain foods, but not allowed to smell any other kind of food.[58] In Palestine (Canaan 1927a: 185) a child with measles was encouraged to eat lentil soup, which makes the rash develop more quickly.

FIGURE 2.5 Sage is an herb used to treat stomachache, infertility, and lack of milk for nursing mothers.

Miscarriage (*takhrim*)

A woman told me that she once had had a natural miscarriage. Exactly one year later, she became pregnant again, and in the third month began hemorrhaging lightly. She was hospitalized at Soroka Medical Center in Beer-Sheba, the hemorrhaging stopped, and she was sent home. She began bleeding again and turned to a female healer who treated her by making burns in the shape of an X above her crotch with a needle heated over a flame. The hemorrhaging stopped and she delivered a healthy son.

Other preventives measures for miscarriage include the woman washing herself immediately following her menstrual period with blood taken from a goat or sheep that has been slaughtered for the Feast of the Sacrifice (*Eid al-adha*), mixed with water. Alternatively, the woman washes herself immediately following her menstrual period with water in which gold coins have been placed. The woman may also wash with water in which leaves of Christ's thorn have been soaked. A piece of silver (*maskih*) may be hung around the woman's neck immediately following her menstrual period and throughout pregnancy.

Another method of preventing miscarriage involves hanging an amulet written by a folk healer and containing verses from the Quran and other writings around the woman's neck at the beginning of pregnancy. It is strictly forbidden to open this amulet, which is personal and may not be passed on to someone else. A healer told me that the amulet contains the name of the woman and her mother and may not include a male name. An amulet called the Blessed Seal (*al-khatim al-mubarak*) may be hung on the woman's body. The woman may take a cord or string from Nabi Musa's tomb, and wind it around her belly in a circular[59] shape or drink a medication made of forty (*arba'in*) kinds of herbs and special ingredients prepared by a healer.

Mother's Hysteria/Aphasia (*khabal, makhbulih*)

In order to treat this condition, the Bedouin burn incense and read phrases from the Quran or hang special amulet. In Kuwait and Bahrain, according to Dickson (1949: 173) "It happens that immediately after birth the mother becomes mad (*mukhabbala*), and unable to speak. [In such cases] a mare is hastily sent for and brought to the woman's side and offered barley from her lap. If the mare eats, the woman's tongue is loosed and her reason returns. If not, the woman is sure to die."

Mouth Thrush/Herpes/Acne (*habb al-shabab/habatah*)

Thrush is an inflammation that affects the mouths of children and causes a patchy white appearance of the tongue, palate, and lips. The Bedouin give the affected children crystalline plant sugar to suck on or a cup of water with which to wash out the mouth several times a day. Other treatments include soaking tamarind (*Tamarindus indica* [*tamr hindi*]) or *Matricaria aurea* (*babunaj, rabil*) in a cup of water and washing the mouth with the infusion or drinking it several times a day; rinsing the mouth with leaves of *Artemisia herba-alba* (*shih*) or onion; soaking the leaves of *Eucalyptus bicolor* (*keina, kina*), *Achillea fragrantissima* (*gaysum, qisum, gisum*), or *Artemisia herba-alba* (*shih*) in water, gargling and washing the mouth and lips several times a day; or boiling hyssop leaves in water, drinking the brew and washing the mouth and lips for forty days. During this period, one should eat bread and honey without salt, smear the mouth and lips with olive or black cumin oil, or smear *samnih* (processed butter of livestock or cows) on the mouth, lips, and face. In Arabia, treatment of mouth sores, tender gums, mouth blisters in children, and mouths sore from scurvy involves boiling the leaves of *Heliotropium ramosissimum* (*ramram*) in water and washing the mouth and the skin. The crushed leaves of *Heliotropium ramosissimum* are soaked with kermes (*girmiz*—the dried bodies of the female insect, *Coccus ilicis*, which yield a red dye) in water and used to wash the mouth and skin, and applied to the mouth sore with a finger (Dickson 1949: 160, 467; Mandaville 1990: 253).

Mumps/Parotitis (*abu-dghaym/dghim*)

The Bedouin relate seriously to this illness, since it can cause future infertility in boys. Treatments include rubbing the neck area with lukewarm olive oil, dressing the patient in warm clothes, and keeping him isolated to prevent the disease from spreading.[60] The Bedouin of Galilee (Hilf 1985) collect the soot (*shahbar*) that sticks to the bottom of an old bowl or pan and smear it around the neck, while reciting Quranic phrases.

Muteness (*kharas/akhras*)

The healer takes a pot (*magr*) from which chickens drink, cleans it, and fills it with fresh water to be given to the baby to drink. The underlying idea behind this method is the belief that an evil eye or a spirit has entered the baby's body and caused his/her muteness. The fact that s/he is drinking from the same pot as the chickens implies that he is no longer human, so the evil eye or the spirit will leave his body. The baby could also be given water in which leaves of hyssop and anise have been boiled. According to Shinnawi (1982), the Bedouin of the Negev make burns on the baby's buttocks to treat muteness.

Nosebleed (*ra'afa, nazif khashm*) and Nose Wounds (*jarh khashm*)

Treatments for nosebleeds include washing the head with cold water and placing drops of liquid prepared from the leaves of *Achillea fragrantissima* (*gisum*) in the nose. The Bedouin of the Negev and Sinai (Bailey and Danin 1981: 145–62) sniff the powder of dried leaves or burnt roots of *Lycium shawii* (*'awasaj*). The Bedouin of Galilee (Hilf 1985) place drops of olive oil mixed with fresh coffee (liquid) in the nose. The Bedouin of the Negev (Abu-Khusa 1979: 106–11) sniff a powder prepared from a burnt mat (*hasira*) made from palm tree leaves (*burdi*). It is also possible to sniff this powder mixed with vinegar (*khall*). Among the Rwala (Musil 1928: 443), it is told that Belhan ibn Mnazzel brought his flock to the same well and tried to drive Medbagh away. Enraged, the latter attacked Belhan, fell upon him with a saber, and cut off his nose, so that it hung only by a bit of skin and later had to be sewn on with the hair of a virgin.

Osteomalacia (*marad al-'Idham*)

Ben-Assa (1974: 73–74) attributes walking problems among the Bedouin of the Negev to the existence of osteomalacia. The primary sources of vitamin D were milk products (butter), eggs, and figs. Among Bedouin who lived near the sea (Cole and Altorki 1998; Levi 1987; Shuqayr 1916), fish were a good source of vitamin D.[61] Vitamin D is very important for healing bones and teeth, for proper assimilation and balances of calcium and phosphorus, and for preventing rickets (Lust 1980: 499). Among the weakest and poorest segments of the population, one can find night blindness, rickets in children, osteomalacia, and periodontal disease as a result of vitamin D deficiencies (Groen et al. 1964: 37–46; Groen, Duyvensz, and Halsted 1960).

In a retrospective survey of hospital admissions conducted at Soroka Medical Center in Beersheba from 1980 to 1989, primary nutritional osteomalacia was diagnosed in twenty patients, all of whom were Bedouin women. Patients suffered from bone pain and proximal muscle weakness, while fixed skeletal deformities were common. This investigation shows that primary nutritional osteomalacia, a preventable disease, still occurs, causing severe morbidity, and may be a manifestation of endemic subclinical vitamin D malnutrition in the Bedouin community in the Negev (Lowenthal and Shany 1994: 520–23).

Piercing/Perforation of the Ears/Earlobes/Nose (*kharm, khurm, khurum*)

In order to prevent infection or to keep the hole from closing after piercing the nose or the earlobe, the spot is rubbed with lukewarm olive oil and table salt with onion boiled in olive oil or *samnih,* or with fat from a sheep's tail. Alternatively, a *miswak*—a small stick made from the *Dianthus strictus* (*slayslih*) or *rgaygih/irgaygih*—is inserted into the piercing. The Bedouin of the Negev and Sinai (Bailey and Danin 1981: 145–62) also treat and prevent infection in the nose or earlobe by inserting a small *Dianthus strictus* (*slayslih*) stick in the hole (*kharm*) until it heals. The Bedouin of Southern Sinai (Levi 1978: 67, 1987: 301) also insert a *miswak,* but one made from

Farsetia aegyptiaca (*jirbih, jraybih*), *Zilla spinosa* (*sleis, seili*), or *Pergularia tomentosa* (*ghalqa, demia*). They also use olive oil.

Piles/Hemorrhoids (*basur*, pl. *bawasir, msammil*)

Treatments for hemorrhoids include heating pieces of onion with olive oil and inserting them into the rectum during the night or lightly massaging the rectum with salty lukewarm olive oil. The patient may also sit in a hot bath with medicinal herbs every night before bedtime for a month. The patient may be given olive oil or laxative herbs to drink daily. Laxative food plants include *Malva* spp. (*khubbiza*) and *Corchorus olitorus* (*mlukhyah*). The patient should avoid eating dry dishes and instead consume laxative foods. Rice and the fruit of the *Opuntia ficus-indica* (*sabr*) should be avoided mainly in the morning. Another treatment consists of drinking water in which the fruit of carob (*Ceratonia siliqua* [*kharrub*]) has been soaked overnight in the morning. Drinking a soup made of goat or sheep meat is also recommended. The Bedouin of Galilee (Hilf 1985) heat a piece of earthenware (*fukhkhar*) over a fire, place a cloth on the rectum and then insert the earthenware, with no direct contact with the rectum, in order to avoid burning, or sit the patient indirectly on the hot shard for an hour a day for two weeks. The Bedouin of the Negev (Abu-Khusa 1979: 106–11) boil leaves of *Ruta chalepensis* (*ruta, fayjan, sadhab*) in water and wash the rectum with this liquid. Krispil (1986: 241) names twelve plants used to treat piles among the Bedouin of the Negev. A suppository (*tahmila*) made from the inner part of *Citrullus colocynthis* (*handhal*) is also used. Among the Rwala Bedouin (Musil 1928: 667), a piece of clay is kneaded, shaped like a large nail, allowed to dry, burned to a white heat and then inserted into the rectum in order to burn out the hemorrhoid.

Placenta/Afterbirth (*sala*), Burial of Placenta

Among the Bedouin of Sinai, women who have just given birth blow air forcefully into a bottle while pushing with their abdominal muscles in order to accelerate the expulsion of the placenta. Some midwives put their hand smeared with *samna* in the womb and pull the placenta loose. When the placenta has been expelled, the umbilical cord is tied ten centimeters from the navel and cut above the knot. All tissue secreted during the delivery—the membrane of the fetal sac, the umbilical cord, and the placenta—is collected in a piece of cloth and buried in the earth a distance from the encampment. There are those who leave a 2–3 centimeter piece of the umbilical cord protruding above ground to serve as a blessing for mother and child. A bough of white broom (*ratam*) or another bush is thrust through the protruding piece of tissue, and is believed to appease the local angel and to bless the newborn. It is thought that any demon that wishes to harm the child will be fooled into casting its spell on the umbilical cord rather than the newborn (Levi 1987: 263–64). In Palestine, when the afterbirth is not expelled quickly, they tie a thread to the cord of the afterbirth and the big toe and make the mother blow into a bottle in order to expell the afterbirth. Alternatively, they burn a blue rag and let the smoke rise into her face and administer snuff, which causes the mother to sneeze and cough, and expel the placenta. The midwife[62] may also fold a thick cloth, put it on her head, and press her head against the mother's stomach to encourage the expulsion of the placenta. This custom is also practiced in Nablus. There, in the mid-twentieth century, a midwife explained that "if the afterbirth is delayed, they give the confined woman olive oil to drink and the midwife puts her own finger in the mother's mouth. Then the afterbirth comes" (Granqvist 1947: 71).

Granqvist reported (1947: 97–98) that in Palestine in the mid-twentieth century the custom was to put salt on the afterbirth and hang it inside the doorpost to ward off *qarinas*.[63] There they also preserved the afterbirth, and also hung a piece of ass's meat above the doorpost. They believe that if a *qarina* wants to harm the child, she would be frightened away by the rotting meat. In most cases, the midwife buries the afterbirth with the earth that was spread in front of the stone on which the woman in labour sat, and which she collected in a sack, to prevent cats from eating it or someone stepping on it, which might hinder her bearing children in the future. The afterbirth must be buried very deep, so that dogs cannot eat it, in which case she would become barren. The earth, with blood and all, is buried with the afterbirth. The midwife is bound to bury the afterbirth.[64] It is put in a rag and she digs a hole and buries it. The place where she buries it must be noted by her. If the mother does not become pregnant again, she unearths it and washes herself with water in which it has lain (Granqvist 1947: 97–98). Interestingly, among Jews the placenta was traditionally buried in the ground. It seems this act was symbolic and believed to ensure long life, and perhaps stemmed from respect for something that is part of the body, that no longer has any function, just as body parts are buried with the dead. That is the earth is ensured that what was born will return to dust when the day comes (Rubin 1995: 65). Similarly, during the pre-Islamic period, among Central Asian people and in Turkey healers believed that it was dangerous to leave the placenta of the newly born baby outside, exposed to evil spirits, so they would bury the placenta of the newly born under the ground, in cult spots, for example under a tree (Bayat 2002: 52).

Poisoning by Plants (*tasammum min nabatat*)

The leaves, unripe seeds, and fruit of *Hyoscyamus* (*sakaran*) or mandrake (*Mandragora autumnalis* [*mjininih, yabruh, tuffah al-majanin*]) are poisonous. In cases of accidental ingestion, vomiting is induced, milk or olive oil is administered orally, and rest is recommended. According to Urkin et al. (1991: 714–16) Bedouin children from the Negev have been hospitalized as a result of eating the leaves of *Hyoscyamus* (*sakaran*), which caused ataxia and other symptoms.

The Bedouin of Southern Sinai (Levi 1978: 75) give the patient sweet tea to drink, while those of the Negev (Dafni and Dafni 1975: 235) make the patient gargle with tea made from *Matricaria aurea* (*babunaj*) (Abu-Khusa 1976: 71), induce vomiting with a tablespoon of salt in lukewarm water, or administer a laxative to induce diarhhea, in order to cleanse the stomach and bowels of the remnants of the poisoned food.

Ben-Assa (1974: 73–76) reported that if a Bedouin from the Negev suspected another person of trying to poison him with a special drink (*sagwa/saqwa*), he would induce vomiting several times a year and ask a Western physician to take X-rays of him. In such cases, the best treatment would be to refer to a dervish.

Porcupinefish Sting (*gunfud al-bahr/qunfud*)

Treatments include drinking olive oil and rinsing the sting with it, and boiling leaves of hyssop, mint, and *Heliotropium* (*dhanab al-'agrab*) in water and drinking the solution. Oil of black cumin (*habbit al-baraka*) may also be drunk.

Pregnancy Bead (*kharazat al-haml*)

The pregnancy bead, which contains a sign that resembles a fetus, is hung on a woman during pregnancy to prevent miscarriage.

Premature Baby (*khdajih, ikhdajih*)

Treatment consists of making a tiny, cradle-sized tent (*khulla*), wrapping the baby in a gray, red, or black cloth and placing the premature baby inside this tiny tent until the ninth month, in order to give him the feeling that he is still in his mother's womb. Pinczuk (1994) describes a similar custom among the Bedouin of the Negev.

Prostate Problems (*mutha, iltihab al-masura*)

The Bedouin of the Negev treat prostate problems by eating hot pepper (*filfil, shattah*) (Ihmid Abu-Naja, personal communication, 1 June 2007). Olive oil is the predominant oil used in Arab culture and one study suggested that olives have some protective effect against cancer. A comparative study between Arabs and Jews in Israel reveals that the striking differences between the prevalence of cancer are the result of different dietary patterns, which may include nutritional factors that serve as cancer-inducing or cancer-protective mechanisms. Olive oil and olives have protective effects against gastric cancer (Abu-Rabia 2005: 404–7; 2015: 124–135; Bitterman et al. 1991: 501–8).

Psychological Trauma from Food Deprivation (*'ashman*)

This psychological trauma occurs when a child is prevented from eating a desired food, such as candy. The symptoms are frequent crying, repeated requests for the particular food, disinterest in other foods, unusual behavior, restlessness, sad eyes, or constant salivation. The treatment consists of giving the child the particular food he craves. If it is unavailable, some of the child's urine is collected and he is unknowingly made to drink it. The Bedouin believe the child's soul (*nafs*) has been bruised and has left the body with his urine or through his rectum. Drinking the urine will return his soul to his body and restore him to his former self. It is important to use the first urine after the first symptoms appear. Placing a cloth beside his rectum is believed to prevent the soul from leaving the body. It is believed that if a child smells cooked food it must partake of it or fall sick. The mother generally dips one finger in the food and touches the lips of the baby (Canaan 1927a: 170–71). The peasants believe that a child's unfulfilled cravings will result in disease. The child may suffer from fever or diarrhea or waste away. Mothers are often heard excusing themselves for giving the child every prohibited thing by saying, "He asked for it." Similarly, all the wishes of a pregnant woman must be satisfied, for it is firmly believed that any unsatisfied desire will have some negative effect on her unborn infant. If she craves an apple and does not get it, we were told that somewhere on the skin of the new-born a representation of an apple will show itself. Such a mark is called *shahweh* (desire). In English,

it is still called a "mother mark," which shows clearly that a similar belief was once prevalent in Europe (Canaan 1927a: 183).

Pustule/Abscess/Boil Bead (*kharazat al-hboun, hibin, habatah*)

Treatments for these ailments include the application of a medicine produced from the skin of the honey badger (*Meles meles* (*am ka'yb*) steeped in olive oil on the boil or pustule or using a boil bead (*kharazat al-hboun*) to treat an abscess or boil on the arm or leg of a person or animal. The bead is tied to the boil, pustule, or abscess, causing it to burst, drain out, and disappear within a week. The bones of a dead dog may be burned and the ashes applied to the inflammation. A churn[65] made from livestock skin may be scraped and the scrapings applied to the pustule. The pustule may be smeared with henna or with *Rhus coriaria* (*summag*). The patient may be given a mixture of olive oil, wheat bread, and milk.

A 22-year-old man told me he had been treated unsuccessfully by several doctors in Beer-Sheba for boils (*hibin*) on his genitalia, and finally turned to a Bedouin healer. After examining him the healer told him to catch a mole (*khlund*) in a trap baited with an onion, put the mole in a 30-centimeter-deep hole, cover it with soil, and roast it by indirect heat from a fire on top of the soil. Two to three hours later he was to put the mole in a bottle, being careful not to lose the fluid oozing from the mole's body, to make an ointment from the liquid and Bedouin butter, and to smear it on the boils in the morning and evening. The boils completely disappeared within 10 days.

Bedouin of the Negev (Abu-Khusa 1979: 106–11) put tuber of onion on the pustule. The Bedouin of Southern Sinai (Levi 1978: 64, 74) scratch the pustule with garlic and *Trigonella foenum-graecum* (*hilbih*). The Bedouin of the Negev (al-'Aref 1933: 244–45) treat pustules by eating pure honey mixed with oil of black cumin or *Lepidium sativum* (*habb al-rashad, hurf*). Alternatively, burns are made around the pustules.

Rabies (*sa'ar*)

Rabies spreads among the domestic animals and wild animals in the Middle East, with no regard for political borders (Awerbuch-Friedlander 2005: 451–85). However, some countries, such as Israel, are more vigilant than others and stringently enforce anti-rabies regulations.

The Bedouin believe that the eyes of a rabid dog (*mas'ur*) are red and that it is frightened away from drinking water because when it looks at the water it sees its own red eyes and flees. It wanders around and its saliva foams from its mouth. There is no treatment for rabid dogs. Usually the Bedouin shoot the animal and bury it far from their tribal encampments, making sure to keep their animals far away from it.

The healer takes *Mylabris syriaca* (*dhirnah*), an insect that appears in spring and early summer and lives on flowers and plants. The Bedouin hollow out the stem of *Nerium oleander* (*defla*) or *Phragmites australis* (*gasabah*) with a piece of wire, force a *Mylabris* insect into the hollow stem, and close both ends. Then, when a person is bitten by a dog suspected of being rabid (*sa'ar*), or when a person is unable to urinate, the dried insect is removed from the stem, placed in a dried fig or piece of bread and eaten. This treatment, which turns the urine red, is administered only once. As protection from rabid dogs, the Bedouin dress in red.

In Palestine (Hareuveni 1930: 120), they used roots of *Anagyris foetida* (*khseiwat al-kalb*),[66] crushing and pounding it until a liquid was obtained. This liquid was mixed in a cup of water and given to the patient. In North Africa (Boulos 1983: 187–91), leaves of *Alisma* spp. (*mizmar al-raa'y*) or the dried roots of *Thapsia garganica* (*diryas al-abdan*) were boiled in water and the resulting tea was administered by mouth. The Bedouin of Sinai use a medicinal liquid (*sharbah*)[67] to treat a person who had been bitten by a rabid dog (Shuqayr 1916: 411). The Arabs in the pre-Islamic period believed that the blood of a murdered king or prince was an effective antidote against rabies and a few drops mixed with water were drunk by a person bitten by a rabid dog (al-Shatti 1970: 5–10; Ullmann 1970: 185–89, 1978: 1–6). There is a significant custom in Arabia (Dickson 1949: 191) among the Birzan tribe, who "having been blessed by the Prophet Muhammad himself for their kindness and hospitality, were rewarded by being told that even their blood was blessed—hence it is believed that to drink a Birzani's blood will cure a man of impotence, cause a woman to conceive, and counter the poison of a mad dog." According to Dickson (1949: 540) "if a person is bitten by a dog suffering from rabies, he must immediately find a man of the Birzan section of the Mutair, and drink a coffee-cup full of his blood (which he pays for). The blood of a Birzani so taken is regarded among all the tribes of North-Eastern Arabia as an infallible cure."

Among the Rwala, Musil (1928: 326) heard the following anecdote about a poet, a member of the Dahamshe tribe, who had been bitten by a mad dog. His relatives dragged him to a water hole, gave him salt, flour, and dried dates to last him forty days, and threatened him with death should he leave the place and come near them before the forty days had expired. They believed that the rabies would resolve itself after this period of time. The injured man had to stay in the desert alone. His faithful comrade, Hmud, was on a raid at the time. Hearing on his return of the misfortune that had befallen his friend, he rode to him despite his kinfolk's warning of the contagion, thirty days having passed since the accident. The sick man is supposed to have composed this epigram for Hmud: "O Hmud, take care of me who has been ensnared, for among my kin is no honest man who would think of me."

Sir Richard Burton (1893: 389) pointed out that Arab Bedouins interpreted rabies as occurring when "a bit of meat falls from the sky and a dog eating it becomes mad." If a man was bitten by such a dog, his fellows had to "shut him up with food, in a solitary chamber, for four days." However, if he continued barking like a dog, they would "expel the demon from him, by pouring over him boiling water mixed with ashes."

Louis Pasteur's invention of the rabies vaccine on 1885 had a significant effect on human health. The battle against rabies began with the use of a rabies vaccine and the gathering and killing of stray dogs. During the World War I, rabies was a great problem. The medical team of the Ottoman Red Crescent Society conducted public vaccinations everywhere they went. A hydrophobia laboratory was established and rabies vaccine was produced in Sivas as well as in other locations at Turkey (Ozaydin 2002: 194–213). Similar procedures were adopted in other hospitals around the Middle East.

Rash (*smat, ṭafah*)

Babies who suffer from diaper rash/redness on their buttocks or between their legs are treated by rubbing a mixture of olive oil, black cumin or *Nigella sativa* (*habbit al-barakah, qazhih*), and lemon juice on the affected area twice a day, morning and evening. The Bedouin of Galilee[68] (Nejidat 1984: 29) treated skin diseases and *smat* by rubbing the affected areas with the roots of asphodel (*swai*). A special red clay called *simmag* can be used to rub the infected area. It is worth mentioning that such clay (Creyghton 1992: 46), or Cimolian earth (Bos 1997: 37; Ibn al-Baytar 1992: 149–50) is widely used for medicinal purposes in the Middle East as well as in other parts of the world, and that red clay treats red rash (*smat*), according to the theory of "like on like," or "like cures like" of sympathetic magic (a form of homeopathy). Notably, tiny bricks or small bags of holy earth from Mecca or Kerbala may be used as charms for protection against disease (Doumato 2000: 149). Among the Rwala (Musil 1928: 126), the hips of a baby are plastered with dry camel manure (*dimne*). The baby is then wrapped in a long shawl tied with a thin string and fastened by two ropes of camel's hair to the main tent stakes, and the cradle is ready. It is said that the dry manure absorbs the baby's urine and excrement and prevents the red rash.

Rashes/Dried Skin (*nasaf, gashab*)

Treatments include rubbing the affected areas twice a day with olive oil that has been heated with salt, especially in winter when diaper rash is more common. The baby should be dressed in warm clothing during the winter and should not be exposed to the eastern wind (*shargiyih, am-Salih*). The hands and face should be washed with lukewarm water and rubbed with olive oil, oil of black cumin, or even with melted sheep fat tail (*dhanaba, himit*) as a preventive measure.

Rheumatism/Leg and Joint Pains (*waja' rijlin/waja' mafasil, 'asab, rih al-'asab*)

To treat rheumatism or leg and joint pains, the roots of *Asphodelus microcarpus* (*swai*) are pounded, placed in a pot, and boiled with two liters of water over a slow fire. The pot is removed from the fire and placed on embers, and the patient, who is nude from the waist down, stretches his legs above the pot so the steam covers them. After half an hour he dresses without washing, rests for a week or two, and may repeat the treatment after a week if necessary. The bran (*nkhala*) or crushed roots of *Anchusa strigosa* (*ihmim*) may be boiled in water, the mixture placed in a cloth and wrapped around the painful spot once a day for one week. A bath/sauna is prepared in which the following plants have been soaked or boiled: *Achillea fragrantissima* (*gisum*), *Capparis* (*lasaf*), *Phagnalon* (*qadih, sufan*), and *Peganum* (*harjal*). Cabbage is boiled in water with onion, to absorb bitterness, and the water is replaced and boiled. The water is drunk when it has cooled and the cabbage leaves are eaten five times a day. Leaves of *Origanum dayi Post* (*za'itri, hnaydih*) and *Reaumuria negevensis* (*millihi*) are boiled and then cooled, to be drunk twice a day for two weeks. Tea made from hyssop and *Varthemia iphionoides* (*slimania, ktilih*) is drunk. The roots of *Anchusa strigosa* (*ihmim*) are crushed and boiled in water, wrapped in a heavy cloth, and placed on the painful limb.

Other treatments include drinking tea made from *Origanum* leaves (*mardagoush*), *Tamarix* (*ithil, tarfa*), and *Mentha*; eating honey on a empty stomach early in the morning; heating the fruit of *Citrullus colocynthis* (*handhal*) on coals and wrapping it around the painful limb; or rinsing the painful limb with sheep tail fat, table salt, and vinegar. Burns are made with a small needle round the painful limb.

In cases of sprain, the Bedouin of Jabaliya in Sinai (Ben-David 1981: 125) recommend burns and complete rest for one week. The Negev Bedouin (al-'Aref 1933: 248) used to treat the patient with complete rest (*hijbih*) for two weeks. They also eat honey (Abu-Khusa 1979: 106–11). The Bedouin of Galilee (Hilf 1985) inhale steam (*hablih, 'argih*) and take saunas, rinse the affected area with sheep tail fat, or use burns around the painful limb. The Bedouin in Egypt (Osborn 1968: 165–77) treat rheumatism by using *Citrullus colocynthis* (*handhal*). The Bedouin of Sinai (Levi 1978: 70–72, 1987: 303) use a sauna with steam made from the following plants: *Hammada scoparia* (*haddad*), *Hammada salicornica* (*rimth*), *Capparis cartilaginea* (*lassaf*), *Ochradenus baccatus* (*kurdhy, kurdy, gurdi*), *Ziziphus spina-christi* (*sidrih*), *Reaumuria negevensis* (*millih*), *Atriplex halimus* (*gataf*), *Tamarix aphylla* (*ithil, tarfa*), *Peganum* (*harjal*), *Mentha* (*na'na'*), and *Juncus litoralis* (*samar*). Alternatively, they heat *Capparis cartilaginea* (*lassaf, lussayf*) or *Citrullus colocynthis* (*handhal*) on a fire and apply these to the painful spot. The Bedouin of the Negev and Sinai (Bailey and Danin 1981: 145–62) use *Scrophularia xanthoglossa* (*zeita*), *Capparis cartilaginea* (*lassaf*), *Phagnalon rupestre* (*gadih*), and *Citrullus colocynthis* (*handhal*). According to Bailey (1982: 65–88), they may also wear a bracelet (*swar*) made of camel's wool (*wabar*).

Musil (1928: 667) mentions that among the Rwala Bedouin, rheumatic pains (*rih*), especially in the *sferi* season (October–December), was treated by burning the affected limb. The Rwala also hunted the vulture (*nisr*, pl. *nsur*) and ate its flesh. Seven pieces of its flesh dried in the sun were the preferred remedy for rheumatism and hemorrhoids. The patient was instructed to eat these seven pieces at once, cover himself with seven quilts, and sweat (Musil 1928: 36).

Scabies (*jarab*)

Treatment for scabies may consist of the application of olive oil that has been stored in a bag made from the skin of the *Varanus griseus* (*waral*) (a type of lizard). This oil is also used for the treatment of eczema, impetigo (*goubah*), and other skin disorders, including rashes. The body may be rubbed with the green leaves of *Thymelaea hirsuta* (*mitnan*). The Bedouin of the Negev (Abu-Khusa 1979: 106–11) rub the body with a mixture of olive oil and sulphur (*al-zayt wal-kabrit w-atla' ya jarab*). In the Arabian Peninsula (Dickson 1949: 507), scabies on children's scalps (*agra'*) were treated with a mixture of clarified butter and charcoal.

Sciatica (*'irq al-nsy, 'irq al-nnasa*)

Sciatica is diagnosed by folk healers, usually men, who treat it with cauterization, which is followed in all cases by forty days of complete rest.

In addition, the wool-like leaves of *Phagnalon rupestre* (*gadih, sufan*) are collected and dried, laid on a flint[69] (*sowwan/suwwan*), and ignited with sparks from a piece of hard steel (*znad*). The burning leaves are placed on several parts of the body: the hip (*wirk*), the leg, behind the knee (*rukba*), and above the ankle (*rummanih*). Sometimes burns are made in different locations of the body. A piece of burning cloth, red-hot iron, or hot stone[70] may also be used. During my fieldwork, I met Sheikh Salman 'Ali al-Huzaiyil of the Bedouin Negev, who was the most famous healer of sciatica. Patients flocked to him from all over the country and even from abroad. His son, Sheikh Jaddu', followed in his father's footsteps. They used the dried leaves of *Phagnalon rupestre* (*qadih, sufan, qray'i*) to cauterize[71] (*kay, kai, kawi, makwa*) the area of pain from the sole of the foot to the thigh of the patient. Following this treatment, the patient was required to rest for forty days,[72] consume a special diet, and refrain from sexual activity. According to Ben-Assa (1974: 73–76), healers among the Negev Bedouin treat certain diseases by making burns or scorches on various parts of the body; this treatment is related to a method that employs "counterirritants" and is used among different cultures in the world. The Bedouin of Galilee (Hilf 1985) also treat sciatica by making burns along the leg, as do the Bedouin of the Negev (Shinnawi 1982), using leaves of *Phagnalon rupestre*.

Scorpion Sting/Snake Bite (*garsit 'agrab/garsit ham*)

Treatments for scorpion sting and snake bite include administering a glass of olive oil, especially one that has been blessed by a dervish with verses from the Quran. When a dervish, functioning as a *hawi*,[73] is called in to treat a scorpion or snake bite, he drinks olive oil and gives some to the stricken person to drink. He makes a cut near the bite with a razor heated in a fire and sucks out the blood, which the Bedouin believe is the venom, and spits it out.[74] While he is doing this, he chants verses from the Quran and other sources, prays, and asks for the mercy and aid of Allah, the prophets, and the angels, to help him heal the victim. The dervish gives the victim tea and camel's milk or other milk to drink, and instructs him not to drink water for two days, since doing so is believed to stimulate the action of the poison in the blood. The leaves of *Ballota undulata* (*ghassih*) or *Heliotropium* (*dhanab al-'agrab*) are boiled in water and the liquid is drunk.

In Palestine (Hareuveni 1930: 120), the ashes of burnt *Eryngium creticum* (*kursannih*) and *Carlina lanata* (*kharshuf, shouk*) are applied to the sting. The bite or the whole body is massaged with olive oil from a bag made of *Varanus griseus* (monitor lizard [*waral*]) skin. Drinking a glass of oil from this bag is considered effective medicine for a victim of a scorpion sting or snake bite.

The Bedouin also use a special bead called a sting bead or bite bead (*kharazat al-hwaia*)[75] to treat patients; half a teaspoon of sugar is put on a scorpion sting or snake bite and the bead is put on the sugar. The Bedouin believe that the bead draws the venom from the afflicted person and relieves pain. The sugar acts as a paste to keep the bead in place, and relieves pain. A finger that has been stung by a scorpion or bitten by a snake may be placed in a lizard's mouth (*Agama pallida* [*am brays*]) for about half an hour. A *waral* skin bag may be filled with olive oil and hung from one of the tent poles. One to two tablespoons of this oil are ingested.

Another treatment involves killing a honey badger (*Meles meles* [*al-gharir, al-ghariri, am ka'yb*]) if possible. A bag made from the animal's skin is filled with olive oil, which is taken orally (one teaspoon) as a remedy. Some Bedouin give this medicine to their children prophylactically. The Bedouin may also kill an Egyptian vulture (*rakhamah*), cut the carcass into small pieces, grind it, and cook it in a pot with 2–3 tablespoons of Bedouin butter, saffron, onion, black cumin, and a liter of water. They each drink a small glassful of the soup as a preventive medicine against scorpion and bee sting, snake bite, spider bite, or food poisoning. The Bedouin of the Negev (Shinnawi 1982) drink olive oil several times a day.

The Jabaliya Bedouin in Santa Catharina-Sinai (Ben-David 1981: 126) treat scorpion sting/snake bite with the saliva of a *hawi*. There is a Bedouin proverb that says, "the *hawi* of snake bite can't heal himself" (*al-hawi ma biyhwi nafsih*) meaning that a healer who is endowed with the rare ability to suck out snake poison and provide this essential service to others is unable to use it to help himself (Bailey 2004: 109). The *hawi* has the ability to suck poison from scorpion stings and snake bites; this process is transferred by the *hawi* mouth and called *hwaya* (Bailey 1982: 84).

The Bedouin of Southern Sinai (Levi 1978: 75, 1987: 296, 305–6) appeal to the *hawi* to treat snake bites and scorpion stings, make burns around the sting, or administer tea made with *Cleome droserifolia* (*samwih*) or *Tamarix*. Another treatment consists of placing a cowrie that has solid black colour on its back or placing a mixture of flour, onion, and olive oil on the sting, or administering oil from a *waral* skin bag by mouth.

Among the Bedouin of the Negev and Sinai (Bailey and Danin 1981: 145–62), burns are made by placing smoldering dried leaves of the *Phagnalon rupestre* (*gadih*) around the sting. The Bedouin of Galilee (Hilf 1985) also make burns around the sting, while the Bedouin of the Negev (Ben-Assa 1970: 218) spread sugar on it. The Negev Bedouin (Abu-Khusa 1976: 70; 1979: 106–11) use burns on the head, and give the patient milk and olive oil to drink.

Among the Rwala Bedouin in Syria (Musil 1928: 669), in cases of snake bite, the healer (soothsayer) is sent for and cures the stricken man with his saliva. The healer learns this art from a member of the Rifaiye order,[76] in the *an-Nukra* in the neighborhood of Damascus. No snake can harm a healer.

In Arabia (Dickson 1949: 505, 513), in cases of snake bite, the bitten spot is deeply cut with a knife and bled. Two tourniquets must be applied to the limb (arm or leg) above the bite. A sheep must be slain at once, and the bitten person wraps his whole body in the skin to make him perspire. After twenty-four hours, the skin is removed and the patient drinks tea made from *Heliotropium cignosum* (*ramram*), while the bitten spot is covered with its leaves. In Iraq (Dickson 1949: 505), a stone called "cat's eye" (*sulaimaniyah*) is used to extract the scorpion venom. According to Lawrence (1979: 277), "the Howetat treatment of snake bite was to bind the affected part with a snake-skin plaster and read chapters of the Quran to the sufferer until he died. Three of our men died of snake-bites, four recovered after great fear and pain, and a swelling of the poisoned limb."

According to the Prophet Medicine, the Prophet allowed the treatment of poisonous stings such as snake bite and scorpion stings with *Ruqya.* The Bedouin hunt a bird called the short-toed eagle (*Abu al-doud*)[77] and feed its liver and heart to their babies to immunize them against snake bite. The healer recited Surat al-Fatiha, gathered his saliva, and spat on the scorpion sting or snake-bite (al-Bukhari 1974: 424–27). Bailey (2004: 34) cites a proverb that suggests using caution after a bad or tragic experience in the desert: "He who is bitten by a viper will jump from a spotted rope."

The Greeks believed in a stone that cured snake bites, and hence was named the snake stone. To test its efficacy you had only to grind the stone to powder and sprinkle the powder on the wound (Frazer 1962: 257–58).

"Shifted Liver" (*makbud, makboud, mkawshikh*)

A "shifted liver" is diagnosed when the liver is found to have moved downwards. According to the Bedouin, shifted liver is one of the most serious liver diseases. Symptoms include aching shoulder; severe pains in the legs; knees that prevent the patient from walking up an incline or climbing stairs; white eyes; pale complexion; loss of appetite, especially for fatty foods; and lack of thirst. The person tires easily, and has pains in the hands, elbows, and back and general weakness in the limbs and body. Bedouins believe that this illness is a result of a blow to the ribs during a fight, lifting a heavy object, or trauma to the ribcage or liver by a strong blow. It may also be caused by falling off a horse, camel, or donkey.

Shifted liver is a serious illness and is treated by a special healer, usually a woman. Treatments consist of complete rest and several additional actions. Olive oil is rubbed over the area of the liver. Burns are made around the skin on both hips with a red-hot iron. The patient is made to stand on his head for a few minutes, three times a day for a week. A strap is tied around the patient's abdomen at the height of the liver for three to seven days, and fatty food is avoided. A comb is tied in a scarf and placed over the liver for a week. This special lightweight comb is made from animal bone and has dense teeth on both sides. The Bedouin believe the comb functions as an external support, keeping the liver in place, like a cast or splint applied to mend broken bones.

Treatments consist of the following: leaves of *Anthemis pseudocotula* (*rbayan*) finely ground and mixed with honey and taken three times a day for a week; a salted, dried, and minced wolf's liver[78] is mixed with olive oil and eaten early in the morning; camel's milk is mixed with camel urine and drunk.[79] The tongue of a hyena may be salted, dried, and eaten raw or grilled on an open fire and eaten.

The diagnosis and treatment of suspected shifted liver varies for adults and children. In the case of an adult, the healer instructs the patient to lie on the ground with his feet and legs elevated and resting on an object about thirty centimeters high. The healer pours lukewarm olive oil in her hands, tells the patient to breathe deeply, and proceeds to examine the region of the liver. If the ribs are compressed as a result of trauma and are pressing on the liver (*mkawshikh*), the healer massages the area (*takbiyd*) with slow upward movements. If the ribs are bent inwards, she straightens them with her fingers—a painful procedure that is executed very slowly. When the massage is completed, the healer ties pieces of cardboard or cloth over the area with a scarf to secure the liver in place and prevent it from moving downwards. The liver should then move slowly back to its natural position.

The healer performs the massage for twenty to thirty minutes, twice a day, in the morning and evening, for fifteen days in serious cases, and seven days in milder cases. During this period, the patient stays with the healer and is forbidden to move except to tend to his physical needs. Following the morning massage, he eats a light breakfast of hard-boiled eggs, potatoes, honey, and flat bread made from wheat or barley. He rests for another two to three weeks at home, during which time both men and women are instructed not to engage in sexual intercourse. This treatment and the rest period of up to forty days is called seclusion or confinement (*hijbih*). The degree of seclusion and content of the diet vary according to the healer. Some healers prescribe complete seclusion and no fatty or sour foods. Other do not insist on seclusion and allow the patient to eat fatty and sour foods in limited quantities, since every case is individual and should be judged on its own merits.

If the patient also suffers from a common cold, he is given an egg yolk to drink every morning. If he coughs frequently, he is given a brew of *Artemisia herba-alba,* Bedouin processed butter, and ground coffee to drink every morning. More serious colds and coughs that complicate shifted liver are treated by drinking half a cup of a brew made from the seeds of *Lepidium sativum* (*habb al-rashad*), onion, safflower, and nutmeg (*Myristica fragrans* [*jouzit al-ttib*]) boiled in water every morning for a fortnight. This medicine helps heal the liver condition and stops the cough. Young boys and girls under the age of fifteen are not treated with massage, because their livers and intestines are more tender and sensitive than those of an adult. Instead, the boy (or girl) is lifted onto the woman healer, back to back, with his head down and his legs on her shoulders. She walks around her house two or three times (about 150 meters) twice a day, in the morning and evening. The hands and legs of both adults and children are shaken or snapped briskly several times after each treatment to improve blood circulation. The patient stays in the healer's house for this seven- to fifteen-day treatment, and rests at home for another two to three weeks, during which he may not work or exert himself. He consumes a diet of hard-boiled eggs, potatoes, honey, chicken, wheat or barley flatbread, fruit, vegetables, and biscuits, both for their medicinal and nutritional value. Am Salem, a Bedouin woman healer, told me that she treated a patient who had been hospitalized several times until he finally came to her. "After examining him, I found he had a shifted liver. I treated him and he recovered." She said that doctors sometimes refer patients to her and she could not recall a case of shifted liver she was not able to help. She continued:

> I treat all those who turn to me without payment. If someone brings me a gift of food, I accept it because this is the custom among Bedouin. I learned this profession from one of my female relatives. When I was young I had a shifted liver and my female relative treated and healed me. Afterwards, I used to visit her and watch her work. She saw that I was suited to learn her trade and taught me. I have been treating people for more than forty years. I teach other women. I have convinced three other women to learn the profession and they now treat people. They consult me in serious cases and sometimes I go to see their patients and counsel them. This profession is only for women. I don't know of any men who practice it. I mainly treat relatives and friends, but if strangers request my help I ask my husband for permission to treat them and he always agrees. You should remember that I am an old woman, Allah has given me a *baraka* in my hands, with this *baraka* I heal sick people; it is not human to refuse treating and healing these people, I heal them with the help of Allah.

Al-'Aref (1933: 245–46) describes treatment among the Bedouin of the Negev similar to the one mentioned above. The Bedouin of the Negev (Shinnawi 1982) also use massage and olive oil, burns, and eating cloves to strengthen the liver (Abu-Khusa 1979: 106–11). The Bedouin of Southern Sinai (Levi 1978: 68) use cupping and burns round the navel and drink tea made with *Zygophyllum coccineum* (*rotrayt*) and *Cleome chrysantha* (*sufira*). The Bedouin of Galilee (Hilf 1985) use burns on the shoulders or on the chest. Ben-Assa (1964: 451) notes that Bedouin women often complained that the liver was "swinging" (*kibdi mlawlah*), i.e., moving backwards and forwards or from one side to side.

Shock/Fright[80] (*khilia'h, khawf, khuf, rajfih, rajjih*)

Symptoms of undefined anxieties and sudden fear and are treated by a female family member or healer. Treatment is carried out with a "fright cup/shock pot/ shock pan" (*tasit al-rajjih/rajfih, ru'bih*). The original pot was a human skull, but today it is made of copper or silver, decorated with verses from the Quran (1:1–7; 2:255; 37:1–7; 84:1–4; 113:1–5; 114:1–6) and God's names,[81] Muhammad's family name,[82] and the names of the angels.[83] The best pots are brought from Mecca. The pot must not be exposed to sunlight, even indirectly, or its power will be diminished. The procedure is carried out between the thirteenth and twentieth days of the lunar month, to maximize the effect of the moon and stars (*tanjim*).[84] The pot is filled with water, yogurt, or milk and placed on top of the tent during the night. Verses from the Quran are recited and prayers are offered for the healing of the patient. The patient is awakened before dawn, made to drink the liquid from the pot and is suddenly told, "Know that you are drinking from a human skull." Fearful, the patient throws away the pot. The Bedouin believe this sudden fright cures the patient of his anxiety. The pot may not be touched by a woman for forty days after childbirth or miscarriage, by a menstruating woman, or by an unclean woman or man (after sex). Only women perform the treatment and most of the patients are women, boys, and girls, although a man can also be treated. Women who fail to conceive because of a sudden shock are also treated in this manner. Another treatment involves drinking a tablespoon of olive oil from a *waral* skin bag in the morning.

In Palestine (Hareuveni 1930: 122–23), the leaves of *Adiantum capillus-veneris* (*sha'ar al-ghulih*) are steeped in water and the liquid is drunk. The rationale behind this therapy is that the leaves of this plant shake most of the time from any wind or movement around them, like a frightened person. Ben-Assa (1970: 220) reports that the Negev Bedouin believe that this kind of fear (*khilia'h, khawf, khuf, rajfih, rajjih*) is caused by a jinni and best healed by a dervish, who is often more successful than Western physicians in these matters.

The Jabaliya Bedouin (Ben-David 1981: 128) use *tassit al-rajjih* to treat shock and fright. They administer a liquid made by boiling leaves of *Ruta chalepensis* (*faijan, fijan, shadhab, ruta*) in water. They also place the leaves under the pillow. The rationale behind this therapy is that the name of this plant means jinni (like cures like). Verses from the Quran are also chanted to treat the patient. (Quran 37:1–7; 84:1–25).

Sinusitis (*waja` ras muzmin*)

Treatments for sinusitis include wetting a handkerchief with cold water containing ground roots of *Anchusa strigosa* (*ihmim*) and tying it around the patient's head or lightly salting slices of potato skin and tying them on the forehead with a headscarf. The head may be washed with a liter of water in which the leaves and pounded roots of *Lycium shawi* (*'awsaj*) have been boiled, three times a day; this mixture may be used to make tattoo (*washm*) marks between the eyes and the ears, and on the forehead. The boiled leaves of *Achillea fragrantissima* (*gisum*) may be placed in a bowl of water and their vapor inhaled.

The Bedouin of Galilee (Nejidat 1984: 30) treat sinusitis by making burns on the head, between the eyes and the ears. Ben-Assa (1964: 452) reported that sinusitis was very rare among the Bedouin of the Negev in the 1960s.

Skin Diseases/Allergic Diseases (*amrad jild, hakkih, hikikih, hasasiyih*)

Allergic skin diseases and dermatitis are treated by rinsing the body once a day for one week with water in which *Asphodelus microcarpus* (*swai*) roots or the leaves of *Zygophyllum* (*'adhbih*) have been boiled. Other methods of treatment include squeezing the juice of the fruit of *Citrulus colocynthis* (*handhal*) on the affected body, rubbing a compound of sulfur mixed with lemon juice on the body once a day for a week, and rinsing the body in *Convoluvulus* sap (*middaidy, maddaidy*). The patient may also wash with a new bar of soap seven times in a row and after each washing say: "I bear witness that there is no one worthy of being worshipped except Allah and I bear witness that Muhammad is the messenger of Allah." *Achillea fragrantissima*, hyssop, *Artemisia herba-alba*, and *Pituranthos tortuosus* may be boiled in water and given to the patient to drink. A child's body may also be washed with this solution or with *Achillea fragrantissima* soaked in warm water once a day for a week. Olive oil mixed with parched wheat grains (*jiriyshih*) may be spread on the skin. The Bedouin in the Arabian Peninsula eat wolf's flesh as a treatment for skin diseases (Doughty 1921: 372). The Rwala Bedouin (Musil 1928: 667) treat eruptions[85] on the body and itchy skin by drinking *hebbhar*[86] and garlic (*tum, thum*) in milk.

Children's skin diseases may be treated in several ways. A lotion made from the ash of a goat's horn (*garin 'anz*), dried chicken droppings (*warass*), and a little water may be applied daily for a week. The body may be rinsed daily for a week with water in which the roots of bugloss (*Anchusa strigosa* [*ihmim, lisan al-thur, hemhem*]) have been boiled. A mixture of olive oil and a little salt may be applied to the skin once a day for a week. The body may be rinsed with water from the Dead Sea once a day for a week. Olive oil that has been kept in a receptacle made from the skin of the monitor lizard (*Varanus griseus* [*waral*]) may be applied to the skin. A sick child may drink a brew made from barley (*Hordeum* [*sha'air*]) boiled in water, or be washed with this liquid to lower fever. The Bedouin of the Negev (Dafni and Dafni 1975: 238) squeeze the roots of *Asphodelus microcarpus* (*swai*) on the body or use lemon juice. The Bedouin of Sinai (Levi 1978: 63) give the patient water in which leaves of *Artemisia judaica* (*b'aythran, bu'aythiran*) have been boiled. A drink made from the leaves of *Reaumuria negevensis* (*millih*) and *Farsetia* (*jirba, jraybih*) soaked in water is administered.

Skin Rashes from Spoiled Food (*tafah al-shariya*)

A person who eats spoiled food may experience an allergic reaction, including a red rash on his body. Treatments include rubbing the body with lukewarm olive oil or oil of black cumin mixed with table salt twice a day and rubbing a mixture of lemon juice, vinegar (*khall*), and table salt on the body. The Bedouin of Galilee (Hilf 1985) allow the patient to inhale the smoke of roasted dried *Rumex* (*hummad saghir, hummidhah, hummidh*) several times a day. The Bedouin of the Negev (Abu-Khusa 1979: 106–11) rub the body twice a day with a mixture of crushed garlic and table salt.

Sleeplessness/Insomnia (*galag*)

Treatments for insomnia may involve hanging a written amulet on the upper part of the body or placing it under the pillow. A small Quran may be placed under the pillow to induce sleep. Drinking a concentrate of boiled black tea made from the leaves and flowers of *Matricaria aurea* (*rabil*) is also recommended.

Smallpox (*jadrah, jadari, jidri*)

The leaves of *Salvia fruticosa/triloba* (*marmarya, miramia*) are boiled in water and taken as a drink. The leaves of *Achillea fragrantissima* (*gaysum, qisum*), *Retama raetam* (*ratam, ratama*), or *Ballota undulata* (*ghassih*) are boiled and the liquid is used to wash the body. The body may be rubbed with lukewarm olive oil mixed with table salt. Another treatment involves diluting red clay (*hamra*) in water and then pouring the liquid into the patient's eyes or washing the body in the Dead Sea. Bedouin used to take pustules (*bathr,* pl. *buthur*) from the patient during his recovery, mix them with camel milk, and give the milk to humans to drink, in order to immunize them against smallpox (Abu-Rabia 2005b: 421–29). In Palestine (Hareuveni 1930: 124), they would soak leaves of *Eucalyptus bicolor* (*keina*), or *Umbilicus intermedius Boiss* (*mukhallidah*) in water and give it to the patient to drink. The Bedouin of Southern Sinai (Levi 1978: 65, 1987: 300) wash the body with boiled water and *Cleome droserifolia* (*samwih*). When they have smallpox, the Bedouin of Galilee avoid salty food (Hilf 1985). In Arabia (Dickson 1949: 507), when children caught smallpox (*jidri*), they were segregated in a distant tent. The healer inoculated the patients with serum taken from another smallpox victim. This drastic treatment was often fatal, but was sometimes effective as a cure.

Spider Bite (*garsit 'ankabout*)

A spider bite causes pain, fever, sweating, headaches, and blurred vision. Medical treatments for spider bite include drinking olive oil from a *waral* skin bag and drinking camel or livestock milk. In addition, the following ceremony is performed by a dervish, a *hawi,* or a known folk healer: the spider is examined and a white sheep or black goat is slaughtered, according to whether the spider's back is white or black. A small grave-like ditch is dug approximately 50 centimeters deep from the tent. A fire is lit in this ditch and quenched with water or sand. The patient is stripped, lain on his back in the ditch, and the viscera (*kirsh*) of the sheep or goat are poured over him. His body is then covered with straw or clothing and he is made to lie, perspiring profusely, for twenty to thirty minutes, after which he is taken out of the ditch, washed with lukewarm water and soap, dressed and put to bed. He may drink only tea and milk and eat only light, nutritious food for the next twenty-four hours.

This ceremony derives from a Bedouin tale about how the female spider, after copulating with her husband, bit and killed him. According to this story, the husband's last words were, "Oh, widow, God will blacken your face for killing your husband," to which the female replied, "I swore to God that anyone I sting must go to his grave." The Bedouin believe that the female's oath cannot be broken, but she can be cheated of her victim if a mock burial is conducted. Like a real burial ceremony, the mock burial is followed by feasting on the slaughtered animal. Neither the word spider (*'ankabut*) nor the stung person's name is spoken throughout the ceremony in order to trick the spider and avoid arousing its suspicion.[87]

The Bedouin believe that a spider carrying several offspring on its black[88] back at the beginning of winter signifies a wet winter and a plentiful harvest. While the Bedouin know that some spiders are poisonous, they will not destroy a spider's web out of gratitude for the generous act performed by a spider for the Prophet Muhammad. When Muhammad was fleeing his enemies in the early days of Islam, he hid in a cave. A spider spun a web over the cave entrance, leading Muhammad's pursuers to conclude that no one was inside. This story is recorded in the Muslim oral tradition (hadith), and there is an entire Sura devoted to the spider (Quran 29).

In Palestine (Hareuveni 1930: 120), *Pallenis spinosa* (*bakhkhur maryam, shabath*) is used because the shape of the flowers' crown resembles that of a spider. Among the Rwala (Musil 1928: 669), bites of scorpions and poisnous spiders are cured by wrapping the wounded limb in a raw animal skin or by laying the patient in an oblong pit whose bottom is covered with camel manure thrown over camel urine, then covering the patient up to his head with clay or sand and building a small fire at his side to make him sweat thoroughly. To prevent him from falling asleep they shout at him, "O thou who has been bitten by a spider, wilt thou live or wilt thou die?" He must answer: "I shall live, I shall live, not die."

Spleen (*thal, tihal, ithal*)

Treatments for spleen include oral administration of olive oil or black cumin mixed with salt, performing light massage with this mixture, as well as boiling the leaves of *Pituranthos tortuosus* (*zaqquh, zagguh*) and administering it as a drink. According to Levi (1987: 301) the Bedouin of Southern Sinai make burns round the spleen with a needle or boil the leaves of *Zygophyllum dumosum* (*'adhbih*) and *Cleome droserifolia* (*samwih*) in water to be taken by mouth.

Stomachache/Abdominal Pain (*waja' batin, maghs batin*)

Stomachache and abdominal pain are treated by eating or drinking the following substances or mixtures as indicated, repeating the treatment the following day if the pain continues: water in which leaves of *Teucrium polium* (*ja'adih*) have been boiled, three times daily for three days; a glass of water in which fenugreek (*Trigonella foenum* [*hilbih*]) has been boiled, once a day for two to three days; a glass of water in which the resin of frankincense (*Boswellia carterii* [*luban*]) has been boiled; a cup of yoghurt (*laban, marisa*) produced by dissolving dried cheese (*'afig, 'afyg*) in water twice a day for one to two days. Alternatively, a piece of *'afig* may be placed in the ashes of the hearth for ten minutes and eaten hot.

Eating meat and soup made by boiling hyena (*dhabi', daba'*) meat in water is said to be good treatment for diarrhea and dysentery. Bitter coffee (*gahawa*) with a little Bedouin processed butter (*samnih, samin, samn*)[89] is drunk in the morning before eating or drinking, for three days. Water in which a piece of hyena skin has been soaked is drunk. Water in which roots of *Anchusa strigosa* (*hmim, ihmim, lisan al-thour*) have been soaked is another treatment for stomachache. Eating garlic on an empty stomach, in the early morning, or mixing it with *laban* is also recommended. A glass of camel's milk[90] (*halib nagah*) may be taken daily for two to three days. Other treatments include drinking tea with lemon five times a day for three days, a glass of water in which the leaves of *Achillea fragrantissima* (*gisoum*) have been boiled twice a day for two days, or a glass of water or tea in which the leaves of *Artemisia arborescens* (*shiba*), *Artemisia herba-alba* (*shih*), or *Artemisia judaica* (*b'aythiran*) have been boiled two to three times a day for two or three days. A glass of water or tea in which the leaves of *Eucalyptus globulus* (*keina*) have been boiled may be drunk twice a day for three days. A tablespoon of pure honey may be swallowed three times a day for three to five days. The Bedouin consider honey a holy medicine (Quran 16:68–69; al-Bukhari 1974: 397–98).

In Palestine (Hareuveni 1930: 118–22), bowel pain is treated with water or tea in which sage (*Salvia triloba* [*marmariyih*]) leaves and *Teucrium polium* (*ja'adih*) have been boiled, two to three times a day for three days. Nursing mothers who suffer bowel pain are given a glass of water in which leaves of *Matricaria chamomilla* (*rabil, babounaj*) have been boiled. The Bedouin of the Negev (Shinnawi 1982) drink sage or *Teucrium polium* (*ja'adih*). Making burns on the chest and belly is another treatment method.

The Bedouin of Southern Sinai (Levi 1978: 56–57, 1987: 296) drink tea prepared from one or more of the following plants: *Varthemia iphionoides* (*slimaniya, ktilih*), *Artemisia herba-alba* (*shih*), *Teucrium polium* (*ja'adih*), *Achillea fragrantissima* (*gisum*), *Scirpus litoralis* (*diys, dis*), *Tamarix chinensis* (*tarfa*),

Artemisia judaica (*ba'aythran*), *Mentha*, *Rhus coriaria* (*summag, summaq, dbagh*), *Cleome droserifolia* (*samwih*), *Retama raetam* (*ratam, ratama*), *Ochradenus baccatus* (*kurdhy, kurdy, gurdi*), *Pulicaria incisa* (*ra'ra'*), *Pituranthus tortuosus* (*zagguh*), *Thymus decussates* (*za'tar barry, zu'taran*), *Hammada salicornica* (*rimth*), *Reseda luteola* (*dhanab al-kharuf*), *Suaeda asphaltica* (*swida, suida*), hyssop, or *Solenostemma argel* (*arghel*).

The Bedouin of Galilee (Hilf 1985) drink tea made from *Matricaria chamomilla* (*rabil, babounaj*), sage, and/or *Eucalyptus bicolor* (*keina, kina*). The Bedouin of the Negev (Dafni and Dafni 1975: 236; Seligman et al. 1959: 378) drink *Artemisia herba-alba* (*shih*). According to Abu-Khusa (1976: 70; 1979: 106–11), they drink sage, *Micromeria fruticosa* (*gurnia, qurnya*), *Matricaria chamomilla* (*rabil, babounaj*), *Teucrium polium* (*ja'adih*), and *Artemisia herba-alba* (*shih*). The Bedouin of the Negev and Sinai (Bailey and Danin 1981: 145–62) treat indigestion, called *marrah*, by boiling leaves of *Cassia* (*kasiah, sinamakky*) in water. Among the Rwala Bedouin (Musil 1928: 666), *sharba*—stomach pain combined with fever and endless thirst—is treated by cutting the root of the nose so that it bleeds copiously, and then burning the shoulders. Sometimes a stick is pulled through the skin of the shoulder and left there until the wound suppurates. The disease appears in winter, especially after drinking cold water.

In Arabia (Dickson 1949: 510–11), there have been cases of general stomach disorders caused by drinking muddy or infected water, especially among those who go on the pilgrimage (*haj*). These afflict both men and women, who return with dysentery, colitis (inflammation of the colon), and so forth. Doughty (1921: 80) reported the following: "After marching above one hundred miles in forty-three hours we came to the water—water-dregs teeming with worms. The hot summer nights are fresh here after the sunset, they are cold in spring and autumn, and that is a danger to the health of the journeying pilgrims especially when they return jaded from tropical Mecca."

Stomach Ulcers/Colic (*gurhat al-mi'dih*)

Treatments consist of drinking one of the following mixtures: one quarter-spoonful of myrrh (*Commiphora myrrha* [*mur batarikh*]) in a glass of goat's or camel's milk in the morning for a week; half a spoonful of resin produced from the dragon's blood tree (*Dracaena draco*/*Pterocarpus* [*dam al-akhawain*])[91] in a glass of water; a glass of milk with half a spoonful of the powder of the mastic tree/lentisk (*Pistacia lentiscus* [*mustaka*]) every morning for one week; a spoonful of the juice of the carob-locust tree (*Ceratonia siliqua* [*kharroub*) for one week; camel's milk or the milk of a black goat several times a day for one week; one small cup of honey with *Rhus coriaria* (*summag*), anise, and rinds of pomegranates crushed very well together, then added to water, boiled, and cooled, each day in the morning; *Lepidium sativum* (*habb al-Rashad*) with *Nasturtium officinale* (*jarjir*) and honey; a tincture made from the leaves of *Artemisia herba-alba* (*shih*) or *Artemisia judaica* (*b'aythiran*); or a cup of black tea with *Trigonella foenum-graecum* (*hilbih*). A pomegranate may be eaten before breakfast. The Bedouin of the Negev (Shinnawi 1982) boil Artemisia herba-alba (*shih*) with Bedouin processed butter (*samin, samnih*) and eat it. The Bedouin of Southern Sinai (Levi 1978: 58, 1987: 297) drink a tincture prepared from *Teucrium* (*ja'adih*), *Cucumis prophetarum* (*heneidhalan*), and *Cassia italica* (*kasiah, sinamakki*). The Bedouin of Galilee (Hilf 1985) eat pita bread with milk and avoid pepper and foods pickled in salt or vinegar. The Bedouin of the Negev (Abu-Khusa 1976: 70; 1979: 106–11) ingest a mixture of cinnamon, butter, and honey. They also drink water boiled with sugar and *Rhus coriaria* (*summag*). To strengthen the stomach, they drink water in which cloves have been soaked or eat ripe pomegranate and quince (*safarjal*). Among the Rwala (Musil 1928: 538), *debayel*—ulcers or abscesses—are thought to make eating unpleasant and interfere with digestion.

Stridor (*madhiub, dhibih, dhybih*)/Hoarseness (*mabhuh*)

The dried windpipe of a wolf (*'agalat al-dhib*) is hung on the patient's throat. The rationale behind this practice is that when a baby coughs, his voice resembles that of a she-wolf (*dhybih*); the use of the wolf's windpipe follows the principle of "like cures like." Other treatments include administering tea with hyssop, ginger (*zanjabil*), or cinnamon (*girfih*) and burning incense and letting the baby smell it. In Palestine (Hareuveni 1930: 122), the leaves and stalk of *Limonium sinuatum* (*khubayzit sayyiadih*) were boiled and the solution was drunk, and sage (*Salvia triloba*) was used as a gargle. The Bedouin of the Negev (Dafni and Dafni 1975: 235) gargle with *Matricaria aurea* (*babunaj, rabil*) boiled in water and suck on crystalline sugar (*sukkar fadhdhi*) several times a day (Abu-Khusa 1979: 106–11).

Stuttering (*ṭaram*)

Stuttering is treated with donkey milk, which is believed to cure a child who stutters or fails to start speaking at the proper age. It is believed that the milk of a female donkey has the power to untie the tongue of such a child. "Tongue-twisting" is viewed as the doing of a jinni or the evil eye. Other measures to cure stuttering include hanging a special amulet prepared by a dervish on the baby, drinking tea prepared from anise or hyssop, making a pilgrimage to a holy tomb, and sacrificing an animal.

Sudden Stomachache (*waththab*)

Sudden stomachache is treated by a healer having the adult patient, male or female, lie on the belly with arms extended alongside the body. The healer massages him or her vigorously, by grasping and releasing the muscles of the left shoulder until the patient screams with pain. The healer then pulls the patient's left hand and hits the upper muscle of the left arm. He wraps that arm in a head-scarf and places it under the patient's head for ten to twenty minutes, until the hand becomes numb. Following this treatment, the patient drinks tea, puts on warm clothes, and sleeps.

Sunburn (*darbit shams*)

Sunburn is inflammation of the skin caused by overexposure to the sun (*shubih*), while sunstroke is heat stroke brought about by excessive exposure to the sun. The pastoral nomadic Bedouin have acclimatized to the desert, having learned to deal with excessive heat by adapting their pattern of living to the climate (Sohar 1980: 157–58) such as refraining from strenuous work in the sun. In order to prevent sunburn or sunstroke the Bedouin wear heavy clothing, cover the head and neck, and refrain from exposing themselves to the sun during the hottest hours of the day. They begin working early in the morning and rest in the heat of the day, moving as little as possible to avoid dehydration from sweat and conserving energy so they can renew their work in the late afternoon. To treat sunburn, the Bedouin rubbed the body with a tincture produced from the leaves of *Inula viscosa* (*tayun*), with the leaves and fruit of *Calotropis procera* (*'ushir*), or put yoghurt on the affected areas. The Bedouin of Galilee (Hilf 1985) drink yoghurt and rest.

Syphilis (*firjal, franji, bajal*)

Treatments for syphilis include boiling the leaves and flowers of *Retama raetam* (*ratam*) in water, drinking a cup of the liquid and washing the body and the genitals with it. Another method of treatment involves roasting the seeds of *Asparagus stipularis* (*tgaytgih*) in a pan, pounding them, mixing them with alum and water, and washing the genitals with the mixture, mainly at night. The leaves and flowers of *Matricaria aurea* (*rabil*) may be boiled and the liquid used to wash the body and the genitals. The bulbs of *Colchicum ritchii* (*wada'*) may be roasted in hearth ashes and eaten, or its dried bulbs may be soaked in water and the infusion drunk. Likewise, the bulbs of Cyclamen persicum (*sabunit al-ra'ay*) may be roasted in hearth ashes and eaten, or soaked in water that is used for washing the genitals. The Bedouin of the Negev and Sinai (Bailey and Danin 1981: 145–62) roast the seeds of *Asparagus stipularis* (*tgaytgih*) in a pan, pound them, and let the patient inhale the powder. Al-'Aref (1934: 269) found that the Bedouin of the eastern Negev Desert in the early 1930s were afflicted by syphilis (*franji*—the disease of the Franks, i.e., white men).

In Palestine (Canaan 1927a: 166) in the 1920s, it was believed that a man should never have sexual intercourse with his menstruating wife as the begotten child will be leprous or syphilitic. In Arabia (Dickson 1949: 508–9) the disease was known as *balash* among the Bedouin, and *fringi* among townsmen, as it was common among them. Philby (1933) related that it was rare in Najd. Dickson (1949: 508) assumed that the sea-coast towns gave the disease to Najd, from whence it spread to Mecca and Riyadh. He also believed that the Turks brought it to the province of Hasa prior to 1912, though some of it must have also come from Bahrain. In Kuwait, the tent of a sufferer who has contracted the malady is placed far apart from the others, and no one is allowed to go near it or to leave it except to take food and water that are placed there for the occupants by friends, some 300 yards from the tent.

Teeth/Dental Problems (*waja' snun*)

Dental problems are treated by gargling and washing the mouth with lukewarm salt water several times a day; gargling with a brew made from leaves of *Polygonum equistiforme* (*gudhdhab*) several times a day for a week; gargling several times a day with salt water in which sage has been soaked or with a brew made from *Salvadora persica* (*arak, siwak*); wearing a special seashell as a necklace; inserting *Salvadora persica* (*arak, miswak, siwak*) leaves in the left nostril; applying the ripe fruit of *Solanum nigrum* (*'anibet al-dhib*) to the sore teeth for five minutes, removing it, and rinsing the mouth with lukewarm water and salt; or drinking tea made from chamomile or hyssop several times a day.

Teething pain in children is treated with olive oil, safflower, butter, or sheep's fat massaged into the gums. These are purported to slow the growth of the teeth and reduce pain. Bleeding or pain in the gums or teeth was treated by rubbing them with bituminous material (*hummara*).[92]

In Palestine (Hareuveni 1930: 123) they used *Solanum nigrum* (*'anibet al-dhib*) or *Populus alba* (*safsaf abyad*) to treat dental problems. The Bedouin of the Negev (Bailey 1982: 65–88) dissolve plant sugar in water (*sukkar fad-hdhi*) and garlic (*thum*) and put drops of this liquid into the mouth, morning and evening. The Bedouin of the Negev and Sinai (Bailey and Danin 1981: 145–62) use *Lycium shawi* (*'awsaj*), *Peganum* (*harjal*), and *Hyoscyamus* (*sakaran*). The Bedouin of Galilee (Hilf 1985) treat gum infection by making burns on the gums using a small needle. The Negev Bedouin (al-'Aref 1933: 246) treat toothache, dental caries, or dental "holes" caused by *susih/sousih*,[93] (a tiny worm)[94] by applying resin of *Ferula asafetida* (*hiltit, jiddih*) to the tooth to relieve the pain. They also use burns on the tooth.

The Bedouin of the Negev (Abu-Khusa 1979: 106–11) put cloves (*grunful*) on the tooth for fifteen minutes, remove them and rinse the mouth with lukewarm water and salt. The Bedouin of Southern Sinai (Levi 1978: 59–60, 1987: 298) use seeds of *Peganum* (*harjal*), *Zygophyllum dumosum* (*'ad-hbih*), *Citrullus colocynthis* (*handhal*), *Solenostemma argel* (*arghel*), roasted coffee powder, palm, *Thymus decussatus* (*za'tar barry, zu'taran*), *Avicennia marina* (*girm, qurm*), *Ochradenus baccatus* (*kurdhy*), *Hammada salicornica* (*rimth*), *Pergularia tomentosa* (*ghalqa, demia*), or burns on the tooth.

Usually when a milk tooth comes out, the child throws it in the direction of the sun and says: "O sun, take a donkey tooth and give me a tooth of a gazelle." There is a similar custom in many countries, for example in Palestine. A child must throw his or her milk teeth away towards the rising sun and say, "God, take the brown teeth and give me white ones, so that I may drink calf's milk."

In Arabia (Dickson 1949: 157), women clean their teeth with the bark of a tree called *darum*, which enhances their beauty by turning the lips saffron-red. When a boy's tooth fell out, the Arabs in the pre-Islamic period believed he could guard against an ugly one growing in its place by taking the tooth between his index finger and thumb and throwing it at the sun saying, "O sun! Replace it with a better one" (al-Shatti, 1970: 5–10; Ullmann 1970: 185–89, 1978: 1–6).

Thirst (*'atash*)

Treatment methods include giving the baby honey or honey mixed with camel milk to drink, and boiling leaves of *Pituranthos tortuosus* (*zagguh*) or *Coridothymus capitatus* (*zahayfy*) and drinking the liquid. Levi (1987: 286) notes that the main reason for cutting the uvula among the Bedouin of Sinai is to allow them to bear thirst for a long time. Bailey (1975, 1982) found among the Bedouin of the Negev and Sinai that they protect their children from thirst by giving their babies honey, which causes the throat to be moist all the time.

Tick Fever (*dalam*); Brucellosis (*humma maltya*)

Humans as well as animals (livestock,[95] partridges) who live in abandoned caves are liable to contract tick fever or brucellosis. A Bedouin rids a cave of ticks (*dalam*) by burning *Thymelaea hirsuta* (*mitnan*), *Sarcopoterium spinosum* (*billan*), or rubber (*kawshak*), which also drives off or kills scorpions, spiders, and other dangerous insects. A person suffering from tick fever is given large quantities of sweet food such as candy, honey, halva, or grape honey (*dibs*), which is believed to drive out the fever. Another option is to make a brew from the roots of *Achillea fragrantissima* (*gisum*), bring it to a boil, and put in a confined space, such as a bathroom. The patient takes off his clothes, lets the steam cover his body, and dresses without washing or drying himself. This procedure is carried out two or three times a day for about a week. In some cases, the patient is also given a brew of *Achillea fragrantissima* (*gisum*) to drink. His body is massaged with olive oil or oil

FIGURE 2.6 *Badan* meat is considered to be nutritive, and is used as a diuretic and to treat paralysis.

of black cumin to prevent itching and scratching, and he rests for two to three weeks.

The Bedouin of the Negev treat brucellosis (Malta fever [*humma maltya*]) in humans by eating garlic and onion. For afflicted animals, they mix garlic, onion, and naphtalene (*funik*) in water and put a cup of the mixture in the animal's mouth (Ihmid Abu-Naja, personal communication, 1 June 2007). Ben-Assa (1968: 13–18, 1974: 73–76) mentions that the Bedouin of the Negev were frequently bitten by animal ticks and get tick fever/brucellosis. Despite exposure to modern medicine and education campaigns, one still encounters brucellosis due primarily to the use of unpasteurized milk; according to Hakhmon et al. (1998: 3–7), there were 151 newly diagnosed cases of brucellosis in Israel in 1997. Forty-four percent were in the Negev and 20 percent in the north of Israel. Most of the cases diagnosed at the Soroka Medical Center in Beer-Sheba were Bedouin, reinforcing the impression that there is a connection between brucellosis and the unique living patterns of the Bedouin.

Tongue Infection (*imdhafdi'*)

When the baby has an infection of the tongue while nursing, he sounds like a frog, so this infection is called *dhifdi'* (frog), and the afflicted baby is referred to as *imdhafdi'*. Treatments include boiling olive oil with crushed seeds of black cumin and rubbing the baby's tongue once a day, usually at night before sleeping, and rubbing the tongue with oil of black cumin once a day. The Bedouin of Galilee (Hilf 1985) dip cotton wool in indigo dye powder (*nilih*) and rub the underside of the tongue, twice a week; they hang from the baby's head material made from a seashell/clamshell (*sadafah*), or a stone that looks like a frog.

Tonsillitis (*bnat adhan tayhat*)/ Peritonsillar Abscess/Quinsy (*habbih mikhtiyih*)

Lukewarm olive oil is smeared on the neck and a scarf tied around the chin and head and knotted on the top of the head. Other treatments include eating garlic or onion with salt, drinking a brew of hyssop several times a day, and hanging special beads around the patient's neck. A healer who possesses a *baraka* spits on his/her hands and massages the neck, in order to "bring back" the tonsils and cure the tonsillitis. Gargling with lukewarm water and table salt or sodium bicarbonate is also recommended. The healer attempts to squeeze out the pus using his little finger smeared with onion. Sometimes, in difficult cases, the Bedouin make a cauterization in the shape of X on the head of the patient using a needle.

The Bedouin of the Negev use massage and hang special beads around the neck (Shinnawi 1982). They also eat *samnih* or gargle with lukewarm water mixed with chickpea (*hummas*) seeds (Abu-Khusa 1979: 106–11). The Bedouin of Galilee use massage in addition to gargling with salt water as well as burns on the neck, under the lower jaw near the tonsils in cases of *am/um al-hlug* (peritonsillar abscess) (Hilf 1985). Hilf mentions another disease called *al-shwihija,* in which the patient feels as though he is being strangled from inside his neck; the treatment is drinking milk of a black ass/donkey without prior boiling.

Tuberculosis (*sill*)

Tuberculosis (*maslul*) patients must eat nourishing food, stay in the fresh air (*hawa shafa*) and keep away from children. Remedies include tea prepared from one of the following plants: black cumin, fenugreek, *Lepidium sativum* (*hab al-rashad*), *Achillea fragrantissima* (*gisum*), *Retama raetam* (*ratam*), *Inula* (*tayun*), and *Lycium shawii* (*'awsaj*). Garlic and onion are eaten. The Bedouin of Sinai (Levi 1978: 63, 1987: 299) drink tea prepared from *Asparagus stipularis* (*tgaytgih*). Ben-Assa (1964: 452) comments that the Bedouin in the Negev during the 1950s and 1960s contracted tuberculosis as a result of new contacts[96] with the Jewish population that had immigrated from abroad to the new State of Israel in part of Palestine in 1948.[97] Before that time, the Bedouin had never been exposed to tuberculosis, so their resistance to it was low and they had not developed any kind of immunity. Their low resistance to this disease was accompanied by a lack of medical care, poor nutrition, and unsanitary water. Malnutrition, dust and sand, sandstorms, and sleeping in close proximity to one another inside the nuclear family all caused tuberculosis to spread.

In Arabia (Dickson 1949: 160) in the mid-twentieth century, tuberculosis was treated by branding/burns. Two small straight brands are branded on the left wrist opposite the thumb, and if this treatment is ineffective after fifteen days, two additional brands are placed on the right wrist.

Tumors[98] (*khlund, sartan, dummal*)

A black tumor with hairs inside it is called (*hizam nari*). It is treated by mixing seeds and oil of black cumin (*habbit al-barakah*), lemon juice, and sap from the leaves of *Convoluvulus* (*middidy*) and rubbing the tumor with this tincture twice a day for three weeks. Other treatments include making burns round the tumor using a small needle and rubbing the tumor with high-quality henna powder mixed with water. Tumors on the body or on the neck are treated by rubbing them with a tincture produced in the following way: burning the skin of a young calf (under the age of one year), adding to it processed butter (*samnih*) made from cow's milk, a liquid called *qitran* produced from *Juniperus communis* (*'ar'ar, 'itran*), verdigris[99] (*junzara*), and *Psychotria ipecacuanha* (*'irq al-dhahb*). The tumor is rubbed with this mixture twice a week for one month.

Ben-Assa (1964: 453) comments that among the Bedouin of the Negev, cancer seems to have been very rare; the first breast cancer was reported in 1964. The Bedouin of Southern Sinai (Levi 1978: 64, 74) wash the tumor (*dummal*) with a tincture produced from the following plants: *Asparagus stipularis* (*haliyun*), onion (*basal*), *Lepidium sativum* (*habb al-rashad*), and *Cleome droserifolia* (*samwih*).

Dickson (1949) reported a case in which the patient had initially consulted one of the Kuwaiti doctors in 1939, who attributed the patient's symptoms to a brain tumor and pronounced the condition hopeless. The Bedouin woman healer shaved the Bedouin's head and burned a cross from ear to ear and from the nape of the neck to the forehead. At the end of the burning process she uttered words from the Quran and then ordered the spirit out. Dickson found the patient in healthy condition weeks after the time the doctor had told him he would be dead.[100]

Uncontrolled Yawning (*tathawib*)

Treatments for this ailment include burning incense (*bakhkhur*) on Monday and Tuesday evenings and inhaling the smoke, hanging a special amulet on the body, and drinking and massaging the face with olive oil or oil of black cumin. The Bedouin of southern Sinai (Levi 1987: 299) boil the leaves of *Fagonia* (*shki'ya*) in water and drink the potion. Among the Rwala (Musil 1928: 399) in the early twentieth century, it was thought that when yawning the Rweyli (Rwala man) must be very cautious, as the throat opens wide during this process and a demon then may let a drop of its urine fall into the man's throat, causing various diseases.

Undescended Testicle/Cryptorchidism (*khuswah mirtafa'ih*)

A Bedouin told me his son was born with an undescended right testicle. He took the child to a doctor in Beer-Sheva, who told him the child would have to undergo surgery. The father opposed this and took the child to a Bedouin healer, who heated a needle over a flame and made burns behind the child's right ear (on the artery or vein behind the ear [*'irg idhin*]), shoulder, and spine.[101] A week later the right testicle began to descend slowly until it was at the same level as the left one. A man who has a defect in one of his testicles[102] is called *abu-khuswa.* If he is impotent as a result of the defect, he is called *makhsy*, which means "castrated." According to Shinnawi (1985), the Bedouin treat swollen testicles with cauterization on the legs.

Urinary Tract Illnesses: Urine Retention/ Urethral Obstruction (*hasir boul*)

To treat urine retention, the leaves of one of the following plants are boiled in water and drunk twice daily: *Ammi visnaga* (*khall, khillih*), *Paronychia argentea* (*rijl al-'asfour, rijl al-hamam*), *Achillea fragrantissima* (*gaysum, qisum, gisum*), *Petroselinum sativum* (*bagdunas*), *Teucrium* (*ja'adih*), *Artemisia herba-alba* (*shih*), *Trigonella foenum-graecum* (*hilbih*), and barley. The seeds of *Lepidium sativum* (*habb al-rashad, hurf*) are mixed with egg yolk and eaten early in the morning. Two tablespoons of olive oil are drunk, one in the morning and one before bedtime. In Palestine (Canaan 1920–1921: 155–65), water taken from cisterns and from certain springs and wells are used for various medical and magical purposes. For example, the water of *'iun al-hasr* (springs of suppression of urine) is used to cure the suppression and retention of urine. There is a folk belief that any person who urinates in flowing water will contract a urogenital disease. *Ein [En] al-farkha waddik* in Salt (Jordan) has a curative action in the suppression of urine (Canaan 1920–1921: 170). Among the Rwala (Musil 1928: 408), it is believed that if someone has been bewitched, he will experience difficulty in urinating. To help him, the Bedouin shoot a porcupine from which they extract the gall bladder, and, pressing out its contents into a little water, drip it into the nostrils of the sick person. The Bedouin of the Negev (Abu-Khusa 1979: 106–11) treat retention/obstruction of urine by eating ripe quinces (*safarjal*) or drinking tea prepared from the seeds of *Trigonella foenum-graecum* (*hilbih*) or barley.

Uvula (*khlyjy, ikhlyjy, ukht al-dh'uf*)

Ben-Assa (1974: 73–76) reports that Bedouin mothers believe all baby's diseases are caused when the uvula—the small piece of soft tissue that can be seen dangling down from the soft palate over the back of the tongue—

"falls down" inside the throat. The symptoms are of this illness are dry nostrils and twisted eyelashes (*al-rmush maftulih*). Treatments for this ailment include making a tiny incision in the uvula, in order to "shock it" and to cause it to contract, so it returns to its original position. Neck massage by a special healer using lukewarm olive oil may also be employed to bring the uvula back to its original position. These healers are blessed by a *baraka* from God. In certain circumstances, the uvula is cut and removed by special surgical blades (*shafra*), a razor (*muss*), or forceps (*malgatt*).

Shinnaw (1982) reports that the Bedouin of the Negev use massage. Levi (1987: 286) states that the main reason for cutting the uvula among the Bedouin of Sinai is to enable the person to bear thirst for a long time (see above section on thirst). The Sinai Bedouin believe that removing the uvula also "vaccinates" the baby from various childhood ailments and immunizes him from thirst in harsh and hot desert weather. Dr. Hillel Nathan (1980: 156) found that among the Bedouin of Southern Sinai, almost all preschool age children undergo throat surgery in which their uvula is removed. Nathan et al. (1982: 774–78) found that many Bedouin in South Sinai "believe that it increases their ability to tolerate thirst, while others say that it prevents upper respiratory tract diseases or certain mechanical difficulties, such as obstruction of the larynx due to a hypertrophic uvula."

Over the years, this operation has been transformed into a ritual undergone by all members of the tribe. Such operations were also known in Ethiopia, Tanzania, the Barbary Coast, and Saudi Arabia (Sarnelli 1940: 288–93). The procedure is self-conducted by tribe members (healers) with a spatula-shaped spoon used to support the uvula in order to cut it off with a knife. Certain tribes in Tanzania do this with a looped piece of string, sometimes employing a hair from the tail of a mule, knives, razor blades, or scissors.

Vaccination/Immunization (*tat'ym*)

The Bedouin use different methods to vaccinate themselves against poisonous stings and bites. The *hawi* (who is immune), places sugar[103] in his mouth, moistens it with his saliva, then places it in the mouth of the baby (usually during its first six months of life). This practice is supposed to protect the baby from scorpion, hornet, and wasp stings and snake bites. The mother crushes a hornet and mixes it with sugar, water, or milk, and gives it to her baby to drink. Alternatively, she crushes a burnt scorpion mixed with water and places it on her nipple, so that her baby will suckle it with her milk. This process is called "sucking the scorpion" (*ridha'at al-'agrab*).

Vaccination from Wounds (*dhra'ih, madhru', dhra'*)

Among the Bedouin of Southern Sinai, Levi (1978: 29) found that the mother makes a tiny incision in her baby's left arm (*dhra'*) and places there about one centimeter square of "seborrhea capitis/vernix." [104] This material is absorbed into his body and vaccinates against illness. The baby is then called *madhru'*, while the vaccination is called *dhra'ih*. Sometimes *dhra'ih* is carried out by amulet: the "seborrhea capitis/vernix" is placed in small bag made from animal skin, and is hung on the baby's neck. The Bedouin believe that babies vaccinated in this way will not suffer from blows, his arms will not be broken, and no bullet will be able to penetrate his body.

Vomiting (*gdhaf*)

Treatments for vomiting include soaking the following plants in water and administering drops of the liquid as nose drops three times a day: mint (*na'na'*), *Teucrium polium,* bugloss, *Anchusa strigosa* (*ihmim, lisan al-thur, hemhem*), *Noaea mucronata* (*sirr*), *Solanum dulcamara* (*hulwa murra*), cloves (*grunful*), hyssop, and sage. In children, rennet is placed on the stomach (see Abdominal Sprain) or a vomiting bead (*kharazat al-glazz*) is hung on the child. If the baby vomits during or after nursing, it is given tea made with one of the following plants: lemon, *Matricaria aurea* (*babunaj, rabil*), hyssop, *Teucrium* (*ja'adih*), *Varthemia iphionoides* (*slimaniya, ktilih*), salvia, *Mentha,* or *Thymus decussates* (*za'tar barry, zu'taran*) several times a day.

The Bedouin of the Negev (Abu-Khusa 1979: 106–11) soak two or three cloves in water (*qurunful, grunful*) and drink the liquid or eat the ripe fruit of quince (*safarjal*). According to al-'Aref (1933: 244), burns are made on the stomach and shoulders. The Bedouin of southern Sinai (Levi 1978: 57, 1987: 297) drink tea made with *Cleome droserifolia* (*samwih*), *Teucrium* (*ja'adih*), *Hammada salicornica* (*rimth*), *Mentha, Thymus decussates* (*za'tar barry, zu'taran*), or *Rhus tripartite* (*'irn*).

Vomiting and Diarrhea (*taraf, mitrif, gdhaf wa-hrar*)

Babies afflicted by *taraf,* a combination of vomiting and diarrhea, are called *tarfan.* As a preventive medicine measure, the mother may expose her baby to many scents during the first week of his life in order to prevent him from developing allergies, nausea, vomiting, vertigo, or dizziness from scents he will encounter as he grows up. Therefore, he is introduced to a resin from asafoetida (*Ferula assafoetida* or *Ferula narthex* [*jiddih,*[105] *anjudan, haltit*]) with its very pungent scent.[106] The following plants are collected before dawn, placed in water, and set on the roof of the tent overnight to allow the stars[107] to act on them: *Anchusa strigosa* (*ihmim, lisan al-thur, hemhem*), *Eryngium creticum* (*kursannih*), *Polygonum equistiforme* (*gudhdhab*), *Pituranthos tortuosus* (*zagguh*), *Noaea mucronata* (*sirr*), *Solanum dulcamara* (*hulwa murra, sabra murra, 'inab al-dib*), and crystalline plant sugar (*sukkar fadhdhi*). Early each morning for a week, the solution is absorbed with a piece of cotton or sheep's wool and used as nose drops for babies.

The Bedouin of the Negev (Shinnawi 1982) attribute this disease to the baby having smelled something bad or impure (*al-'ayyl mistarwih'*). The baby is treated by allowing him to smell a mixture of plants in a clean cloth soaked in a small amount of water several times a day, drinking this liquid, and being washed in it. This medicine is supposed to cancel the effect of the bad smell. It consists of *Tamarix aphylla* (*ithil, tarfa*), *Phragmites australis* (*gasabah*), cinnamon (*girfih*), *Lepidium sativum* (*habb al-Rashad, hurf*), crystalline plant sugar (*sukkar fadhdhi*), *Achillea fragrantissima* (*gisum*), *Trifolium arvense* (*nafal*), *Teucrium polium* (*ja'adih*), *Cleome droserifolia* (*samwih*), *Malva parviflora* (*khubbiza, khubbayza*), *Launaea tenuiloba* (*lbynih, lubynih*), *Convolvulus* (*middaidy, maddaidy*), *Eryngium creticum* (*kursannih*), *Matthiola livida* (*shugayra, shugira, fijjayli*), and *Anthemis* (*rbayan*).

Warts (*thalul*, pl. *thawalil*)

The treatment of warts (*thalul*) varies according to their number and location. A piece of flesh or spleen is rubbed on the wart and then buried in the ground in the belief that when this flesh decomposes in the earth, the wart will disappear from the body. For a wart on the finger, the finger is put in the mouth of small lizard, *Agama pallida* (*am brays*), for fifteen to thirty minutes, while the lizard sucks on it, after which it is buried alive. The Bedouin believe that the wart disappears as the lizard decomposes. Alternatively, the lizard is killed, its blood is smeared on the wart (also on boils), and the lizard is buried. The lizard's belly may also be rubbed on the warts or on the largest wart, after which the lizard is wrapped in a rag and buried.

Other treatments include inserting two thorns into the wart, forming the shape of a cross. If they are left for one week, the wart will disappear. Ashes of burnt *Phragmites australis* (*gasaba, bous*) or a burnt mat (*hasira*) made from palm-tree leaves (*burdi*), or earth from a holy tomb may be rubbed on the wart.

According to Shinnawi (1982) the Bedouin of the Negev cut the upper side of the wart with a razor blade, while the remaining part is burnt with

Phragmites australis (*gasaba, bous*). Levi (1978: 64, 1987: 300) reports that the Bedouin of Southern Sinai stab the warts using thorns taken from palm trees, then put earth taken from an ancient tomb in the wart, or place a praying mantis (*sayf rabna*)[108] on the wart and let it lick the wart, leaving its saliva.

According to Stavi (1946: 329–47), the Palestinians believe that warts appear on the body as a God's punishment for counting the stars at night. In Andjra, Morocco, if lighting strikes a tree and splits it, a piece of its wood is taken and the wart is rubbed with it (Westermark 1926).

Weaning (*ftam, iftam*)

It is believed that the longer a child is breastfed, the stronger it will become. Moreover, prolonged lactation is said to postpone the next pregnancy. If a woman becomes pregnant soon after the last delivery, she is afraid to suckle much longer, believing that pregnancy changes the composition of her milk completely. Any ailment of the baby is attributed to this milk. Among pastoral nomadic Bedouin, cooked foods available for infants would also have enabled mothers to shorten the period of weaning. To wean the baby, mothers smear their nipples with a bituminous substance (*hummara*), *Teucrium* (*ja'adih*), *Artemisia herba-alba* (*shih*), *Brassica oleracea* (*malfuf*), *Solanum* (*hulwa-murra*), *Vinca minor/heracea* (*'anaqyya*), *Alnus glutinosa* (*hawrah rumiya, maghth*), *Stellaria media* (*'ayn al-jamal*), *Salvia officinalis* (*marmarya, miramya*), pepper, *Launaea spinosa* (*kbath*), *Acacia negevensis* (*talh*), or *Citrullus colocynthis* (*handhal*). In all cases, the offensive taste causes the child to abandon the mother's breast. The Bedouin women of Southern Sinai (Levi 1978: 30) use the droppings of a black goat for this purpose.

Whooping Cough (*gougih*)

Patients suffering from whooping cough (usually children) are fed a diet composed of hot food and soup and no sweets. The child may be given hot asses' milk to drink twice a week. Burns may be made on the exterior trachea. A brew made with the leaves of *Hedera helix* (*'ulyg*) in water and drunk twice a day. The Bedouin of the Negev (Shinnawi 1982) use burns on the wrist and between the fingers. In Arabia (Dickson 1949: 507) in the mid-twentieth century, whooping cough (*abu hamaiyir*) was common among the children in spring and autumn, and usually ran its course with no serious consequences.

Womb Contraction (*inkimash al-rihm*)

Pinczuk (1994) found that among the Bedouin women of the Negev, in order to encourage uterine contractions following delivery, mothers drink several cups a day of an infusion of the following plants for two to three weeks: *Teucrium* (*ja'adih*), *Salvia triloba* (*marmariyih*), *Artemisia judaica* (*b'aythiran*), *Tamarix aphylla* (*tarfa*), *Matricaria chamomilla* (*rabil*), and *Trigonella foenum-graecum* (*hilbih*). They also eat a dish of dates with olive oil called *makhtum*, *Portulaca oleracea* (*farfahina*) cooked with rice, or dried leaves of *Eminium spiculatum* (*irgita*) cooked with egg.

Women among the Negev Bedouin also wear a special red belt or girdle made of sheep's wool (*sufiyih*), a symbol of fertility, for forty days following childbirth (Abu-Rabia 2011). The girdle (*sufiyih*) indicates a woman's being at the height of her fertility and sexual activity.[109] This belt is worn in order to encourage uterine contractions and to prevent a "fallen womb."[110]

In Kuwait and Bahrain (Dickson 1949: 173) women traditionally treated the womb by packing it with salt following childbirth. To return the size of the vagina to normal, after the birth of a baby, they rub it with alum.

Wounds/Sores (*jarh*, pl. *jruh*)

Wounds and sores are treated by boiling leaves of *Ballota undulata* (*ghassih*) or *Artemisia herba-alba* (*shih*) in butter, applying it to the wound and holding it in place with a cloth. A powder of crushed roasted coffee or the scrapings of the inside of a leather belt (*jilditt hzam*) may also be applied to the wound to stop bleeding.[111] An ointment may be made by boiling an onion or the juice of leaves of *Cleome droserifolia* (*samwih*) in olive oil or Bedouin butter. Alternatively, dried droppings of a donkey or ass from the previous spring are boiled and strained and the liquid put on the wound. In early twentieth-century Palestine (Hareuveni 1930: 121), powder made from *Ceterach officinalis* (*'ishbit al-juruh*), Inula *viscosa* (*tayun*), and Malva sylvestris (*khubbayzih*) was used to treat wounds. In the Nabi Rubin area, Palestinians used the fruits of *Typha domingensis* (*turraysh*) and *Herniaria hirsuta* (*maker, mkur*). The Bedouin of the Negev (Shinnawi 1982) put kohl on the wound. The Bedouin of Southern Sinai (Levi 1978: 73, 1987: 304) drink tea made from *Hammada scoparia* (*haddad*), *Hammada salicornica* (*rimth*), *Retama raetam* (*ratam*), *Cleome droserifolia* (*samwih*), and *Achillea fragrantissima* (*gisum*) or wash the wound with water with salt, coffee, or human, livestock, camel, or donkey urine. The Bedouin of the Negev and Sinai (Bailey and Danin 1981: 145–62) use *Cleome droserifolia* (*samwih*), *Solenostemma argheln* (*arghel*), and *Fagonia* (*shki'ya*).

The Bedouin of the Negev (Dafni and Dafni 1975: 237) use *Marrubium vulgare* (*roubia, qriha*) boiled in olive oil or the roots of asphodel and salt. Among the Bedouin of the Negev (al-'Aref 1933: 244) flesh wounds are sewn together with ordinary needles and silk thread (*harir safi*). Sometimes, the needle is left in part of the wound until it is healed. A paste compounded of pure olive oil and soap (*sabun bikr*)[112] is used for gunshot wounds, after the bullet has been removed. The soap is boiled in oil until it becomes elastic. It is then smeared on the wound and bound tightly to prevent bleeding. If the bullet is not near the surface, they take a pigeon,[113] tear it until it bleeds, and place the bird's bloody side next to the wound. The bird and the wound are then bound while the patient and healer tell themselves that the bullet will be absorbed by the pigeon's flesh. If the bullet has entered a man's chest or intestines, efforts are made to rush him to a doctor, if possible.

The Bedouin of the Negev (Abu-Khusa 1976: 70; 1979: 106–11) apply *samnih,* honey, or ashes from a burnt mat[114] (*hasira*) made from palm-tree leaves (*burdi*) or powdered roasted coffee to wounds.

Among the Rwala in the early twentieth century (Musil 1928: 26), the skin of the young antelope (*Oryx leucoryx* [*maha*]) is used for making water bags or coverings, and from the fat skin at the back of the neck (*'ar'ur*), the Bedouin sew gauntlets (*daraga/darake*) for protecting the hand against saber wounds. The wounded person stops his nose with *ketaran* or *hantita* drug as a protection against injurious odors. He must deny himself sweet dishes, which, according to local belief, would cause the wound to fester.

At first soap is applied to the wound. The urine of young children is also used to clean wounds (Musil 1928: 668). Among the Rwala (Musil 1928: 97) camel's fat, known as *shahm,* is cut up and boiled into suet (*makhlu'* or *widak*). *Widak* is a good remedy for boils and suppurating wounds. They use pork fat in healing both wounded men and animals (Musil 1928: 395).

When treating wounds, the Bedouin also carefully observed the stars, since they believe that their influence on man is more unfavorable than favorable. Wounds would not heal, it was thought, when pierced by the rays of either the stars or the sun. Therefore the wounded person is laid, wrapped in all sorts of covers, in some corner of the tent so as to keep the rays from him (Musil 1928: 399).

Urine may be used as an antiseptic for cleaning wounds as well as for other purposes. In Arabia (Dickson 1949: 159), the urine of the she-camel is used as a purgative, eye-wash, wash for wounds, hair wash, and general tonic among the Bedouin. It kills head lice instantly. During a raid (*ghazu*) by a war party, the companions of a wounded man will wash his wounds with their own urine for the same reason. But to gain the best results it must be urine of young fighters, not elderly men (Dickson 1949: 512).

When a man is suffering from a wound, certain scents (*riha*) or smells harm the wound and cause it to open again. It is harmful for a man who has had sexual intercourse and not yet had time to wash to approach a wounded man. Similarly, a menstruating woman is a danger. Both are considered unclean (*najsih*) and thus harmful.[115] In Arabia (Lawrence 1979: 443) urine was also used as an antiseptic.

Notes

1. Rennet contains renin, an aspartic proteinase structurally homologous with pepsin, formed from prochymosin, the milk-curdling enzyme obtained from the glandular layer of the stomach of the calf (Stedman 2000: 349).
2. For more methods for abortion in Egypt see Morsy 1982: 157–58.
3. This *rishush* contains cloves, resin of *Boswellia carterii* (*luban, bakhur*), rice, lentils, incense, *junzara,* cumin (*Cuminum cyminum* [*kamun*]), anise seeds, black cumin seeds, *Lepidium sativum* seeds (*hab al-rashad*), and wheat and barley seeds.
4. Compare to magical rituals in Nigeria (Maclean 1971: 79–80).
5. *Wasitt al-bayt* is the symbol of male sexual organs (for more details about this term see Havakook 1986: 69).
6. There are similar beliefs among other peoples in the world. For example, in Ponape, one of the Caroline Islands, the umbilical cord is placed in a shell and then disposed of in a way as that will best adapt the child for the career that the parents have chosen for him. Among the Cherokees, the navel-string of a boy is hung up on a tree in the woods, in order that he may be a hunter (Frazer 1962: 260; Blom 1992: 37).
7. Compare this ritual to that found in Egypt (Morsy 1982: 165) and among the Slayb tribes in Syria (Jabbur 1995: 429–30).
8. *Asafetida/asafoetida* is bought in the market from a perfume vendor (*'attarin*). It is remarkable for its unpleasant odor. In Algeria, the plant is used against sorcery, demons, or jinn because of its smell (Hilton-Simpson 1922: 17). In Yemen, after childbirth, the resin of asafoetida is burnt and the smoke placed between the mother's legs to contract the vagina (Ghazanfar 1994: 208). Among the Rwala (Musil 1928: 375) when a mare gave birth to a filly, the owner of the mare smeared the filly with tar to protect it from the effect of disagreeable smells.
9. In the Indies, the herb called *Perebecenuc* is used: "When this herb is ground, the juice is extracted and then strained. It is used to wash the penis and the lower parts and all around the pubic region, especially where the pain is most frequently felt. When everything is thus washed, the ground herb with its juice is taken and put in those places mentioned, and in a few hours, before a natural day of 24 hours passes, the patient can urinate, the stone is broken and the suffering is totally relieved" (Valdes 1992: 122).
10. Foreskin in Arabic is *ghulfe*; the insulting name for an uncircumcised person is *Abu-ghulfe,* means "father of the foreskin." In the Bible, too, "uncircumcised" is a derogatory term (Granqvist 1947: 207).

11. See also Kazaz 1990; Marx 1973: 411–427.
12. The aborigines of Central Australia believe that under certain circumstances, the near relations of a wounded man must grease themselves, restrict their diet, and regulate their behavior in other ways in order to ensure his recovery. Thus, when a child has been circumcised and the wound is not yet healed, they may not eat opossum, or a certain kind of lizard, or a carpet snake, or any kind of fat that would retard the healing of the boy's wound. Every day the mother greases her digging-sticks and never lets them out of her sight; at night she sleeps with them close to her head. No one is allowed to touch them. Every day also she rubs her body all over with grease, as in some way this is believed to help her son's recovery (Frazer 1962: 261).
13. *Rshush/rishush* means to spread a powder.
14. *Dhrur* means to sprinkle powder.
15. *Artemisia* spp. has the active constituent santonin that heals wounds and infections (Tal 1981: 152–53).
16. Burying the foreskin in the earth was one method common in Babylon: circumcision was performed over a receptacle of water in which the blood dripped and the foreskin was dropped. The congregation attending the circumcision would dip their fingers or hands into the water and wet their faces for luck. When the circumcision took place over bare ground and the blood was absorbed, they covered the foreskin with the earth. As cited above, two customs cite two different approaches to the foreskin: removal and disposal of the foreskin by burying it or the opposite—drawing near for physical contact with it, as is customary vis-à-vis an object associated with holiness—such as the Jewish custom even today of dipping one's fingers in the wine that drips from the Saturday-night Havdalah cup and smearing the drops on one's eyelids (Rubin 1995: 105–6). The custom of using myrtle and the circumcision water is in keeping with another custom tied to myrtle. This shrub symbolized renewal and revival—thus one finds it used in other ceremonies. We see it used in marriage ceremonies—to make wreath of myrtle for grooms, dancing before the bride with cloth of myrtle (*Babli, Ktovot Yod-Zyin Eyin-Aleph*). In Babylon it was customary to sprinkle myrtle on the bed of the dead (*Babli, Bitza, Vav Ayin-Aleph*), perhaps as an expression of the continuity of life. The myrtle remains green for a long time even without water, and after the shrub is burned it sprouts triangular branches and even thicker foliage than before (Rubin 1995: 106; Rubin 2008). Perhaps for this reason it has become a symbol of renewal and growth (Hareuveni 1980: 82–83).
17. See Raz 2005; Panter-Brick 1991: 1295–302.
18. "The original wellspring of these marriages was almost certainly the Arabian camel Bedouins, who evolved a preference for both cousin marriage and virtual consanguineous marriage due to a process of gene-culture coevolution. In fact, at the same time that Arabs were breeding their camels for greater milk production, ancient Arabian camel nomads were breeding themselves via consanguineous marriage and virtual consanguineous marriage to ensure that their kin would continue to survive on milk in the waterless desert" (Reilly 2013: 374–85).

19. Compare that to Egypt (Morsy 1982: 152–53), where traditional contraceptive methods include nursing and insertion of a cube of sugar after sexual intercourse "to absorb the semen."
20. See "The Effectiveness of Symbols" in Lévi-Strauss 1963: 206–31.
21. See also the use of this plant in Medicine of the Prophet (al-Jawziyya 1998: 230–32; Rispler-Chaim 1992: 13–20).
22. Prof. Michael Alkan, director of the Institute for Infectious Diseases, Soroka Medical Center and Ben-Gurion University of the Negev, *Opinion on the Subject of Public Health, Water Supply to Unrecognized Locales in the Negev.*
23. Levy et al. 1998: 179–86.
24. For more details regarding the evil eye, see Abu-Rabia 2005e: 241–54.
25. Compare this with an acephalous society, the Mkako of Cameroon: "He stole some items of clothing, some nail cuttings and hair from his elder agnate ... to be used in sorcery to kill his elder agnate ... then, he caught a chameleon and hung it up with a medicine made from the stolen things" (Copet-Rougier 1986: 55).
26. The ancient Turkish tribes believed that good health and illness were strongly related to the good and evil spirits in nature, so the healer—*kam*—would enable contact between the spirits and the people. The healer treated the patient whose soul was taken by evil spirits, accompanying the souls during their journey to the world. The healer would wear a special robe bearing symbolic figures and a mask, and perform the ritual by playing his magical drum and dancing around the sick person, who would be laid by the side of a fire. Music was a fundamental element of such rituals as a mystical and magical method (Bayat 2002: 51). For more details regarding the use of music as a therapy to expel jinn from the body, or during trance, see Rouget 1985; Turner 1967.
27. See Abu-Rabia (1994c: 215–18, 2012: 157–66).
28. The use of the shoe and spitting: the shoe is considered to be unclean, and with its help, devils are exorcised. Spitting in the face is intended to humilate the devils and drive them out. What seems a curse to one it may be a blessing to another (Abu-Rabia 2012: 157–66).
29. According to Dickson (1949: 540): "If a person is bitten by a dog suffering from rabies, he must immediately find a man of the Birzan section of the Mutair, and drink a coffee-cup full of his blood (which he pays for). The blood of a Birzani so taken is regarded among all the tribes of North-East Arabia as an infallible cure." Compare treating a mad dog with al-Shatti 1970: 5–10; Ullmann 1970: 185–89, 1978: 1–6.
30. Even in ancient Arabia, when a sheikh wished his only son to divorce a barren wife, the sheikh had first to vow that he would never speak to his son, and then to call in all the elders and warriors of the kindred group to persuade him (Smith 1903: 68).
31. A marmot (Musil 1928: 28).
32. In prehistoric skulls that have been collected in all parts of the world, holes made by trepans can be found. These are holes cut out of the bone with flint instruments to obtain access to the brain. It would appear from the evidence of the Stone Age skulls of thousands of years ago that these holes could have

been used to treat a localized condition—migraine, epilepsy, or even brain tumours. The positioning of the holes may support such an assumption (Ritchie Calder 1958: 42–43)

33. The Baganda (Uganda) believe that a barren wife infects her husband's garden with her own sterility and prevents the trees from bearing fruit; hence a childless woman is generally divorced. Based on the theory of homeopathic magic, a person can influence plants (by his act or condition) either for good or for evil: a fruitful woman makes plants fruitful, a barren woman makes them barren (Frazer 1962: 250). See also Eickelman on a similar belief about barren women in Oman (Eickelman 1993: 652–66).
34. "We give you to drink of that which is in their bellies, from betwixt the refuse and the blood, pure milk palatable to the drinkers" (Quran 16:66).
35. For more details about breastfeeding see Abu-Rabia 2007: 38–54.
36. African pastoralists also use many plants with thick, juicy leaves or milky sap to promote lactation because of the resemblance to the udder or to milk (Ibrahim 1986: 189–203). The Palestinians used the soft, whitish stones of the Milk-Grotto in Bethlehem to increase mother's milk. The stones are rubbed in water and the milky liquid is given to nursing women. It is believed that the Holy Family took refuge in this cave where a drop of Virgin Mary's milk fell onto the floor (Canaan 1927b: 110).
37. The term *dirrih* means mother breast or cattle/livestock udder. This bead/coral's shape resembles the shape of the breast and the udder.
38. On *kabsih/kabseh*, see Bailey 1982: 65–88; Canaan 1927b: 170; Inhorn 1994a: 487–505.
39. Pastoral nomadic Bedouin in ancient Arabia and early Islam ate the *wabr* (Amin 1969: 9) and continue to eat its flesh as a food and for medicinal purposes, since its blood, urine, and droppings are considered having medicinal properties for their livestock.
40. Ants appear in a Bedouin proverb as symbolic of hard work: "I will tire you till you are tired as an ant" (Bailey 2004: 21).
41. On the significance of this blood see Bailey (1974b: 105–31).
42. In the Bedouin cosmology, the sea is a symbol of fertility and a source of affluence.
43. Among the Bedouin of Cyrenaica, it is dishonorable for a woman to remain married to an impotent man. She cannot divorce him, but her father can insist on a witnessed test of impotency, and, if it is proven, the husband is compelled to divorce her (Peters 1990: 193, 293). The same is true among the Bedouin of the Negev and Sinai.
44. For more details about rituals of male circumcision among the Bedouin see Kazaz 1990; Marx 1973: 411–27; Shuqayr 1916: 393–95.
45. In ancient Arabia, the mother plaited the hair of her daughter, put rings in the side-locks (*jadayil*), and strung them with sea-shells; put on her a chain of cowries; and gave her a necklace of dried dates (Smith 1903: 291).
46. *Salvia multicaulis* is also used as a flavoring for tea, and as a drink with boiled water and sugar (Bailey and Danin 1981: 155–56); for details about its chemical composition see (Senatorea et al. 2004: 237–40; Bagci and Kocak 2008: 13–18).

47. For more details see Abu-Rabia 2005f: 295–300.
48. Compare to Avitsur 1976: 115, 158.
49. On incense (*bakhkhur*): "Incense is a traditional perfume that is commonly used in the Arabian Gulf area. It consists of charcoal, starch, karaya gum, aromatic chemicals, plant wood, perfume, and essential oils. Incense has appeared in many forms: raw woods, wood chips, resins, powders, and even liquids or oils. The people of the Arabian Gulf use various perfumes on their body and clothes. A common ancient tradition to keep their houses and offices filled with fragrance is burning incense on hot coals in a special type of incense burner (*mabkhara*). The most commonly used incense for burning is *oud*. The tree referred to as *oud* is *Aquilaria agallocha*, and is also known as lignum aloes, aloes wood, agarwood, or eaglewood. The unique aroma is due to a fungal infection of the heartwood, which causes the tree to secrete [an] aromatic protective resin that has long been used in the Middle East as a source of incense and perfume. Other types of incense are derived from sandalwood and are usually mixed with other ingredients such as agarwood, natural oils, and other natural ingredients. Frankincense is a resin produced by small pine-like trees of the genus *Boswellia*. The gum oozes out, hardening in lumps. These lumps are then gathered and stored in mountain caves for six months to dry" (Abdul Wahab and Mostafa 2007: 476–77). Combined together, or with other spices such as cinnamon, cassia, and iris, they create a myriad of scents (Groom 1981).
50. See also Melling and Forsythe 1999.
51. Compare this with the treatment of psychotic patients by a healer among the Yoruba of Nigeria. When the patient is deemed ready for release, a "discharge ceremony" may be held on the banks of a river, involving blood sacrifice, symbolic cleansing of the patient of his illness, and perhaps symbolic death and rebirth into a new life (Prince 1974: 138–45).
52. The psychological literature shows that religious identification tends to increase when an individual's control over his or her circumstances weakens (Korf and Malan 2002: 149–69).
53. In the context of a *zar* ceremony: "the *ma'zur*- excused (not obliged as a result of being sick) is the vehicle of communication. Having reached an altered state of consciousness through the stimulations of a variety of musical instruments and through the rhythmic, exhausting swaying of dancing to a rapid beat, the afflicted person starts to speak in an unfamiliar tone of voice. The sound is immediately recognized as the *asyads*' response to the sheikh's calling. Speaking through the mouth of the *ma'zur*, the *asyad* then proceeds to explain the circumstances that led to their association with their host. They also set the conditions for reconciliation and for sparing their host from the ravages of illness; many of their demands are directed to the patient's personal advantage" (Morsy 1978: 601).
54. Abu-Rabia 2005b: 421–29.
55. Compare to Abu-Rabia 2001: 44; Bresslavsky 1946: 254; Saliternik 1978: 518; 'Iyd Sayyah al-Majnun, personal communication, 1 January 1993.
56. Sufian 1999; Haj Salamih Sbayyih Abu-Rabia served as a police officer during

the British mandate in Palestine, and his brother, Sliman Sbayyih Abu-Rabia, was a wireless operator] personal communication, 2 January 1993.

57. See note 20. Its chemical formula is lead sulphate (PbS), but it varies in appearance due to traces of various metals including arsenic (As), antimony (Sb), silver (Ag), copper (Cu) and gold (Au). Kohl reacts with tears in the eye to produce a lead compound and hydrogen sulphate, which gradually break down into water, lead, and sulfur; these work as cleansing and antiseptic agents. The chemical process of the breakdown of kohl in the fluid of the eye is: $PbS + 2H_2O \text{ -> } Pb(OH)_2 + H_2S \text{ -> } PB + 2H_2O + S$. For more details, see Duri 1982; Cohen 1982: 45–97; al-Tamimi 1976: 17–44.
58. Dickson does not supply details about this kind of food.
59. It is worth noting that "rings and other circles are life symbols among the ancients and one of the earliest forms was made of a knotted cord or piece of wire turned into a knot" (Fielding 1945: 34).
60. There are similar practices in rural Greece (Blum and Blum 1965: 53).
61. It should also be noted that some plants contain compounds called sterols, which can be irradiated with ultraviolet to make vitamin D. Human skin contains sterol, which is converted to vitamin D by the ultraviolet part of sunlight.
62. For general cross-cultural perspectives on midwifery, see Cosminsky 1976: 229–48.
63. For more details about *qarina*, see chapter 4.
64. The concept of blood is cited in Mkako explanations of the taboo connected with kinship, alliance, and violence: procreation originates from a mixture of the blood from the man's sperm and from the woman's uterus at the end of the menses. If the mother's blood is stronger than the father's, then the child will be a girl, and vice versa. Sometimes the sex of the child is inadequate because the blood of the sexually opposed parent is so strong and continues to fight. If such inadequacy is not remedied, the child will die. However, Mkako themselves identify incest with the eating of one's own blood, and regard both actions as the same. In short, "same" linked with "same" leads to death, life stemming only from the coupling of differences. Eating kin is self-anthropophagy, and self-anthropophagy is incest. Thus, the reason why the Mkako bury the placenta is that, should it be thrown into a river and eaten by a fish which is subsequently eaten by a relative of the child, that person has eaten his own blood and will die, as the case if someone eats his own kinsman (Copet-Rougier 1986: 60–61).
65. For more details about production of churns or livestock skins, see Abu-Rabia 1994: 105.
66. The term *khseiwat al-kalb* is diminutive for a dog's testicle.
67. *Sharbah* is a general term for drug-liquid; Shuqayr did not specify its components.
68. The northern district of Israel is called Galilee (*al-Jalil*).
69. The use of the flint is very ancient. "The earliest non-mythical records of acupuncture date from the Stone Age in China; they are inscribed on tortoise shell and explain how flint needles were used to cure diseases. Jade and bamboo later became popular, and as Chinese metallurgy progressed, iron, bronze,

silver and gold needles found their way into the acupuncturist's armory. As an alternative to needles practitioners sometimes use a technique called moxibustion, which consists of putting small cones of the dried herb artemisia on the acupuncture point, lighting it and letting it burn down almost to the skin" (Eagle 1978: 129–30).

70. It is worth noting that "using stones in medicine is mentioned among Upper Paleolithic peoples [the first people of modern appearance, who lived in the last part of the Old Stone Age]; as a new technique was used to manufacture blades. The stone is broken to create a striking platform, then vertical blades are flaked off the sides to form sharp-edged tools. It is amazing that Western medicine used scalpels in heart surgery in USA [1986] made from obsidian [a naturally occurring volcanic 'glass'] by the same technique used by the Upper Paleolithic peoples to make blades" (Haviland 1996: 79–83; Sheets 1987: 231).
71. The Prophet said: "If there is any healing in your medicines, then it is in cupping, a gulp of honey or cauterization that suits the ailment, but I don't like to be cauterized" (al-Bukhari 1974: 397).
72. Usually the patient is isolated in a solitary place such as a tent, hut, or room. The place should be a dark, and no daylight should enter it. Being in a dark place should evoke the sense of being in the grave. The isolation/seclusion/retreat is normally limited to periods of forty days. Compare this method with the *khalwa* ritual among the Sufis (Suhrawardī 2005: 125–27; Enc. of Islam 1978: 990–91).
73. For more details about the *hawi*, see Abu-Rabia 1999a: 54, 77; Bailey 1982: 65–88; Lane 1981: 170, 370–81.
74. Attempting to extract the active cause of a disease by sucking it out through a hollow tube and spitting out the poison is a common medical practice (Calder 1958: 45–46).
75. The Arabs in the pre- and early Islamic periods believed that certain precious stones and beads bore magical healing powers, prevented diseases, and brought good omens. Among these stones are emerald (*zumurrud*) and jade (*yashm*), considered to be a cure for epilepsy (*sara'*) and carnelian/cornelian (*'aqiq*), which was thought to cure animal bites. Emerald (*zumurrud*) was used as an amulet against the evil eye. An amulet (*tamima*), a spotted or speckled bead, was hung on children to ward off the evil eye, death, and disease. Solace (*sulwana*) was a white shiny bead hung around the neck or placed in a cup of water and given to a lover to drink to quench his ardor. A sinking bead (*ghatsa*) caused the enemy to be "sunk" in disease. The sterility bead (*'uqra*) was hung on a woman's loins to prevent conception. A red bead (*wajiha*) was like the carnelian that was hung on a person to prevent disease and ward off the evil eye. Antimony (*kahla*), a black bead, was hung on boys to prevent disease. The witchcraft (*tuwla/tiwala*) bead was hung on a person as protection against witchcraft, misfortune, and evil spirits. Cameos (*sadafa manqusha*) were hung on the breast or neck to treat face spots, freckles, or pustules (al-Najjar 1994: 52–53; al-Shatti 1970). For more details regarding the use of beads among the Arabs, in different centuries, see Tifashi 1977; Kunz 1915: 131–33, 281–324, 360–78; Ibn Zuhr 1992; Holbeche 1989; Clark 1984).

76. For a long time Ahmad al-Badawi (1200–1276) was a Sufi (a mystic) authority (*qutb*) in Egypt, as were 'Abd al-Qader al-Jilani (1078–1166), Ahmad al-Rifa'i (1106–1183), and Ibrahim al-Dasuqi (1235–1278), in what is called the *qitaba* (*Shorter Encyclopedia of Islam* 1974: 22–23).
77. The short-toed eagle (*Circaetus gallicus*) favours soaring over hill slopes and hilltops on up-draughts, and it does much of its hunting from this position at heights of up to 500 meters. Its prey consists mainly of reptiles, for the most part snakes, but also some lizards. Sometimes these eagles entangle with larger snakes and battle on the ground. Occasionally they prey on small mammals up to the size of a rabbit, and rarely on birds and large insects. The Bedouin call this bird *abu al-doud,* which means "the eagle that eat snakes." See Jabbur 1995: 140–41).
78. On the homeopathic magic principle of "like cures like," see also izzutherapy/isotherapy (Calder 1958). One common practice of medicine men is to try to extract the active cause of a disease by sucking it through a hollow tube and spitting out the poison. The identification with animals has also a deep medical-biological significance: the totem, the identification of people with an animal symbol, is universal—it exists in the coats-of-arms of noble families. In some cases eating the totem animal is part of a healing rite. Certain organs of certain animals are regarded as seats of the spirits—the heart, the liver, and the brain. If eaten raw they are supposed to be powerful therapeutics. This eating of organs to treat similar organs in patient-isotherapy (like-curing-like) persisted in the sacrificial rituals of the Romans and the Greeks and was still extant in the pharmacopoeias of Western Europe as late as the eighteenth century. In religious rituals, they have become the sacrificial cakes and sacramental wine (body and blood of Jesus) (Calder 1958: 45–46).
79. Compare with Yasin 2003.
80. For more details see Abu-Rabia 1999a: 55–56; Canaan 1923: 122–31; Harari 2007: 55–85.
81. Al-Rahaman, al-Rahim, al-Hanan, and al-Rian; God has ninety-nine names.
82. Muhammad, 'Ali, Fatema, al-Hasan b. 'Ali b. Abi Talib, the eldest son of 'Ali and Fatima, the daughter of the Prophet, al-Husain, the second son of 'Ali and Fatima.
83. Michail, Jabrail, and 'Izrael.
84. Compare with Ben-Assa (1974: 73–76).
85. It is worth comparing this with similar treatments in Germany: "a stick of red sealing wax carried on the person cures the red eruption" (Frazer 1962: 250).
86. The meaning of the term *hebbhar* may be *'abhar,* which is the Arabic name for the *'abhar* plant (styrax, *Styrax officinale*), whose resin, called *'abhar,* roots, and seeds are used in Bedouin folk medicine as treatment for skin and venereal diseases.
87. The technique of treating spider bites by "burying" the patient is mentioned among the Bedouin of the Negev (Ben-Assa 1970: 220), among the Rwala Bedouin in Syria (Musil 1928), and in Egypt (Morsy 1982: 147–74).
88. Black in this context signifies black clouds that bring plentiful rain.

89. In Yemen, a woman after childbirth should eat honey and *samn/samin* to strengthen her. Newborn babies have *samin* smeared in their mouths and on their noses in order for them to get used to it. *Samin,* which is considered to have healing and purifying properties, has many ritual uses, and is regarded as something of a cure-all (Maclagan 2011: 163–64).
90. Treatment with camel's milk is mentioned in the hadith (oral tradition of the Prophet) (al-Bukhari 1974: 408); Yasin 2003.
91. According to Johnstone 1975 and Prof. Allan Witztum, personal communication, 1992. Both kinds of *dam al-akhawain* are sold, bought, and used by the Bedouin. Personal observations of the Bedouin healer Abu-Skik 1982–1992.
92. See more details on bituminous material (*hummara*) in Chapter 3.
93. The Bedouin believe that small holes in the teeth are carried outmade by tiny worm called *susih.*
94. Patients' culturally constructed explanatory models of teeth rotted by "tooth worms" differ substantively from the dentists' model of dental decay by *Streptococcus mutans,* while western medicine finds a striking similarity between the tooth worms and the caries-causing microorganism, *Streptococcus mutans.* Regarding beliefs about a myriad of topics, from what causes tooth decay to the meaning of rotten teeth, see Nations and Nuto 2002: 229–44. Through the ages, "dental worms" were believed by the Aztecs, Babylonians, Greeks, and Romans as well as other nations to cause tooth decay (Ring 1998).
95. See also Ben-Assa 1974: 73–76; Hakhmon et al. 1998: 3–7.
96. Compare this with the Yanomamo of Venezuela and Brazil when they were afflicted by measles: McElroy and Townsend 1996: 8–33.
97. The British Mandate in Palestine was terminated in May 1948 as a result of United Nations Resolution (29 November 1947) to divide Palestine between Jews and Palestinians (Abu-Khusa 1994: 274–86; Abu-Rabia 2001: 58; al-Dabbagh 1991: 360).
98. For more details see Abu-Rabia 2005a: 404–7.
99. Verdigris is a green or greenish blue substance obtained artificially by the action of dilute acetic acid on thin plates of copper (*Oxford English Dictionary,* 2nd ed., 533); its chemical formula is $Cu(C_2H_3O_2)_2 \cdot H_2O$ (Abu-Rabia 1999a).
100. See Doumato 2000: 165n58.
101. A similar treatment method is found among the native tribes in Mexico (Femia and Aguilar 1993).
102. The theory of the vein that conveys the sperm from the brain along the ear to the testicles was well known among the Greeks and Arabs: "There are two great vessels running through the whole cavity of the body on either side of the spinal column, downwards to the legs and upwards under the collarbone through the neck to the brain. A pair of vessels called spermatitis run from the kidneys to the testicles" (Philips 1973: 25; Lloyd 1950: 150–51, 268, 318–19; al-Tabari 1928: 31).
103. In Samarkand, women give babies sugar candy to suck and put glue in the palm of their hands, so that that when they grow up their words may be

sweet and precious things may stick to their hands as if they were glued (Frazer 1962: 258).

104. See also Ben-Assa 197473–76; Pinczuk 1994 and 2 July 2007 correspondence).
105. *Jiddih* means the baby's grandmother. *Ferula* is remarkable for its bad odor. It is bought in the market from a perfume vendor (*'attarin*). *Ferula*'s active constituents is sulfur (Lust 1980: 501–6). The oleo-gum resin asafoetida is obtained from the plant's rhizome, whose volatile oil contain sulfur compounds; the resinous portion includes asaresinol ferulate and free ferulic acid (Appendino et al. 1994: 183–86; Evans 1998).
106. In Algeria, it is used against sorcery, demons, or jinn because of its smell (Hilton-Simpson 1922: 17). In Egypt, if an infant was very still after delivery, the midwife would ask for an onion and put it on the infant's nose, whereupon the infant would sneeze (Morsy 1982: 169). In Yemen, after childbirth, the resin of asafoetida is burnt and the smoke placed in between the mother's legs to contract the vagina (Ghazanfar 1994: 208).
107. Compare this to al-Razi on the relations of the stars to the disease. Some physicians, like 'Ali Ibn Ridwan, were also astrologists. Several writings address the the astrological knowledge of the physician. 'Adnan al-'Ainzarbi, for example, refers to Hippocrates, who said that the knowledge of the stars is a part of medicine. Galen also pointed out the significance of knowledge of the stars for medicine. He explained that each planet in a determined position indicated a particular disease. The knowledge of such matters would help the physician in diagnostic and prognostic matters. But for therapeutic measures, the star constellation should also be considered. The influence of the heavenly bodies on health is beyond any question. Al-Biruni mentions single stars in specific constellations that are harmful to the eye (Ullmann 1970).
108. The praying mantis (*Mantis religiosa* [*sayf rabna*]) is a large greenish-brown predatory insect with long forelegs that are raised and folded at rest, as if in prayer. For more details see Amitai 1987: 54–58.
109. For more details aout *sufiyih* see Abu-Rabia 2011; Weir 1990.
110. Many Mexican-American women believe that "fallen womb" can be prevented if they swaddle themselves with a tight sash following their first birth and for duration of their child bearings years (Foster and Anderson 1978: 75–76).
111. There are similar treatments in various places. For example, "In Germany [it is thought that] a blood-stone with its red spots allays bleeding" (Frazer 1962: 250).
112. The preferred soap is *sabun Nabilsi* (from Nablus). On the preparation process of soap, see: Abu-Rabia 2001: 47; Doumani 1995: 122, 187; al-Nimr 1961: 288–89.
113. A blood pigeon used in the ancient medicine of Galen (Ibn al-Baytar 1992: 293).
114. According to *The Medicine of the Prophet,* the ashes of a mat made of palm-tree leaves stop bleeding. Sahl bin Sa'd related the following: "When the helmet of the Prophet was smashed on his head and blood covered his face and one

of his front teeth got broken, 'Ali brought the water in his shield and Fatima (the Prophet's daughter) washed him. But when she saw that the bleeding increased more by the water, she took a mat, burnt it, and placed the ashes on the wound of the Prophet and so the blood stopped oozing out" (al-Bukhari, Hadith 4:152).

115. Compare this with a similar belief in Palestine (Granqvist 1935: 161) that if a person with poor vision or a menstruating woman gazes at the person it was detrimental to the subject's eyesight. A similar belief is found among Awlad 'Ali tribes in Egypt: to appear before children in the clothes worn during intercourse is believed to cause them eye problems (Abu-Lughod 1988: 144).

Chapter 3

General Treatments

Agama pallida (A Small Lizard) (*am brays*)

This lizard is used to treat warts (*thalul*). The treatment varies according to the number and location of the warts. A wart on the finger is put in the lizard's mouth for fifteen to thirty minutes while the lizard sucks on it, after which it is buried alive. The Bedouin believe the wart disappears as the lizard decomposes. Alternatively, the lizard is killed, its blood is smeared on warts and boils, and the lizard is buried. Allergies (*hasasiyih*) are treated by rubbing the lizard's belly on the patient's body, or letting the lizard suck the patient's finger. A finger bitten by a scorpion or suffering a snake bite is placed in the lizard's mouth for about half an hour.

Beetle (*khunfisanih*)/Roller Beetle (*ja'al*)

Among the Bedouin of the Negev (Abu-Rabia 1983: 25) the women crush *Mylabris syriaca* (see entry below) together with a bit of olive oil and place this substance, in the form of a suppository, in the woman's vagina as a remedy for infertility with a mixture including a particular beetle (*khunfisanih*) (Abu-Rabia 1983) that contains canthradin.

In Arabia in the spring (Dickson 1949: 469), the roller beetle[1] (*abu-ja'al*) rolls fresh bits of dung (camel, horse, or other livestock) into a perfect ball to bring it to a soft spot, where it starts to dig a sloping hole sufficiently large to contain its manure ball. The manure ball, so carefully placed underground and shut in, is used by the female to lay her eggs in, so that when her progeny hatch they have the manure ball to feed on till they can fend for themselves.

Bitumen/Bituminous Material (*hummara*)

Natural asphalts/bituminous materials (*hummara*) were widely used in the ancient world, as far back as about 9,000 BC. Asphalt was commonly used in ancient Mesopotamia in building materials, such as mortar and cement, paving for roads, waterproofing pipes, and in insecticides, as well as for making fire, medical uses, and magic rituals. Dead Sea bitumen was an ingredient of the balms in Egyptian mummies (Connan, Nissenbaum, and Dessort 1992: 2,743–59; Nissenbaum 1978: 837–44).

According to Bedouin sources (Hajj Hammad Salem abu-Rabia, personal communication, 21 August 1998), the Bedouin called the asphalt *hummarah.* Asphalt, which is congealed petroleum, would be collected by the Bedouin at least once a year, in the form of blocks floating on the Dead Sea. The petroleum would flow into the Dead Sea with springs or ground water, and then congeal into bright reddish-black blocks with a pleasant odor. An easterly wind would blow the asphalt blocks towards the western shore. The Bedouin would break the large blocks into smaller blocks that could be loaded onto camels. They would sell these blocks to Arab traders in Hebron, Jerusalem, and elsewhere. The Bedouin would make tar pastes out of the asphalt, which would be spread on tree and vine stumps after pruning, as well as on cracks in pottery. It would also be boiled in olive oil over a flame and chewed like gum. Medicines were made out of the asphalt for dental therapy. It would be used to hold the jaws or to treat inflammation of the gums; to treat children's stuttering, by freeing their tongue, so they could speak more easily; and to treat fever, diarrhea, and inflammation of the uterus. Asphalt was also used to treat skin diseases in animals and humans being (Abu-Rabia 2001: 56–58).

In Palestine, very small quantities of asphalt were also collected, a fact reflected in its price: in 1872, a camel-load of asphalt fetched 500 *grush* in Jerusalem and Bethlehem. Such trade was an important source of income for the Bedouin tribes that controlled the western shore of the Dead Sea (Avitsur 1976: 274–77).

In contrast to meager asphalt production, larger quantities of oil were produced from "Moses rocks" (*ihjar Musa*), the oil-bearing bituminous shale rocks found in the locality of the large building on the traditional burial place of Moses, near Jericho. The Bedouin, who maintain ritual visits to Moses' tomb, believe that God blessed the place where Moses was buried with "fire rocks" and water wells (*nareh men ihjareh wa-mayteh men ibyareh*).

Before the twentieth century, bituminous shale was only rarely used to produce heating fuel and then usually by Bedouin who chanced to be in the vicinity of such rocks. The extraction of fuel from shale on a regular basis began only during the great fuel shortage of World War I. The Germans (in Palestine during the World War I as allies to the Ottomans) produced aviation fuel from bituminous rocks at Makarin, east of el-Hamma, along the Hejaz railway. The Ottomans used petroleum from bituminous shale to fuel locomotives, as well as to power their steamboats on the Dead Sea (Avitsur 1976: 274–77; Bar-Zvi, Abu-Rabia, and Kressel 1998: 50).

According to Canaan (1927b: 88, 110), stones around Nabi Musa are black and contain some bitumen, so they burn when put on a fire. The stones are also cut in square or triangular forms, a protective talisman is inscribed, and they are carried as an amulet (*hijab*).

Camel's Milk (*halib niag*)

Camel's milk has myriad uses in treating illnesses. It is considered to be a remedy for snake bites, scorpion and spider bites, liver illnesses, stomach ulcers, and stomachaches. It is also believed to strengthen teeth and bones and the sexual organs, especially of old men. Camel's milk mixed with camel urine is used to treat liver disease.[2] The Bedouin of Syria allocate the milk of a she-camel for their horses to drink during their nomadic season when water resources and seeds are rare and limited. The women wash their hair using camel urine, to protect it from insect pests and to bleach it. Some Bedouin drink the urine as a treatment for certain diseases (Jabbur 1995: 136). Camel's milk has low fat content and butter cannot be made from it. It is a purgative, and should be taken in moderation by persons not used to it. Camels must eat *hamdh* plant (Dickson 1949: 414); a food for sick camels is dates and barley mixed with milk into a mush, followed by Arab bread broken up into small pieces (Dickson 1949: 416). Camel's milk is mentioned in the Quran: "A similitude of the Garden, which those who keep their duty (to Allah) are promised: Therein are rivers of water unpolluted, and rivers of milk whereof the flavor changeth not" (Quran 47:15). It is also part of Islamic oral tradition:

> Some people were sick and they said, "O Allah's Apostle: give us shelter and food." Then when they became healthy they said: "The weather of Medina is not suitable for us." So he sent them to Al-Harra with some she-camels of his and said: "Drink of their milk" and they became healthy. (al-Bukhari 1974: 398)

Crow (*ghrab, ghurab*)

The Bedouin eat the liver[3] and heart of the crow. Bedouin believe that crow's liver makes babies sharp and attentive like the crow, and when the baby grows up, it will be as difficult for his enemies to trap him through fraud or deception, as it is difficult to capture the crow. With the exception of the heart and liver, which are eaten for medicinal purposes, Bedouin do not eat crow meat, as it is considered tainted (Abu-Rabia 2010: 460).

The crow is mentioned in the Bedouin proverbs: "His heart is like the heart of a crow." It is also considered a bad omen: "He is like a crow that croaks upon ruins" (Bailey 2004: 21); "What blackened the crow was his word" (*alli sawwad al-grab amantih*)—when the crow was sent by Noah to search out dry land, it did not return; but when Noah sent a dove it brought him a succulent blade of grass; Noah cursed the crow and said: "God blacken you" (Bailey 2004: 399).

Egyptian Vulture (*rakhamah*)

A Bedouin elder told me that some eighty years ago his people caught an Egyptian vulture, slaughtered it, plucked the feathers, cleaned the carcass, and hung it on a tent rope in a clean place where unclean animals like dogs, cats, and reptiles could not reach it. Forty days later, when it was dry, they cut the carcass into small pieces, ground it, and cooked it in a pot with 2–3 tablespoons of Bedouin butter, saffron, onion, black cumin, and a liter of water. They each drank a small glassful of the soup as a preventive against scorpion and bee stings, snake bite, spider bite, and food poisoning. Among the Rwala (Musil 1928: 542) defenders of their camps sang: "O Lord! Our gracious Lord! Thou wilt pour forth a captious rain on our lands, whilst we shall pour forth a supper for the circling birds." Circling birds (*yahum*) refers to the white vulture with reddish wings and yellow peak. It accompanies the warriors on almost all their trips and flies above the battle ground untiringly.

Hawk (*sagir*), Falcon, Short-Toed Eagle (*Circaetus gallicus* [*abu al-doud*])

The Bedouin proverb says: "He who knows not a hawk will roast it" (*alli ma yi'raf al-sagir ibyishwih*). This metaphorical proverb implies that an ignorant person will do foolish things. Usually Bedouin do not eat birds of prey and perceive hawks in particular as lacking in meat (Bailey 2004:

381); "If you have muzzled a hawk, you must feed it" (*in kammamt as-sagr lazim ti'allfih*)—the image of muzzling refers to the Bedouin sport of hunting with hawks, which were trained and not allowed to prey naturally, as they had been accustomed (Bailey 2004: 429).

The Short-toed Eagle (*Circaetus gallicus* [*abu al-doud*]) favors soaring over hill slopes and hilltops on updrafts, and it does much of its hunting from this position at heights of up to 500 meters. Its prey consists mostly of reptiles, mainly snakes (90 percent) but also some lizards. Sometimes they entangle with larger snakes and battle on the ground. Occasionally they prey on small mammals up to the size of a rabbit, and rarely on birds and large insects (Wikipedia 2010). The Bedouin call it *abu al-doud* which means "the eagle that eats snakes" (see also Jabbur 1995: 140–41). The Bedouin claim that the jerboa's white meat resembles the breast meat of a chicken and consider it delicious. Falcons also enjoy it, so hunters use the flesh of jerboas as bait in their snares when they are trying to catch adult falcons (Jabbur 1995: 118). Bedouin babies are given its liver and heart to immunize them/vaccinate them from snakebites or scorpion stings.

Hedgehog (*gunfud*)

High fever and malaria are treated by inhaling the smoke from the burning skin of a hedgehog, including its spines. Some of the Bedouin of Syria eat its flesh broiled or grilled. They also use amulets made from its skin. This amulet is hung on a she-camel's neck for a month as a treatment for jumpy, nervous, or timid camels (Jabbur 1995: 117).

The hedgehog is mentioned in Bedouin proverbs as a metaphor for choosing harmful friends or actions. It is said that "the hedgehog opens up only to the vulture," which consequently hunts it for food (Bailey 2004: 20). Among the Rwala (Musil 1928: 28), hedgehog skin was also tied round the necks of timid camels. It is said that when they have worn it for at least a month, they ceased to be afraid.

Honey Badger (*Meles meles* [*al-ghariri, am ka'yb*])

The Bedouin are wary of this animal and consider it especially dangerous at night when it may lunge at men's testicles. They kill it when possible. A bag made from its skin is filled with olive oil, which is drunk (one teaspoon) as a remedy for scorpion stings or snake bite. Some Bedouin give it to their children as a preventive medicine. Some Bedouin cook the meat and bones (without intestines and stomach) in a little water until soft, and eat it to cure boils and varicose veins. In the Arabic texts, the honey badger is renowned for its foul smell (al-Damiri 2005: 2:153). Musil (1928: 22) gives an accurate description of it—its teeth are similar to those of humans and it has a long tail. Its skin has a characteristic smell. Its flesh is eaten by the Rwala tribe members. Among the Bedouin of Syria, it is claimed that the badger comes near the burrow of the stellion lizard and breaks wind noiselessly, and then the stellion leaves its burrow and falls prey to the badger. This smell, when it contacts clothes, will remain until the clothes become old and worn. Some of the Bedouin kill the badger and eat its flesh. In the northern Syrian Desert near the Euphrates they call it *haffar al-gubur,* "gravedigger," since they believe that the badger digs into the graves and eats the dead (Jabbur 1995: 90–91). The same belief exists among the Bedouin of the Negev and Sinai.

Monitor Lizard (*Varanus griseus* [*waral*])

The dry feces of this lizard are separated from the earth in a sieve or headscarf, and the fine dust stored in a bottle or special leather sack. This powder is put in the eyes as a treatment for trachoma or inflammation and is also used to treat eye illnesses in animals. A bag is made from the skin of the *waral,* filled with olive oil, and hung on one of the tent poles. One to two tablespoons of the oil are ingested in case of scorpion, spider, or snake bite. It is also smeared on the body against scabies, eczema, impetigo (*goubah*), and other skin conditions, including allergies. Other uses include: drinking a tablespoon in the morning as a remedy against fear and anxiety; mixing the flesh of the lizard with fenugreek, cooking it, and eating it as a preventive and treatment for stings and snake bites, and for general strengthening of the body; smearing the meat and fat of the lizard on the hair as a remedy for balding and dandruff (*gishrih*), and to make the hair shine.

In Arabia (Dickson 1949: 466), the lizard is called *wurral,* the snake-headed monitor, and its bite is said to be poisonous. If the *waral* is bitten by a poisonous snake, it runs to the *ramram* bush (*Heliotropium cignosum*), rolls itself well in the bush and eats some of the leaves. This is said by the Bedouin to act as an antidote to the snake venom. The Bedouin have thus learned to value the *ramram* as an anti-snake medicine, apparently with satisfactory results.

Mylabris syriaca (*dhirnah*)

This insect appears during the spring season, and lives on the flowers of various plants. A person bitten by a dog suspected of being rabid or a person who cannot urinate, is fed a dried *Mylabris* placed in a dried fig or piece of bread. This treatment, which turns the urine red, is administered only once.

Among the Bedouin of the Negev (Abu-Rabia 1983: 25), the women crush *Mylabris syriaca* together with a bit of olive oil and place this substance, in the form of a suppository, in the woman's vagina as a remedy for infertility.

Bedouin who work with livestock, especially camel breeders who become infected with scabies (*jarab*), mix these insects with Bedouin butter (*samin*), salt, sesame oil, and sulfur and smear the paste on the affected areas.

In Morocco, they cut very fine slivers from white broom (*ratam*), mix it with flour, bran (*nkhalah*), and warm water, and give it to a dog that shows signs of becoming mad/rabid (Westermarck 1926: 112). The Bedouin in *wadi Karm* of Southern Sinai, use it as a medicine for the bite of a mad dog. They also use it to treat baldness (*sala'a*).

The *Mylabris syriaca* was used among the ancient Arab, Egyptians, and Greeks as a medicinal powder to strengthen sexual potency among the men (Kirby 1856: 223). Cantharidin, a vesicant produced by beetles, has a long history in both folk and traditional medicine and in dermatology; topical cantharidin[4] has long been used to treat warts and *Molluscum contagiosum* (Moed et al. 2001: 1357–60; Budenheimer 1961: 445).

Ostrich (*na'ameh*)

In the early twentieth century, the Rwala used the fat of the ostrich, known as *zihem,* as a remedy for various diseases (Musil 1928: 39). The Bedouin mix the egg with flour and clarified butter (*samin*), and fry into an omelet, producing a tasty dish. Bedouin hunters ate the breast meat and saved its fat to sell as a remedy for many diseases (Doughty 1936: I:1973–74).

Owl (*bumeh*, pl. *bum*)

The Bedouin proverb says: "An owl's sustenance is at the mouth of its cave [hole]" (*rizg al-bum 'ala fam juhrah*) (Bailey 2004: 98). The Bedouin of the Negev regarded it as a bad omen, mainly in the morning and when they heard its wails near their tent.

Among the Bedouin of Sinai, tradition holds that if a child's parents wish him to be lucky throughout his life, he must swallow a finely chopped feather of the long-eared or eagle owl, before he tastes his mother's milk

(Morgenstern 1966: 207–8). The owl is considered a bad omen, the embodiment of evil spirits that carries off children at night. According to an Arabic belief:

> [F]rom each female owl supposedly came two eggs; one held the power to cause hair to fall out and one held the power to restore it. Arabs once believed that the spirit of a murdered man would continue to wail and weep until his death had been avenged. They believed that a bird that they called al-Sada (or the death-owl) would continue to hoot over the grave of a slain man whose death had not been avenged. The bird would continue to hoot endlessly until the slain man's death was avenged. (Wikipedia)

Panther (*fahd*)

Ridwan Rwayli relates that he and his companions killed a panther and its cubs; one of the hunters cut open the animal, plucked out its heart, and sucked out its blood so that his strength would increase (Jabbur 1995: 130).

Rock Rabbit/Marmot (*wabr*)

The *wabr* eats the fresh herbs that grow in the sandstone mountains of the Syrian Desert, as well as the leaves of acacia (the tree from which gum Arabica is derived), which the *wabr* can easily climb. The Bedouin eat *wabr* and enjoy its fatty meat (Jabbur 1995: 116). King Solomon described the *wabr* in an adage, saying: "There be four things that are little upon the earth, but they are exceedingly wise: the ants are a people but not strong, yet they prepare their meal in the summer; the conies (*wabr*) are but a feeble folk, yet make their houses in the rocks; the locust have no king, yet go they forth all of them by bands; the spider taketh hold with her animals, and is in king's places" (Proverbs 30:24–28).

Stellion Lizard (*Uromastix aegyptius* [*idhlim, dabb, dhab, dhub*])

Olive oil stored in a bag made from the skin of this lizard is an all-purpose antidote for poisonous stings and bites. The dried feces of this lizard are used as kohl for treating trachoma. In addition, a paste is prepared from its boiled meat and used as a treatment for freckles (*namash*) and acne on the face. The Bedouin in ancient Arabia and in the early Islamic period ate the *dabb* (Amin 1969: 9). The Bedouin of Syria in the early twentieth century ate its flesh grilled on embers. Its skin was used by shepherds as a container for camel milk. Some rural communities would hang its skin filled with straw on their shops for a good luck (Jabbur 1995: 146–47).

In Arabia (Dickson 1949: 467) this lizard is called *dhub* or spiny-tailed monitor. The Bedouin consider the *dhub* fit for human consumption. Throughout Arabia there is a saying that the *dhub* is held in special sanctity by the 'Aniza tribe. It is certain that no member of that tribe will kill, much less eat, this lizard. Among the Rwala (Musil 1928: 41) the *dhabb* was also known as *abu amad.* The flesh of the dead *dhab* twitches for a long time and is said to be very tasty.

Wild Boar (*khanzir barri*)

The Bedouin of Syria make a medicine from its fat for their wounds and those of livestock, horses, and camels. The Bedouin used to regard it as a bad omen. In the desert certain Bedouin do not hesitate to eat its meat, led to do so by their need and poverty. They even treat their wounds and those of their horses and camels with its fat (Jabbur 1995: 113–14). The Rwala referred to the male as *shihl,* and to the female *shiba,* and to the young as *qarnus* (Musil 1928: 28).

Notes

1. Several species of the dung beetle, most notably the sacred scarab, enjoyed a sacred status among the ancient Egyptians. The scarab was linked to Khepri ("he who has come into being"), the god of the rising sun. The supposed self-creation of the beetle resembles that of Khepri, who creates himself out of nothing. Moreover, the dung ball rolled by a dung beetle resembles the sun. The ancient Egyptians believed that Khepri renewed the sun every day before rolling it above the horizon, and then carried it through the other world after sunset, only to renew it, again, the next day. Some New Kingdom royal tombs exhibit a threefold image of the sun god, with the beetle as symbol of the morning sun. The astronomical ceiling in the tomb of Ramses VI portrays the nightly "death" and "rebirth" of the sun as being swallowed by Nut, goddess of the sky, and re-emerging from her womb as Khepri. Some have been used as seals. Pharaohs sometimes commissioned the manufacture of larger images with lengthy inscriptions, such as the commemorative scarab of Queen Tiye. Massive sculptures of scarabs can be seen at Luxor Temple, at the Serapeum in Alexandria, and elsewhere in Egypt (Wikipedia).
2. Compare with Yasin 2003.
3. The identification with animals also has deep medical-biological significance.

In some cases eating the totem animal or certain organs of certain animals is part of a healing rite (Calder 1958: 46).

4. Canthradin is cantharide: "This substance is claimed to enhance genital responsiveness by attraction of local vascular response and increased irritability of the genital organs. It is a peripherally acting toxic substance that irritates the bladder and urethra and may cause the male to experience pseudo-sexual excitement" (Bergerson 1979: 630).

Chapter 4

"Don't Touch My Body"

The Qarina *and Bedouin Women's Fertility*

This chapter focuses on the practices that surround the *qarina* and examines beliefs and attitudes towards the *qarina* within social contexts, specifically with regard to marital relations and the importance of pregnancy and childbearing for Bedouin women. The chapter aims to contribute to a better understanding of the phenomena of the *qarina* through the study of local health traditions, to provide definitions and to describe rituals, symptoms, and preventive and curative measures used against the *qarina*.

Background

According to traditional Bedouin belief, both health and illness are in the hands of the Almighty. Positive powers are associated with God, and are the source of healing. When God wants to punish a person, He uses negative powers or entities, such as jinn (demons). Traditional Bedouin faith holds that spirits and jinn are the most dangerous causes of certain ailments. Jinn will occupy houses and other places when the residents are absent, but prefer to dwell in human bodies. Thus, they constitute a constant threat to the well-being of human beings.

One of these jinn is the *qarina*. The *qarina* is known by twelve different names, including: *tab'a* ("she who follows a person") and *um al-sibyan* ("the mother of children who seduces and kills them") (al-Diyarbi 1343H:

98; al-Suyuti 1899: 236–48; al-Azraq 1948: 183). The most significant finding of my study of this subject is that the *qarina* is considered one of the most dangerous factors in the lives of the Bedouin. Belief in the *qarina* is more prevalent among women than among men. Although men and women are equally subject to the influence of the *qarina,* this chapter focuses in particular on women and children (because they are the most vulnerable members of the community).

The belief in the *qarina* is a logical extension of the Bedouin belief that the predicament of possessed individuals is inextricably linked with the jinn of these individuals. As we have seen in previous chapters, traditional Bedouin medicine combines supernatural elements from popular superstition, such as counteracting the effects of the evil eye and appeasing spirits (Abu-Rabia 1999a: 22, 43, 47–51).

The word *qarina* is derived from the Arabic term *qarana,* which means "to link" or "to join or combine." The term may be used to refer to a wife, a female demon that haunts women, or a woman's soul (Ibn-Manzur 1956: 329, Anis et al. 1972: 731, al-Munjid 1975: 625, Wehr 1994: 890). Both men and women believe that the *qarina* is a female jinni (*jinniya*) that appears from time to time, and that each woman has her own, individual *qarina.*

The *qarina* is often depicted as a beautiful woman, but has also been portrayed with the legs of a she-goat or as a female donkey, or with the legs of a woman and the body of a she-goat, with long sagging breasts filled with blood. It is believed that a child who suckles or touches the *qarina*'s breast will die immediately.[1] The *qarina* has also been depicted as a red dog with a large human head. It has the ability to assume different forms on different occasions. Sometimes it appears in blackface, sometimes with its head and face covered with long hair. The *qarina* is also said to appear occasionally in the form of a bird (al-Diyarbi 1343H: 98; al-Suyuti 1899: 236–48), and may be invisible.

According to popular belief, the *qarina* is extremely libidinous and seeks to seduce handsome young men. Men who succumb to her charms go mad. She may approach a married man disguised as his wife, and then kill him. Or she may approach a married woman disguised as her husband and then "possess" her from within, during sexual intercourse.

Variations on the *qarina* are present in many cultures. According to ancient Jewish tradition, Lilith, who was created from the earth like Adam, and not Eve, was the first wife of Adam (Austen 1990: 123–29). Lilith derived her main characteristics from her earthly origins. Heronimos, in the fourth century, identified Lilith with the lamia, a monster with a head and breasts of a woman, and the body of snake, from ancient Greek mythology. The lamia seduced young boys and men as they slept, sucked their blood, and ate their flesh (Abarbanell 1997: 26; Avery 1972: 318; Grant and Hazel 1979: 208; Grimal 1990: 236; Zimmerman 1964: 146).

The *qarina* is a hermaphroditic[2] jinni (*antha dhakar/khantha dhakar*), that is, it can simultaneously take the form of a male (*jin*) and a female jinni (*jinniya*). It is believed to enter a woman's body at one of the following times: at the moment of her birth, the moment her umbilical cord is severed; during the female circumcision ceremony,[3] during menstruation, on her wedding night at the moment her hymen is torn (defloration), or during childbirth. New brides are considered the most vulnerable. The *qarina* takes advantage of these "windows of opportunity'" to enter the woman's womb. The *qarina* who dwells in a woman's womb can be the source of various phenomena: varying degrees of insanity, miscarriage, the death of an infant in childbirth or shortly afterwards, or the death of a child during its first five years of life. Bedouin women believe that cases of "crib death syndrome"[4] are caused by a *qarina* who enters the body of the infant and strangles it from within, leaving no trace. Notably, the *qarina* cannot be treated until its gender is determined, and the most difficult to cure is the female type.

In ancient Arabia, a woman whose children died at birth was called *miqlat* (pl. *maqalit*), derived from the word *qalita,* literally "expire his life" (al-Bustani 1995: 493). Arabs believed that if "this woman" (*miqlat*) trod on the body of an assassinated man of noble descent (*rajul karim*), her infant would live (al-Shartuni 1992: 1029). The *miqlat*[5] in pre- and early Islamic times would vow that if she had a child that lived, she would give him to another tribe, Jewish or Christian, to be raised with a wet nurse[6] of the same religion and customs as the adoptive tribe. When the Prophet ordered the Banu al-Nadir (who were Jewish) to be expelled[7] from Medina (AD 625), children from the al-Ansar tribes (who were Muslims) were among them.[8] The Arabs in the Arabian Peninsula brought their newborn children to 'Aisha, the wife of the Prophet, to be blessed against diseases, evil eye, and other maladies.[9]

As mentioned, the art of folk medicine is still relied upon by the majority of common people in the Middle East (Doumato 2000; Inhorn 1994a; Stillman 1983: 485). A people's medical beliefs and practices persist because they are effective and serve a function for members of society. Traditional cultures provide their members with many patterns of folkloric behavior and practices that are conducive to dissipating guilt, fear, anxiety, and stress. Some of these folk practices are expressed in the form of religious chants, sacred religious rituals, and folk medicine, include the treatment of spirit possession and exorcism (Abu-Rabia 1999a; al-Krenawi 2000; El-Shamy 1972: 13).

Jinn and spirits are mentioned in Islam, and even today those who do not believe in their existence are considered infidels (*kafir*, pl. *koffar*). Jinn and spirits as a whole occupy a central place in traditional cultures of the Middle East and North Africa. For those born into these cultures, they are tangible entities and an integral part of daily life (Abu-Rabia 1999a: 43; Bilu 1993: 53–60; Crapanzano 1973, 1977). Belief in the *qarina* exists throughout the Middle East and North Africa (Blackman 1927: 54–75; Lewis et al. 1991: 100–117; Makris 2000; Morgenstern 1966: 12–13, 18–21; Morsy 1978: 599–616; Westermarck 1926: 1:402). In traditional societies and cultures, women who are possessed by a spirits are regularly treated not by permanently expelling the possessing agency, but by reaching a viable accommodation with it; the spirit is tamed and domesticated, rather than exorcized (Lewis 2003: 30). Lewis argues that the cult of spirits and spirit possession is part of a "sex-war" on the part of women who are at a disadvantage vis-à-vis their husbands: "Cults protect women from the exactions of men, and offer an effective vehicle for manipulating husbands and male relatives" (Lewis 2003: 31).

In the Quranic tradition, jinn are an intermediate class of beings—between angels and men, but inferior in dignity to both and said to be created from fire (Quran 15:27). Infidels, or unbelievers, are considered devils, of which Iblis is the chief. He is also called *al-shaytan*—Satan. In contrast to him, the angels (*mala'ika*) are created from light, and are believed to be perfect (Quran 21: 26, 27). Muslims believe that a jinni might enter one's body, either in the ardor of love and passion or to cause mischief and harm, or possibly for other reasons (Quran 2:275). By and large, Islam tolerates belief in jinn so long as they are the focus of single treatments, and they are tolerated as "women's religion/medicine," a category separate from men's Islam. Muslim clerics are much less tolerant of spirit-cults, and in today's more fundamentalist communities, such cults are reclassified as "culture," not "belief" and not "medicine" per se.[10] The following two case studies that deal with the *qarina* are typical among pastoral Bedouin women in the Negev.

Case Study I

Silmiyih is a 27-year-old woman. She studied for four years in a tribal Bedouin school and dropped out on her own accord. Silmiyih's fate and that of her children was cruel. Every time she became pregnant she had a miscarriage, and if she bore the child, it died before the age of two. One day Silmiyih turned to a *darwishih*, a traditional female healer, and told her of her problem. When the *darwishih* heard Silmiyih's story, she told her to come back in a week and in the meantime to follow these instructions: to burn incense[11] or *Ferula*[12] on coals and inhale it before going to sleep and to drink a medicine prepared from the following plants:[13] rose of Jericho,[14] mandrake,[15] rue,[16] Christ's thorn,[17] *harmel,*[18] black cumin,[19] olive oil,[20] and pomegranates.[21]

During Silmiyih's second visit, the *darwishih* prepared a tasty meat meal for her and instructed her to finish everything on her plate, for she had put a medicine in the food. After she finished the meal, the *darwishih* told Silmiyih, and several other women who were present, that the meat she had eaten contained the flesh of a donkey. She added that the meat had been cooked with a special medicine. Silmiyih returned home crestfallen, kept to herself, remained in her house, and did not want to participate in festive occasions. The rumor spread throughout the village that "Silmiyih had eaten the flesh of a donkey." After nine months, Silmiyih gave birth to a healthy infant. The infant survived, but she called him Shihdih, which means "beggar from God." Silmiyih felt that pretending to be poor would protect him from the evil eye and evil spirits such as the *qarina.*

The *darwishih* related to the author that eating the flesh of a donkey and making the fact public knowledge has an objective: that the *qarina* should also hear about it and thus be induced to leave the woman alone, for it would not want to cleave to the body of a woman who had eaten the flesh of so unclean and defiled an animal as a donkey. There are also other situations among the pastoral Bedouin where the donkey is used to cure ailments, or relieve particular symptoms. For example, its milk is believed to cure a child who stutters or who fails to start speaking at the right age. There is a belief that the milk of a female donkey has the power to "untie the tongue" of such a child. "Tongue-twisting" is viewed as the doing of a jinni or the evil eye.

The author has been told by different healers that inhaling incense or *Ferula* before going to sleep is very useful medicine that serves a number of purposes. It keeps the evil eye and other bad spirits away from the mother, fills the house with purifying smoke and a pleasant smell, and cures a women possessed by the *qarina.* The burning of incense is called *tabkhir.*

Case Study II

One night, when Mas'uda was in her sixth month of pregnancy, she dreamt that a *qarina* had come to her and told her, "Had it not been for the object on the pitchfork (*minsas*) placed at the entrance to your home that serves as a buffer between me and you, I would have gone into your house and killed the fruit of your womb." In the morning Mas'uda woke up very frightened and told her husband about the dream. She also asked what was on his pitchfork. The husband told his wife that the previous day he had killed a mole (*khlund*) and its blood was on his pitchfork. Mas'uda went to the field and brought the mole home, disemboweled it, sprinkled salt on its carcass, and hung it on the central tent pole until it was dry.[22] Afterwards, she took the dry pieces and put them in her and her husband's pillows. Mas'uda gave birth to a healthy baby boy, who was followed by four younger siblings, all of whom survived. It should be noted that in all her previous pregnancies, Mas'uda's newborn infants had died soon after birth.

This incident emphasizes the Bedouin belief in the mole as a medicinal antidote to and potent prophylactic against the *qarina.* Healers, both men and women, and others told the author that the fertile earth symbolizes the woman, while the mole symbolizes the *qarina*. The mounds of earth that the mole pushes up to the surface as it burrows are viewed as symbolizing the belly of a pregnant woman, while the mole symbolizes the *qarina* entering her abdomen from inside—in pitch darkness, just as the mole lives and burrows its way underground. The subterranean tunnels dug by the mole symbolize the *qarina*'s trail inside the woman's womb.

There is also another way of looking at the same analogy. The mole enters lives and burrows its way underground without permission to do so from the fertile earth, causing damage to the earth, just as the *qarina* penetrates the woman's body without her permission. This intrusion violates and defiles her body and even causes the death of her children. Just as the mole changes the surface of the earth and damages its fertility, the *qarina* changes the behavior of the woman and violently damages her body both internally and externally. In symbolizing the *qarina,* the mole can serve medical purposes, based on the "like cures like" principle of sympathetic magic.

Review of Literature

The conflation of gender and kinship allows people in the Middle East to view women in terms of family, and mediates the family's relationship to women through their roles as mothers and wives (Joseph 1996: 4–10). Marriage is an important cultural institution—one of the factors that give a woman her value. Fertility has great significance in Arab culture (Balfur 2003). Muslim *shari'a* affirms the importance of marriage, the establishment of family, and procreation. Treatment of an infertile couple is therefore encouraged and considered a necessity, since it involves the preservation of procreation by the married couple (Serour 1998: 191–202; Inhorn 2003: 8–11). In Middle Eastern cultures, women's bodies are considered fertile wombs, and become sites for symbolic rituals to increase fertility.[23] In some cases, by following a prescribed ritual or traditional medicine, fertility will be bestowed upon an infertile woman (FadlAlla 2002).

In Bedouin cosmology, jinn are living entities found in a world parallel to the human world.[24] When a jinni has entered a person's body, that person is able to communicate with a dervish healer who reads verses from the Quran. During such healing rituals, the dervishes play music[25] on a drum (*tar*) and place incense in the embers of the fire, since the spirits dislike this smell. The dervish is able to deal with the jinni, extracting a pledge from it that it will leave the person's body and never return. Sometimes the dervish beats the possessed patient with a stick, whips the individual's body or a foot, through which the spirit is supposed to leave the body (Abu-Rabia 1983, 1999). This practice and dialogue with the spirits is comparable to Western notions of spirit exorcism (Morsy 1978: 601;[26] Sharp 1994). When the jinni enters a human body violently, it causes its victim to become insane, suffer epileptic seizures,[27] or be too frightened to speak (al-Krenawi and Graham 1997; al-Krenawi 2000; Johnstone 1998: 46–50; Ibn 'Uthaymin 1991: 80–81). According to Boddy (1988: 11–12), the *zar* ritual, which is used to exorcise spirits in Ethiopian villages, is not trance-like per se, but such paralytic states are firmly situated in a meaningful cultural context and such states of what is seen as possession have medical, social, psychological, and often profound aesthetic implications.

Jinn are creatures with superhuman powers; they can traverse tremendous distances in no time and without effort, and then cause harm with only a light touch. They can also find objects that have disappeared or been hidden. Jinn live underground, although they can be found above ground, as well—in water, including springs, in fire, and in the air, in caves, and in rock crevices. In addition to the various methods of curing a person of a jinni and preventing harm, there are also certain methods by which one can mobilize jinn to serve humankind, employing their powers positively to heal people, solve thefts, and counter witchcraft and sorcery (al-Krenawi 2000; Bilu 1993: 53–60).

The Rwala Bedouin call jinn "spirits"' (*kurta, qurta, qarudh,* or *qaruz*).[28] To appease spirits, a Bedouin buys a rooster with green neck feathers and waits until his wife is pregnant again and close to term. He holds the rooster and draws seven circles within his tent using the bird; then he kills the rooster in the innermost circle and buries it there—within the tent. When his wife is in labor, he has her lie on the spot where the rooster is buried. This practice ensures that his child will not die, because the *qurta* "has been given its due"—*haqq al-qurta* (Musil 1928: 20, 417). Bedouin women in Palestine in the early twentieth century feared that a *qarina* would come and harm their children with its radiance. These women were in the habit of carrying with them the rope with which they drew water from a well or a spring, and every evening after sunset would throw the rope over the tent to prevent the *qarina* from entering and harming their children. According to Ashkenazi (1956: 92), Bedouin women in Palestine recited verses from the Quran and various incantations while throwing the rope (*habil al-dalu*) over the tent. Often they wet the rope—water being a symbol of life, purity, and healing according to the Bedouin.

The Bedouin consider the tent the abode of the new married couple, symbolizing the bride's womb as a dwelling for the new fetus. The central tent pole (*wasit al-bayt*), the strongest pole in the tent, is considered in this context to symbolize the male's penis, and the center of the tent symbolizes the woman's vagina. Thus, to protect the tent is to protect the bride's womb from dangerous and alien agents. As the body has its own sanctity, so the dwelling has its honor. Each dwelling has its own borders; within these borders sanctity must be preserved and protected. This is the honor of the dwelling and its dwellers.[29] Many Bedouins believe that when a woman gives birth to a boy, her son's face looks down because he is ashamed by his mother's genitals; when a woman gives birth to a girl, the infant's face is turned towards her mother's genitals. When the birth is complicated and labor prolonged, it is said that a male infant does not want to leave his mother's belly because he is positioned so that he would face his mother's genitals; when the birth of a girl is prolonged, it is said that she knows she will not be as loved as a male offspring, that much toil awaits her at home when she grows up, and that she is afraid of the *qarina* and evil spirits.

Pastoral Bedouin in the Negev and Sinai assign special significance to sheep sacrificed (*hilliyih*)[30] by the groom as a part of the marriage ritual. In other cases, a sign of the blood of the *hilliyyih* is applied to the forehead and breast of the bride. This act has an intimate association, linking the redemptive sacrifice with the first act of intercourse of the young married couple freeing the bride from the possession of evil spirits such as a *qarina* at the moment she loses her virginity. It seems that the wedding sacrifice is a way of sealing the new familial alliance with blood (Smith 1903: 62–65). The blood upon the bride may have been used in early times to symbolize hymeneal blood, and was thus intended to "deceive" the gullible spirit into believing that the sprit had "already received its due" (Bailey 1974b: 105–31; Musil 1928: 195–205).

Some Bedouin in the Negev and Sinai, after burying their dead, leave the deceased's clothes on the grave for passers-by to take. The Bedouin

FIGURE 4.1 The tomb of Nabi Musa (Prophet Moses), situated near Jericho.

FIGURE 4.2 This site is considered to be a holy place for pilgrimage, as well as for medical, religious, and mystic rituals.

FIGURE 4.3 The author with his son during a pilgrimage (*zwara*) to Nabi Musa.

FIGURE 4.4 The author during a pilgrimage (*zwara*) to Nabi Musa reads a phrase from the Quran: "And to Musa [Moses] Allah spoke directly."

near al-Tur in the Sinai leave the clothes on a tree or rock near the cemetery (Shuqayr 1916: 395–96). It is considered praiseworthy to leave the clothes of a deceased Bedouin on his/her grave in anticipation that a poor person will find them (Bailey 1991: 65). The author found that in the Negev and Sinai, some Bedouin women take from the cemetery pieces from the hem (*dhayl al-thawb*) of the embroidered clothes that belonged to deceased women, to use them in certain rituals to expel the *qarina* and evil spirits. Needless to say, there is a difference between pastoralists' practices—not just Bedouin but also, for example, the Tuareg (Rasmussen 1995)—village practices (Boddy 1988, 1989; Fakhouri 1968), and practices in large cities such as in Omdurman (Cloudsley 1983), Cairo, or Alexandria (Ismail 1976). The variation may well depend on the position of women in the household and in the immediate environment.

It is worth noting that in early twentieth-century Palestine (Canaan 1927a: 185) a newborn child whose brothers had all died would be "sold." Every one of the friends and/or the agnatic group would pay the mother with a copper coin. These were fastened to the child's cap or hung with blue beads and other amulets around its neck. The main idea of this custom is to mislead the *qarina* and to make her think that the child does not belong to its mother.

Additional Methods of Treatment and Protection against the *Qarina*

The pastoral Bedouin in the Negev describe preventive measures and treatments of the *qarina*. One of these involves taking a piece of flesh from the head of a dead wolf, particularly a piece from between its eyebrows or its forehead, and placing it in an infant's headdress. The flesh with the hair symbolizes the head of the wolf, for it is the most prominent part of its face. When the *qarina* comes near the baby to harm it and sees or smells the flesh of the wolf, it will be frightened away.

Parents are forbidden to buy clothes for their newborn by themselves. Clothing is bought by relatives. Thus, the parents of the newborn deceive the *qarina* into believing that the infant is the worthless offspring of a poor family that cannot afford to buy its own baby's clothes. Sometimes the women buy clothing for the child. Sometimes a member of the extended family "adopts" the baby to the extent of buying its clothing and perhaps other things, and when the infant grows up it is expected to serve the "adopting auntie." Children are sometimes allowed to remain unkempt and dressed in the oldest and most ragged clothing, since their parents

believe that the more beautiful a child is, the more exposed he or she is to evil eye and *qarina*.

Among the Rwala (Musil 1928: 412) in the early twentieth century, in order to cure a person afflicted by a *qarina,* a healer was called in, who, after working himself into an ecstasy, commanded the *qarina* to come out, crying: "Crawl out, crawl out." Sometimes, the healer beat the possessed person. The beating was permitted, since the blows were not intended for the patient, but rather for the *qarina,* and it is she who felt the pain, not the afflicted person. Other methods of providing protection against the *qarina* included hanging beads of various colors above the child's bed or on its clothing, particularly blue beads against the evil eye and evil spirits.

Naming may be used to protect against the *qarina.* A male child may be given the name of one of Allah's servants (Abd-Alla, Abd al-Karim), or the name of a prophet (Musa, Mhammad [Muhammad]). Boys are given girls' names such as Ibnaiyih ("little daughter") or the names of animals and beasts of prey: Klayb ("little dog"[31]), Dhib, Dhiab[32] ("wolf," "wolves"), Nimir ("tiger"), and *Wahsh* ("wild beast"), or the names of birds, such as *Sagir* ("falcon") and *Gunbar* ("lark").

Many other practices are employed to provide protection against the *qarina.* A dried turtle (*qurqa'annih*) or the dried head of a fish may be hung at the entrance of the dwelling or on the tent pole to repel it. A vessel filled with water is placed close to the child's head every night during the first forty days of its life, and a net is generally hung at the door or at the back of the tent in the belief that it is from this direction that the *qarina* in the shape of a bird usually enters a dwelling. Likewise, steel—a needle, dagger, sword, saber, or other metal object—may be hung near the baby's cradle, or under the family's pillows. Similarly, women cut pieces of the tomb covering of al-Nabi Musa and hang them as amulets on their new babies as a preventive measure. A Quran or an amulet may be placed under the pillow of a pregnant woman or a newborn.

The Bedouin believe that beads, certain coins, shells, and cowries have magical and healing qualities. Using clamshells (*sadafah*) and cowries (*wada'*) from the sea in ritual bathing ensures that the impurity of the *qarina* is washed away, since clamshells and cowries bear a strong resemblance to the female genitalia.[33] Blue beads, coins, cowries, shells, and amulets may also be hung on the baby's head covering/cap (*augah,* diminutive for a baby's *augayih*) to protect the baby from the evil eye and the *qarina.* Blue beads that contain alum are called *kushshash* due to their shape, which resembles the legs of a baby when the beads are tied with thread. These beads are said to have the ability hit or kick the evil eye and the *qarina.* Similarly, in pre-Islamic times, women protected their children from harm at the hands of the *qarina* with amulets (*'udha*) called *qarina*'s cloth (*thawb al-qarina*) (al-Munjid 1975: 625).

Verses from the Quran are often used in treating or repelling the *qarina*. For example, a piece of silver (*maskih*) inscribed with verses from the Quran (2:255, *ayit al-kursy*) may be hung around on the pregnant woman's neck. A woman may bathe in dried leaves of Christ's thorn mixed with water. The family may make a pilgrimage to locate Christ's thorn, and read verses from the Quran at the site. In addition, the family may make a pilgrimage to a holy tomb where they read verses from the Quran, light incense, and ask God to heal the woman. A sheep or goat is walked around the tomb several times, his ear nicked, and the blood sprinkled on the tomb. In the evening, the animal is slaughtered and eaten at a festive meal. Notably, in Arabia (Dickson 1951: 543) among the 'Ajman tribe, a piece of the ear above the lobe was cut off from the latest-born infant, placed inside a date, and given to the mother to eat. This was done in order to confuse the *qarina*. The child is then known as *al jida'*, "the cut-off one."[34]

Conclusion

The *qarina* threatens the reproductive power of Bedouin women, polluting and violating their bodies. Thus, the *qarina* violates the two inner sanctums: the harem and the bodies of vulnerable females. Among most pastoral Bedouin, *qarina* is the first cause to be considered in cases of woman's infertility or infant mortality, and is an alien agent. Afflicted women are not considered to occupy a peripheral position as a result, since women occupy a very important position in the economy of the pastoral Bedouin household. In such a climate, in a society that places high value on fertility and numerous children, infertility is simply untenable and requires an explanation. Infertility can lead to polygamy or even divorce. The constant threat of divorce or the prospect of one's husband taking a second wife often forces a wife to seek to raise her status in the eyes of her husband and his family, especially his mother, by giving her husband a male offspring as soon as possible.

Traditional therapies are not only a means for curing sickness; they are a means by which specific types of illness are defined and given culturally recognizable forms. While in Western medicine criteria of proof demand more than plausibility, in traditional Bedouin medicine the condition of plausibility seems to be sufficient. It is interesting to note that *qarina* healing and prophylactic practices are practiced by men as well as women, especially dervishes. In some cases, the healer is unsuccessful in driving out the *qarina* from the afflicted woman. When such failure occurs, a woman remains with her *qarina* until she discovers the correct cure from another healer. Healers and patients explain that this is the will of Allah.

For the patient, a failed therapeutic intervention may be considered important because it offers diagnostic information that points to a more appropriate type of healer. That is, some spirits are more powerful than others, just as some healers may be more familiar and effective with a particular problem than others. The *qarina* has been and is today a very important dimension of healing cultures among pastoral Bedouin women.

The most significant finding on this subject is that the *qarina* is one of the most dangerous factors interfering in the lives of Bedouins, who invest much effort in a variety of methods to counteract it. The second significant finding is that women believe in *qarina* more than men. Therefore, most healing methods are practiced by women, although some religious and educated men use amulets and read holy phrases from the Quran as well.

The main objective of the healer is to establish communication with the spirits. The spirit is defined, circumscribed, tamed, and weakened, in order to be expelled from the body. The author has the impression that the Bedouin woman afflicted by the *qarina* makes every effort to get rid of it, to be healthy in order to rejoin her community to take part in her duties, as she did before she became sick. Although this chapter focuses on pastoral Bedouin, the author found that the *qarina* afflicts not only poor and/or illiterate Bedouin, but also educated ones who live in Bedouin towns. Bedouin healers explain that this is because "there is no one fully protected from jinn." It is the author's impression from observation of Bedouin society over an extended period that during the last twenty to thirty years, there is a movement among the Bedouin to "go back to religion" and readopt the folk practices described here, a trend that strengthens the position of religious healers among their own local communities.

Notes

1. Compare this to *Waq Waq*, a legendary island said to be east in the China Sea, or north of Zanzibar. It was supposed to be inhabited by female creatures similar to human women, who cried out "*waq waq*" and died immediately if touched. Other ancient sources mention an Indian tree called the *waq waq* that bears fruit that resembles a human head suspended by the hair (Kocache 1982: 3).
2. In Greek mythology, Hermaphroditus was the son of Aphrodite and Hermes. Aphrodite was the goddess of beauty and erotic love, Hermes the god of fertility, commerce, and flight. Hermaphroditus, a very handsome young man, came to a beautiful lake to swim. The nymph of the lake, Salmacis, fell passionately in love with him, but he spurned her. One day when he was bathing

in her spring, she embraced him and pulled him down into the pool, praying to the gods that she and Hermaphroditus might be forever united. Their bodies joined into one, making him the first hermaphrodite, with both male and female reproductive organs (Avery 1972: 57–64, 273–80; Grant and Hazel 1979: 40–42, 180–83; Grimal 1990: 47,197–99; Zimmerman 1964: 25–26, 124–25, 232).

3. There is a belief that boys born with a short prepuce (a nearly circumcised foreskin) have "an angel's circumcision," also called a "moon's circumcision" (*tuhur qamari*). It is believed that in such cases the *qarina* of the mother has borne a son at the same time. In her great joy, the spirit circumcised the son of her human sister along with her own son (Canaan 1927a: 164).
4. Also known as cot death or sudden infant death syndrome (SIDS, *maut sariri*).
5. The term *miqlat* was cited in pre- and early Islamic times (Amin 1969: 64).
6. In early twentieth-century Palestine, it was customary for a mother who was suspected of having a *qarina* not to suckle her newborn baby with her first supply of milk (*halib liba/ilby*) in order to mislead the *qarina* (Canaan 1927a: 171).
7. The Prophet suspected the Banu al-Nadir of hostile designs when they refused to leave on the same terms as the Banu Qaynuqa' (Hodgson 1974: 190).
8. Parents of these children came to ask the Prophet's advice as to how they could force their children to follow them and accept Islam as their new religion. The Prophet said that God forbade them from doing so, until their children chose Islam of their own free will. Children who wanted to be with their biological parents would be allowed to stay, but those who preferred their foster parents would be allowed to leave with them: "There is no compulsion in religion" (*la ikrah fi al-din,* Quran 2:256; al-Tabari 1992: 15–19; al-Qurtubi1993: 181–83).
9. When she removed the pillows, she would find a razor under them, placed by the head of the child, to protect it from demons (al-Bukhari 1974).
10. Thanks to Murray Last for this comment and information (17 December 2006).
11. Resin of *Boswellia carterii* (*luban, bakhur*).
12. *Ferula asafetida/asafoetida* (*hiltit, semgh al-unjudan,* or *jiddih* [Arabic for the baby's grandmother]) is bought in the market from a perfume vendor (*'attarin*). *Ferula* is remarkable for its unpleasant odor. In Algeria, the plant is used against sorcery, demons, and jinn because of its smell (Hilton-Simpson 1922: 17).
13. All these plants are well known for expelling bad spirits, demons, and jinn, including the *qarina,* and most of them are mentioned as holy plants in the Arabic-Islamic tradition (Ibn-Qayyim 1998: 215–16, 221; Quran 53:13–18).
14. Fruit of *Anastatica hierochuntica* (*kaf al-Rahaman, kaf Maryam*).
15. Ripe fruit of *Mandragora officinalis* (*tuffah al-majanin, imjinynih*).
16. Leaves of *Ruta chalepensis* (*fayjan*).
17. Fruits and leaves of *Ziziphus spina-christi* (*sidrih*).
18. Black seeds of *Peganum harmala* (*harjal*).
19. Seeds or oil of *Nigella sativa L.* (*habbit al-barakah*).
20. Oil of *Olea europaea L.* (*zayt zaytun*).
21. Fruit of *Punica granatum* (*rumman*).

22. Compare this with the custom among the Koryak (indigenous people of Kamchatka Krai in the Russian Far East), among whom dogs were stabbed in the heart and displayed wearing grass collars on poles around the village to guard against evil spirits (Fitzhugh and Crowell 1988: 252).
23. In Egypt, for example, the body is perceived by villagers as a complex, mysterious reservoir that apprehends and experiences the effects of the natural, supernatural, and social environments of an individual. The body is considered a reservoir in which personal problems and interpersonal tensions become clear on an individual level (Morsy 1980: 93–95).
24. Such a belief is similar to that of the *zar* spirit in Ethiopian society (Kahana 1985: 135–43). *Zar* is a form of spirit possession treated by a traditional healer who negotiates with the alien spirit and bestows gifts on the possessed woman patient (Hodes 1997: 29–36). According to local belief, the body is a microcosm of village society. Similarly to village boundaries, body orifices are ambiguous, however necessary and inevitable (Boddy 1989: 9–16).
25. Using music for therapy to expel jinn from the body is the basic objective of the healer, who establishes communication with the spirits. See also Boneh 1985.
26. In the context of a *zar* ceremony: "the *ma'zur*—excused—is the vehicle of communication. Having reached an altered state of consciousness through response to the audial stimuli of a variety of musical instruments and rhythmic swaying and dancing to a rapid beat working up into frenzy on the verge of exhaustion, the afflicted person starts to speak in an unfamiliar tone of voice. The sound is immediately recognized as the *asyad*'s response to the sheikh's [dervish's] calling. Speaking through the mouth of the *ma'zur,* the *asyad* then proceeds to explain the circumstances that led to their association with their host. They also set the conditions for reconciliation and for sparing their host from the ravages of illness; many of their demands are directed to the patient's personal advantage" (Morsy 1978: 601).
27. On the treatment of epileptic seizures, see Abu-Rabia (2012: 157–66).
28. The *kurta* is described as a beast of prey similar to the wildcat, only larger, dark yellow in color, with cropped ears that end in a tuft of long straight hairs. It lies in wait for gazelles and is fond of hiding itself among dry annuals in the field. The breeze blows the hairs on its ears as it moves through the annuals; the gazelles are thus misled and approach it; the cat then leaps on the back of its prey, thrusts its claws into the victim's throat, and sucks its blood (Musil 1928: 20). It preys on birds, including bustards (Jabbur 1995: 91). The word *qurta* in Arabic is derived from *qarata,* which means "dried blood and flesh" or "a dead body" (al-Munjid 1975: 618).
29. Compare this with Bedouin tent honor (al-'Aref 1933: 181–200; Dickson 1951: 133–35); Bourdieu 1979 on the Kabyle house; and Griaule 1972 on the Dogon compound.
30. The word *hilliyyih* is derived from *yihallil*/halal, and refers to making something sacred and the sanctification of marriage (Bailey 1974b: 126–27; Shuqayr 1916: 388).

31. Dorothy Van Ess of the Basra mission writes that "tribal and village people would give their children names such as Dog, Garbage, and Angry, to indicate that they were not worth the attention of a malevolent spirit" (Doumato 2000: 151n14).
32. Among the Bedouin of the Hijaz (in the Arabian Peninsula) during the nineteenth century, *Dhiab* ("wolves") is a man's name. But it is almost certain that such names are connected to the patronymic theory; it is equally consistent with the theory of totem tribes, and much more natural under it (Smith 1903: 19).
33. Couri/courie/cowries, from the side, with their openings facing outwards, look like a woman's vagina, while the color of the couri is white, like a man's sperm, symbolizing fertility and mother's milk.
34. An old Bedouin custom involved cutting off the ears of their dog when the animals were young. A piece was then cooked and given to the dog to eat. This practice was believed to make the dog a good watchdog and especially a good barker at night (Dickson 1951: 543). It may be that the custom mentioned above was practiced in order to cheat the *qarina* into thinking that the new baby was a dog with a cut-off ear.

Bibliography

Abarbanell, Nitza. 1997. *Eve and Lilith.* Ramat-Gan: Bar-Illan University Press.

al-'Abd, Salah. 1965. "ri'ayat al-badw wa-tahdirahum wa-tawtinahum fi al-mamlaka al-'Arabiya al-sa'udiya." In *ri'ayat al-badw wa-tahdirahum wa-tawtinahum,* vol. 1, al-mu'tamar al-tasi' lil-shu'un al-ijtimaa'iyah wal-'amal. al-Quds: Jami'at al-duwal al-'Arabiya.

Abdul Wahab, Atqah, and Ossama Mostafa. 2007. "Arabian Incense Exposure among Qatari Asthmatic Children." *Saudi Med. J.* 28 (3): 476–77.

Abou-Rbiah, Yunis, and Shimon Weitzman. 2002. "Diabetes among Bedouins in the Negev: The Transition from a Rare to a Highly Prevalent Condition." *IMAJ* 4: 687–89.

Abou-Zeid, Ahmad. 1979. "New Towns and Rural Development in Egypt."*Africa* 49 (3): 283–90.

Abu-Helal, Ahmad, Usama Shammut, and Ibrahim Naser. 1984. *Taiysir Ta'lim al-Badw fi al-watan al-'Arabi.* Tunis: Idarat al-Buhuth al-Tarbawiya, al-Munazzama al-'Arabiya li-Tarbiya wal-Thaqafa wal-'Ulum.

Abu-Jaber, Kamel, and Fawzi Gharaibeh. 1981. "Bedouin Settlement, Organizational, Legal and Administration Structure in Jordan." In *The Future of Pastoral Peoples,* edited by John G. Galaty et al. Ottawa: International Development Centre.

Abu-Khusa, Ahmad. 1976. *Bir al-Saba' wal-ḥaiah al-Badawiya.* 'Amman: matabi' al-mu'assasah al-ṣaḥafiyah al-urduniyah. Volume I.

——. 1979. *Bir al-Saba' wal-ḥaiah al-Badawiya.* 'Amman: matabi' al-mu'assasah al-ṣaḥafiyah al-urduniyah. Volume II.

——. 1994. *Mausu'at Qaba'il Bir al-Saba' wa-'Asha'iriha al-Ra'iysiyah.* 'Amman: sherket al-sharq al-awsat le-teba'ah.

Abu-Lughod, Lila. 1988. *Veiled Sentiments: Honor and Poetry in a Bedouin Society.* Berkeley and Los Angeles: University of California Press.

Abu-Rabia, Aref. 1979. "Comparison between Traditional and Western Medicine." Master's thesis, Hadassah Medical School, Hebrew University of Jerusalem (in Hebrew).

——. 1983. *Folk Medicine among the Bedouin Tribes in the Negev.* Sede Boker: Ben-Gurion University of the Negev, Social Studies Center, Blaustein Institute for Desert Research.

——. 1992. Mourning Rituals among the Bedouin of the Negev. *Notes on the Bedouin,* No .23. Ben-David, Sede Boqer: Social Studies Center, pp. 9–17. (in Hebrew).

——. 1994a. *The Negev Bedouin and Livestock Rearing: Social, Economic and Political Aspects.* Oxford: Berg.

——. 1994b. "The Bedouin Refugees in the Negev." *Refuge* 14 (6): 15–17.

——. 1994c. "Cross-cultural Bedouin Medicine." *Collegium Anthropologicum* 18 (2): 15–218.

——. 1998. "The Bedouin Family in the Negev", in, *Israel: A Local Anthropology Studies in the Anthropology of Israel research group.* Abuhav, O., Hertzog, E., Goldberg, H., & Marx, E. Tel-Aviv: Tcherikover, pp. 27–45 (in Hebrew).

——. 1999a. *The Bedouin's Traditional Medicine.* Tel Aviv: Mod Publishing (in Hebrew).

——. 1999b. "Some Notes on Livestock Production among Negev Bedouin Tribes." *Nomadic Peoples New Series* 3 (1): 22–30.

——. 2000. Review of *Zad al-Musafir wa-qut al-hadir* (On Sexual Diseases and Their Treatment by Ibn al-Jazzar). *Middle Eastern Studies* 36 (2): 224–29.

——. 2001. *Bedouin Century, Education and Development among the Negev Tribes in the Twentieth Century.* New York and Oxford: Berghahn Books.

——. 2002. "Negev Bedouin: Displacement, Forced Settlement and Conservation." In *Conservation and Mobile Indigenous Peoples, Displacement, Forced Settlement, and Sustainable Development,* edited by Dawn Chatty and Marcus Colchester, 202–11. Oxford and New York: Berghahn Books.

——. 2005a. "Palestinian Plant Medicines for Treating Renal Disorders: An Inventory and Brief History." *Alternative & Complementary Therapies* 11 (6): 295–300.

——. 2005b. Evil Eye and Cultural beliefs among the Bedouin tribes of the Negev. *Folklore* Vol. 116, No. 3: 241–254.

——. 2005c. "Indigenous Practices among Palestinians for Healing Eye Diseases and Inflammations." *Dynamis* 2005 (25): 383–401.

——. 2005d. "Urinary diseases and ethno-botany among pastoral nomads in the Middle East." *Journal of Ethnobiology and Ethnomedicine* 1 (4): 1–15.

——. 2005e. "Bedouin Health Services in Mandated Palestine." *Middle Eastern Studies* 41 (3): 421–29.

——. 2005f. "Herbs as a Food and Medicine Source in Palestine." *Asian Pacific Journal of Cancer Prevention* 2005a 6 (3): 404–7.

——. 2006. "A Century of Education: Bedouin Contestation with Formal Education in Israel." In *Nomadic Societies in the Middle East and North Africa: Entering the 21st Century,* edited by Dawn Chatty. Leiden: Brill Publishers.

——. 2007. "Breastfeeding Practices among Pastoral Tribes in the Middle East." *Anthropology of the Middle East* 2 (2): 38–54.

——. 2010. "Child-Birth in Traditional Arab-Bedouin Society," in *Perspectives on Israeli Anthropology,* edited by Abuhav, O., Hertzog, E., & Marx, E. Wayne State University Press. Pp. 453–464.

——. 2011. "The Significance of Colours in Pastoral Nomadic Society." In *Serendipity in Anthropological Research: The Nomadic Turn,* edited by E. Hertzog and H. Hazan. London: Ashgate.
——. 2012. Ethno-Botanic Treatments for Paralysis (*falij*) in the Middle East. *Chinese Medicine,* Vol. 3 No. 4, 2012: 157–166.
——. 2015. Key Plants in Fighting Cancer in the Middle East. *Chinese Medicine,* 6, 124–135.
Abu-Saad, K., S. Weitzman, Y. Abu-Rabiah, H. Abu-Shareb, and D. Frazer. 2001. "Rapid Lifestyle, Diet and Health Changes among Urban Bedouin Arabs of Southern Israel." *Food, Nutrition and Agriculture,* no. 28: 1–14.
Abu-Taha, Hamd 1984. Personal communication, 10 June, 1984.
Adair John, Kurt Deuschle, and Walsh McDermott 1969. Patterns of Health and Disease Among the Navahos. In, *The Cross-Cultural Approach to Health Behavior.* L.R. Lynch, ed. Pp. 83-110. Rutherford, N.J.: Fairleigh Dickison University Press.
Alkan, Michael 2001. *Opinion on the Subject of Public Health, Water Supply to Unrecognized Locales in the Negev.*
Ali-Shtayeh, Mohammad.S., Zohara Yaniv, and Jamal Mahajna. 2000. "Ethnobotanical Survey in the Palestinian Area: A Classification of the Healing Potential of Medicinal Plants." *Journal of Ethnopharmacology* 73 (2000): 221–32.
Almi, Orly. 2003. *No Man's Land—Health in the Unrecognized Villages of the Negev.* Tel Aviv: Physicians for Human Rights in Israel.
——. 2005. *The Ramifications of House Demolitions in Israel on the Mental Health of Children.* Tel Aviv: Physicians for Human Rights in Israel.
Amin, Ahmad. 1969. *Fajr al-Islam.* Beirut: Dal al-Kitab al-'Arabi.
Amitai, Pinchas. 1987. *Handbook of Insects of Israel and other Anthropods.* Jerusalem: Keter Publishing House (in Hebrew).
Amitai, Yonah. 2005. *Annual Report on Infant Mortality in Israel for 2004.* Jerusalem: Ministry of Health, Department for the Mother, the Child and the Adolescent.
Angel, Lawrence. 1964. "Osteoporosis: Thalassemia?" *American Journal of Physical Anthropology* 22: 369–71.
Anis, Ibrahim, et al. 1972. *al-Mu'jam al-Wasit.* Cairo: n.p.
Appendino, Giovanni, Silvia Tagliapietra, Gian Mario Nano, and Jasmin Jakupovic. 1994. "Sesquiterpene Coumarin Ethers from *Asafetida.*" *Phytochemistry* 30 (1): 183–86.
al-'Aref, 'Aref. 1933. *Al-Qada bayna al-Badw.* Jerusalem: Bayt al-Maqdes.
——. 1934. *Tarikh Beer al-Saba' wa-Qabai'liha.* Jerusalem: n.p.
——. 1943. *Tarikh Ghazza.* Jerusalem: Matba'at dar al-Iytam al-Islamia.
——. 1944. *Bedouin Love, Lore and Legend.* Jerusalem: Cosmos Publishing.
'Arim, Abd al-Jabbar. 1965. "Siyasat tawtin al-badw fi al-'Iraq." *ri'ayat al-badw wa-tahdirahum wa-tawtinahum,* vol. 1.
Ashkenazi, Tuvia. 1956. *The Bedouin: Origin, Life and Customs.* Jerusalem: Mas.
Assaf, Michael. 1970. *Relations between Arabs and Jews in the Land of Israel 1860–1948.* Tel Aviv: Milali Tarbut ve-Hinukh (in Hebrew).
Aurel, Alexander, and Peretz Cornfeld. 1945. *The Near and Middle East: WHO'S WHO.* Vol. 1, Palestine, Trans-Jordan 1945–1946. Jerusalem: Near East and Middle East WHO'S WHO Publishing Company.

Austen, Hallie. 1990. *The Heart of the Goddess: Art, Myth and Meditations of the World's Sacred Feminine.* Berkeley: Wingbow Press.

Avery, Catherine, ed. 1972. *The New Century Handbook of Greek Mythology and Legend.* New York: Meredith Corporation.

Avitsur, Shmuel. 1976. *Daily Life in Eretz Israel in the Nineteenth Century.* Jerusalem: 'Am Hasefer (in Hebrew).

Awad, Mohamed. 1959. "Settlement of Nomadic and Semi-nomadic Tribal Groups in the Middle East." *International Labour Review* 25: 25–56.

Awerbuch-Friedlander, Tamara. 2005. "Disease Dynamics across Political Borders: The Case of Rabies in Israel and the Surrounding Countries." *Dynamis.Acta Hisp. Med. Sci. Hist. Illus.* 25: 451–85.

al-Azraq, Ibrahim. 1948. *tashiyl al-manafi' fi al-tibb wal-hikma al-mushtamil 'ala' shifa' al-ajsam.* Bayrut: Dar al-Kutub al-'Ilmiya.

Baba, N., K. Shaar, S. Hamadeh, and N. Adra. 1994. "Nutritional Status of Bedouin Children Aged 6–10 Years in Lebanon and Syria under Different Nomadic Pastoral Systems." *Ecology of Food and Nutrition* 32 (3–4): 247–59.

Bacgci, Eyup, and Alpaslan Kocak. 2008. "Essential Oil Composition of the Aerial Parts of Two *Salvia L.* (*S. multicaulis Vahl. Enum* and *S. tricochlada Bentham*) Species from East Anatolian Region (Turkey)." *International Journal of Science & Technology* 3 (1): 13–18.

Baer, Hans, Merrill Singer, and Ida Susser. 1997. *Medical Anthropology and the World System: A Critical Perspective.* Westport, CT, and London: Bergin & Garvey.

Bahhady, F.A. 1981. "Recent Changes in Bedouin Systems of Livestock Production in the Syrian Steppe." In *The Future of Pastoral People,* edited by John G. Galaty, Dan Aronson, Philip Carl Salzman, and Amy Chouinard. Ottawa: IDRC.

Bailey, Clinton. 1974a. "Bedouin Star-Lore in Sinai and the Negev." *Bulletin of the School of Oriental and African Studies* 37 (3): 580–96.

——. 1974b. "Bedouin Weddings in Sinai and the Negev." *Folklore Research Center Studies* 4, *Studies in Wedding Customs*: 105–32.

——. 1982. "Bedouin Religious Practices in Sinai and the Negev." *Anthropos* 72 (1–2): 65–88.

——. 1991. *Bedouin Poetry from Sinai and the Negev: Mirror of a Culture.* Oxford: Oxford University Press.

——. 2004. *A Culture of Desert Survival: Bedouin Proverbs from Sinai and the Negev.* New Haven, CT: Yale University Press.

——. 2009. *Bedouin Law from Sinai and the Negev, Justice without Government.* New Haven, CT: Yale University Press.

Bailey, Clinton, and Avinoam Danin. 1981. "Bedouin Plant Utilization in Sinai and the Negev." *Economic Botany* 35 (2): 145–62.

Balfour, Gail. 2003. "Women's Health Matters." European Society of Human Reproduction and Embryology. *Women Health Matters Network,* October 23.

Bar-Zvi, Sason, Aref Abu-Rabia, and Gideon Kressel. 1998. *The Charm of Graves: Mourning Rituals and Tomb Worshipping Among the Negev Bedouin.* Sede Boker: Ben-Gurion University of the Negev, Social Studies Center, Blaustein Institute for Desert Research.

Bayat, Ali Haydar. 2002. "Medicine in the pre-Islamic central Asian Turkish world," in, History of medicine, pharmacology, veterinary medicine in Anatolia and Turkish cultures. Edited by Nil Sari, Istanbul: Turkish History Society.

Ben-Assa, Benjamin. 1961. "The Medical Work among the Bedouins in the Negev." *Harefuah* 61: 211–13. (In Hebrew, with English abstract.)

——. 1964. "Medical Observations on 2000 Bedouin Patients." *Harefuah* 67: 450–53. (In Hebrew, with English abstract.)

——. 1969. "The Desert's Effect on the Bedouin Health." *Notes on the Bedouin* (1): 13–18. (In Hebrew).

——.1970. "The Desert and the Health of the Bedouin." *Teva Ve'aretz* (12), 5: 218 (In Hebrew).

——. 1974. "The Bedouin as a Patient." *Harefuah* 87 (2): 73–76. (In Hebrew.)

Benatar, S. 1996. "What Makes a Just Healthcare System?" *British Medical Journal* 313: 1567–68.

Ben-David, Joseph. 1981. *Jabaliya, a Bedouin Tribe under a Monastery's Patronage.* Jerusalem: Kanna.

Benenson, Abram. 1975. *Control of Comminicable Diseases in Man.* 12th edition. Washington, DC: American Public Health Association. [Arabic version 1979].

Bergersen, G., 1979. *Pharmacology in Nursing.* St. Louis: Mosby.

Bhattacharya, A.N., and M., Harb 1973. Sheep production on natural pastures by roaming Bedouins in Lebanon. *Journal of Range Management* 26: 266–269.

Bilu, Yoram. 1990. "Jewish Moroccan 'Saint Impresarios' in Israel: A Stage-Developmental Perspective." *Psychoanalytic Study of Society* 15: 247–69.

——. 1993. *Without Bounds, the life and death of Rabbi Ya'acov Wazana.* Jerusalem: Magness Press.

Bitterman W., H. Farhadian, C. Abu-Samra, et al. 1991. "Environmental and Nutritional Factors Significantly Associated with Cancer of the Urinary Tract among Different Ethnic Groups." *Urol Clin North America* 18: 501–8.

Blackman, Winifred Susan. 1927. *The Fellahin of Upper Egypt.* London: G.B. Harrap.

Blom, Franz. 1992. "Conception and Growth of Children." In *Medical Practices in Ancient America,* edited by Miguel Guzman Peredo. Mexico City: Ediciones Euroamericanas.

Blum, Richard, and Eva Blum. 1965. *Health and Healing in Rural Greece: A Study of Three Communities.* Stanford, CA: Stanford University Press.

Blunt, Anne. 1879. *Bedouin Tribes of the Euphrates.* New York: Harper & Bros.

Bocco, Riccardo. 2006. "The Settlement of Pastoral Nomads in the Arab Middle East: International Organization and Trends in Development Policies 1950–1900." In *Nomadic Societies in the Middle East and North Africa: Entering the 21st Century,* edited by Dawn Chatty, 302–30. Leiden: Brill.

Boddy, Janice. 1988. "Spirits and Selves in Northern Sudan: The Cultural Therapeutics of Possession and Trance." *American Ethnologist* 15 (1): 4–27.

——. 1989. *Wombs and Alien Spirits: Women, Men, and the Zar Cult in Northern Sudan.* Madison: University of Wisconsin Press.

Bodley, John. 1994. *Cultural Anthropology: Tribes, States, and the Global System.* Mountain View, CA: Mayfield Publishing.

Boneh, Dan. 1985. "Dehiya: The Social Significance of a Ceremonial Dance and Its Disappearance in the Context of Sedentarization." Paper presented at the International Congress of Ethnologists and Anthropologists. Alexandria, Egypt.

Bos, Gerrit. 1997. *Ibn al-Jazzar on Sexual Diseases and their Treatment (Zad al-Musafir wa-qut al-Hadir).* London and New York: Kegan Paul International.

Boulos, Loutfy. 1983: *Medicinal Plants of North Africa.* Agonac: Reference Publications.

Bourdieu, Pierre. 1979. *Algeria 1960: The Disenchantment of the World: The Sense of Honor: The Kabyle House or the World Reversed.* Translated by Richard Nice. Cambridge: Cambridge University Press.

Bresslavsky, J., 1946. *Do You Know the Country? The Negev.* Tel Aviv: Hakibutz Hameuchad (in Hebrew).

Brynen, R. 1990: 'The Politics of Exile: The Palestinians in Lebanon', *Journal of Refugee Studies* vol. 3 (3), pp. 204–227.

Budenheimer, S. 1961. *General Enthomology.* Jerusalem: Kiryat Sepher.

al-Bukhari.1974. *Sahih al-Bukhari. Arabic-English,* vol. 7, edited by Muhammad Muhsin Khan. al-Medina al-Munauwara: Islamic University.

Burckhardt, John Lewis. 1822. *Travels in Syria and the Holy Land.* London: J. Murray.

——. 1992. *Notes on the Bedouins Wahabys.* 2 vols. Reading, UK: Garnet Publishing.

Burgel, Christoph. 1976. "Secular and Religious Features of Medical Arabic Medicine." In *Asian Medical Systems,* edited by Charles Leslie. Berkeley: University of California Press.

Burton, Richard Francis. 1893. *Personal Narrative of a Pilgrimage to Al-Madinah and Meccah,* vol. 1. London: Tylson and Edwards.

al-Bustani, al-Mu 'allim B. 1995. *Qutr al-Muhit, A Student's Dictionary of Arabic.* Beirut: Maktabat Lubnan Nashirun.

Calder, Ritchie. 1958. *Medicine and Man: The story of the art and science of healing.* London: George Allen & Unwin.

Campanella, L., G. Crescentini, and P. Avino. 1999. "Chemical Composition and Nutritional Evaluation of Some Natural and Commercial Food Products Based on Spirulina." *Analusis* 27: 533–40.

Canaan, Tewfik [Tawfiq]. 1920–1921. "Haunted Springs and Water Demons in Palestine." *Journal of the Palestine Oriental Society* 1: 153–70.

——. 1923. "*Tasit er-Radjfeh*—The Fear Cup." *Journal of the Palestine Oriental Society* 3: 122–31.

——. 1927a. "The Child in Palestinian Arab Superstition." *Journal of the Palestine Oriental Society* 7: 159–86.

——. 1927b. *Muhammedan Saints and Sancuaries in Palestine.* London: Luzac.

CESCR. 2000. Committee on Economic, Social and Cultural Rights, 2000, Article 30 (43). General Comment No. 14, "The Right to the Highest Attainable Standard of Health."

Chatty, Dawn. 1978. "Changing Sex Roles in Bedouin Society in Syria and Lebanon." In *Women in the Muslim World,* edited by Lois Beck and Nikki Keddie. Cambridge, MA: Harvard University Press.

——. 1990. "The Current Situation of the Bedouin in Syria, Jordan and Saudi Arabia and Their Prospects for the Future." In *Nomads in a Changing World,* ed-

ited by Philip Carl Salzman and John G. Galaty. Naples: Instituto Universitario Orientale.

——. 2006. "Multinational Oil Exploitation and Social Investment: Mobile Pastoralism in the Sultanate of Oman." In *Nomadic Societies in the Middle East and North Africa: Entering the 21st Century*, edited by Dawn Chatty, 496–518. Leiden: Brill.

Civil Administration of Palestine. 1922. Report.

Clark, Linda. 1984. *The Ancient Art of Colour Therapy*. Tel Aviv: Or-teva.

Clark, Margaret. 1959. *Health in the Mexican-American Culture: A Community Study*. Berkeley: University of California Press.

Cloudsley, Ann. 1983. *Women of Omdurman: Life, Love, and the Cult of Virginity*. London: Ethnographica.

Coatesworth, A. P., R. J. Addis, and D. W. Beverley. 2002. "Ear Nose and Throat Diseases in the Bedouin of the South Sinai Desert: A Cross-sectional Survey and Discussion of Healthcare Needs." *Journal of Laryngology & Otology* 116: 83–86.

Cohen, Amnon. 1982. *Jews under Islamic Rule: The Jerusalem Community during Early Ottoman Period*. Jerusalem: Magnes Press, Hebrew University.

——. 1989. *Economic Life in Ottoman Jerusalem*. Cambridge: Cambridge University Press.

Cole, Donald. 1975. *Nomads of the Nomads: The al-Murrah Bedouin of the Empty Quarter*. Chicago: Aldine.

——. 2006. "New Homes, New Occupation, New Pastoralism: Al Murrah Bedouin (1968–2003)." In *Nomadic Societies in the Middle East and North Africa: Entering the 21st Century*, edited by Dawn Chatty. Leiden: Brill.

Cole, Donald, and Soraya Altorki. 1998. *Bedouin, Settlers, and Holiday-Makers: Egypt's Changing Northwest Coast*. Cairo: American University in Cairo Press.

Colson, Anthony. 1971. *The Prevention of Illness in a Malay Village: An Analysis of Concepts and Behavior*. Developing Nations Monographs Series II, no. 1. Winston-Salem, NC: Overseas Research Centre, Wake Forest University.

Comaroff, Jean. 1993. "The Diseased Heart of Africa: Medicine, Colonialism, and the Black Body." In *Knowledge, Power, and Practice, The Anthropology of Medicine and Everyday Life*, edited by Sirley Lindenbaum and Margaret Lock. Berkeley: University of California Press.

Connan, Jacques, Arie Nissenbaum, and Daniel Dessort. 1992. "Molecular Archaeology: Export of Dead Sea Asphalt to Canaan and Egypt in the Chalcolithic-Early Bronze Age (4th–3rd millennium B.C.)." *Geochimica et Cosmochimica Acta* 56: 2743–59.

Copet-Rougier, Elizabeth. 1986. " Le Mal Court: Visible and Invisible Violence in an Acephalous Society—Mkako of Cameroon." In *The Anthropology of Violence*, edited by David Riches. Oxford: Blackwell.

Cornfeld, Peretz. 1947. *Palestine Personalia*. Tel Aviv: Sefer Press.

Coss, Richard, 1981. "Reflections on the Evil Eye." In *The Evil Eye: A Folklore Casebook*, edited by Alan Dundes. New York and London: Garland.

Cosminsky, Shella. 1976. "Cross-cultural Perspectives on Midwifery." In *Medical Anthropology*, edited by Francis Grollig and Harold Haley. The Hague and Paris: Mouton.

Crapanzano, Vincent. 1973. *The Hamadsha: A Study in Moroccan Ethnopsychiatry.* Berkeley: University of California Press.

——. 1977. "Mohammed and Dawia: Possession in Morocco." In *Case Studies of Spirit Possession,* edited by Vincent Crapanzano and Vivian Garrison, 141–76. New York: John Wiley.

Creyghton, Marie-Louise. 1992. "Breast-Feeding and Baraka in Northern Tunisia." In *The Anthropology of Breast-Feeding: Natural Law or Social Construct,* edited by V. Maher, 37–58. Oxford and New York: Berg.

Cunnison, Ian George. 1966. *Baggara Arabs: Power and the Lineage in a Sudanese Nomad Tribe.* Oxford: Clarendon Press.

al-Dabbagh, Mustafa. 1991. *Biladuna Filastin.* Beirut: Dar al-Tali'a.

Dafni, Irit, and Amots Dafni. 1975. "Some Aspects on Uses of Medicinal Plants among the Bedouin." *Teva' ve-ha-arets* 17: 233–40.

Dahl, Marilyn. 2004. "Middle Eastern Nutrition." *Health Care Food & Nutrition Focus* 21 (5): 6–8.

al-Damiri, Muhammad ibn Musa. 2005. AH, *hayat al-hayawan al-kubra,* 2 vols. Dimashq: dar al-bashair lil-tiba'ah wal-nashr wal-tawzi'.

Dawodu Adekunle. 2004. "Vitamin D Status of Arab Mothers and Infants." *J. Arab Neonatol Forum* 1: 15–22.

Dickson, Harold Richard P. 1949. *The Arab of the Desert: A Glimpse into Badawin life in Kuwait and Sau'd Arabia.* London: George Allen & Unwin.

——. 1956. *Kuwait and Her Neighbours.* London: George Allen & Unwin.

Dickson, Violet. 1955. *The Wild Flowers of Kuwait and Bahrain.* London: George Allen & Unwin.

Diqs, Isaak. 1984. *Bedouin Boyhood.* New York: Universe Books.

al-Diyarbi, Ahmad. 1343H. *Mujarrabat al-Diyarbi al-Kabir.* al-Qahira: matba'at al-halabi.

Dloomy, Ariel, Orly Almi, and Faisal Sawalha. 2006. *The Arab-Bedouins of the Naqab-Negev Desert in Israel.* A report to the UN Committee on the Elimination of Racial Discrimination (CERD). Omer (Israel): Negev Coexistence Forum for Civil Equality.

Dols, Michael W. 1987. "The Origins of the Islamic Hospitals: Myth and Reality." *Bulletin of the History of Medicine* 62: 367–90.

Doughty, Charles. 1921. *Travels in Arabia Deserta.* London: Jonathan Cape and the Medici Society.

Doumani, Beshara. 1995. *Rediscovering Palestine. Merchants and Peasants in Jabal Nablus, 1700–1900.* Berkeley: University of California Press.

Doumato, Eleanor Abdella. 2000. *Getting God's Ear: Women, Islam, and Healing in Saudi Arabia and the Gulf.* New York: Columbia University Press.

Draz, Omar. 1969. "The *Hema* System of Range Reserves in the Arabian Peninsula: Its Possibilities in Range Improvement and Conservation Projects in the East." FAO/PL: PFC/13.

Dressler, William, Kathryn Oths, and Clarence Gravlee. 2005. "Race and Ethnicity in Public Health Research: Models to Explain Health Disparities." *Annual Review Anthropology* 34: 231–52.

Duba, H., I. M. Mur-Veeman, and A. van Raak. 2001. "Pastoralist Health Care in Kenya." *International Journal of Integrated Care* 1: e13.

Duri, Zakaria. 1982. *Hapukh ve ha henna: The Kohl and the Hena.* Jerusalem: Khemed.

Dutton, Roderic W., John I. Clark, and Anwar Munir Battikhi, eds. 1998. *Arid Land Resources and Their Management: Jordan's Desert Margin.* London: Kegan Paul International.

Eagle, Robert 1978: *Alternative Medicine.* London: Futura Publication Limited.

Eickelman, Christine. 1993. "Fertility and Social Change in Oman; Women's Perspectives." *Middle East Journal* 47 (4): 652–66.

Elgood, C. 1962. "Medicine of the Prophet." *Osiris* 14: 33–192.

El-Shamy, Hasan. 1972. "Mental Health in Traditional Culture: A Study of Preventive and Therapeutic Folk Practices in Egypt." *Catalyst* 6: 13–28.

Encyclopedia of Islam 1978, Leiden: Brill.

Evans, William, C., 1998. *Trease and Evans' Pharmacognosy,* London: Saunders Company Ltd.

Evans-Pritchard, E. 1937. *Witchcraft, Oracles and Magic among the Azande.* London: Oxford University Press.

FadlAlla, Amal. 2002. "Modest Women, Deceptive Jinn: Perceptions of Foreignness, Danger and Disease among the Hadenowa of Eastern Sudan." Harvard Center for Population and Development Studies, Working Paper Series, vol. 12, No. 6, June.

Fakhouri, H. 1968. "The Zar Cult in an Egyptian Village." *Anthropology Quarterly* 41: 12–22.

Falk, Richard. 2009. "Human Rights Situation in Palestine and Other Occupied Arab Territories." Geneva: UN Human Rights Council.

al-Farabi, Abu-Nasr. 1967. *Kitab al-Musiqi al-Kabir.* al-Qahira: Maktabat Anjlo al-Misriya.

Femia, Paolo, and N. C. Aguilar. 1993. "Aportes de Los Hueseros a la Medicina Tradicinal Mexicana: El Caso Nahuas, Maya y Otomies." 13th International Congress of Anthropological and Ethnological Sciences, Mexico City.

Fielding, William. 1945. *Strange Superstitions and Magical Practices.* Philadelphia: Blackiston.

al-Fīlali, Mustafa. 1965. "tajarib idmaj al-badw bil-hayah al-rifiyah fi al-jumhuriyah al-tunisiyah." *ri'ayat al-badw wa-tahdirahum wa-tawtinahum,* vol. 1.

Fitzhugh, William, and Aron Crowell. 1988. *Crossroads of Continents: Culture of Siberia and Alaska.* Washington, DC: Smithsonian Institution Press.

Foster, George. 1962. *Traditional Cultures and the Impact of Technological Change.* New York: Harper & Row.

Foster, George, and Barbara Anderson. 1978. *Medical Anthropology.* New York: John Wiley & Sons.

Fraser, D., S. Weitzman, S. Blondheim, S. Shany, and Y. Abou-Rbiah. 1990. "The Prevalence of Cardiovascular Risk Factors among Male Bedouins: A Population in Transition." *Eur. J. Epidemiol.* 6: 273–78.

Fratkin, Elliot, and Eric Roth. 2005. "The Setting: Pastoral Sedentarization in Marsabit District, Northern Kenya." In *As Pastoralists Settle, Social, Health and*

Economic Consequences of Pastoral Sedentarization in Marsabit District, Kenya, edited by Elliot Fratkin and Eric Abella Roth. New York and London: Kluwer Academic Publishers.

Frazer, James G. 1962: "Sympathetic Magic." In *Reader in Comparative Religion, an Anthropological Approach,* edited by William A. Lessa and Evon Z. Vogt, 247–67. New York: Harper & Row.

Frazer, James. 1950. *The Golden Bough, A Study in Magic and Religion.* London: Macmillan and Co.

Galal, Osman. 2003. "Nutrition-Related Health Patterns in the Middle East." *Asia Pacific J. Clin. Nutr.* 12 (3): 337–43.

Gal-Pe'er, I. 1979. Beersheba and the Bedouin. *Beersheba Book,* edited by Y. Gradus and E. Stern. Jerusalem: Keter Publishing House. (in Hebrew)

Gal-Pe'er, I. 1991. *Beersheba Sights.* Edited by B. Gideon Biger and E. Schiller. Jerusalem: Ariel. (In Hebrew.)

Geber, Marcelle, and R.F.A. Dean. 1956. "The Psychological Changes Accompanying Kwashiorkor." *Courrier* 6: 3–14.

Ghazanfar, Shahina. 1994. *Handbook of Arabian Medicinal Plants.* London: CRC Press.

Goren, Orna. 1994: "The Jewelry of Bedouin Women in the Negev and Sinai." In *Israel: People and Land,* edited by Rehavam Ze'evi. Tel Aviv: Eretz Israel Museum.

Government of Palestine. 1937. Report.

Granqvist, Hilma. 1935. *Birth and Childhood among the Arabs.* Helsingfors: Soderstroms.

———. 1947. *Child Problems Among the Arabs.* Helsingfors: Soderstrom.

Grant, Michael, and John Hazel. 1979. *Gods and Mortals in Classical Mythology: A Dictionary.* New York: Dorset.

Griaule, Marcel. 1972. *Conversation with Ogotemmeli; An Introduction to Dogon Religious Ideas.* London: Published for the International African Institute by the Oxford University Press.

Grimal, Pierre. 1990. *A Concise Dictionary of Classical Mythology.* Oxford: Basil Blackwell.

Greene, Mark. 1975. "Impact of the Sahelian Drought in Mauritania." *African Environment* 1: 11–21.

Groen, J. J., Miriam Balogh, Mina Levy, et al. 1964. "Nutrition of the Bedouin in the Negev Desert." *American Journal of Clinic Nutrition* 14 (37): 37–46.

Groen, J. J., D. Ben-Ishay, and B. Ben-Assa. 1962. "Clinical and Biochemical Observations on Osteomalacia among the Bedouin of the Negev Desert." *Voeding* 23 (1): 49–61.

Groen J.J., Duyvensz F, Halsted JA. 1960. Diffuse alveolar atrophy of the jaw (noninflammatory form of paradental disease) and presenile osteoporosis. Geront Clin 1960: 2: 68–86.

Groom, Nigel. 1981. *Frankincense and Myrrh: A Study of the Arabian Incense Trade.* London: Longman.

Gruner, Cameron 1930. *A Treatise on the Canon of Medicine of Avicenna.* Incorporating a Tradition of the First Book. London:Luzax & Co.

Haddad, Sami. 1975. *History of Arab Medicine.* Beirut: Lebanon.

Hakhmon Rinat, Juri Bar-David, Asher Bashiri, and Moshe Mazor. 1998. "Brucellosis in Pregnancy." *Harefuah* 135 (1–2): 3–7.

Hamarneh, S. 1991. Ibn al-Quff's contribution to Arab-Islamic medical sciences. Hamdard Med. 34(1), 1991, pp. 27–36.

Hameida, J., and L. Billot. 2002. "Nutrition Status of Libyan Children in 2000 Compared to 1979." *Eastern Mediterranean Health Journal* 8 (2 & 3): 261–71.

Hampshire, K. 2002. Networks of nomads: Negotiating access to health resources among pastoralist women in Chad. *Social Science & Medicine* 54: 1025–1037.

Harari, Yuval. 2007. "Jewish Magic Plates in the Modern Period: From the Islamic World to Israel." *Pe'amim* 110: 55–84. (In Hebrew.)

Hareuveni, Efraim. 1930. "Medicinal Herbs and Their Virtues among Palestinian Arabs." *Harefuah* 4 (3): 113–27. (In Hebrew.)

Hareuveni, Nogah. 1980. *Nature and Landscape in the Israelite Tradition.* Kiryat Ono: Neot Kedumim. (In Hebrew.)

Harfouche, J. K. 1965. *Infant Health in Lebanon: Customs and Taboos.* Beirut: Khayt.

Harley, George. 1941. *Native African Medicine: With Special Reference to Its Practice in the Mano Tribe of Liberia.* Cambridge, MA: Harvard University Press.

Hasan, Muhammad. 1965. "tawtin al-badw fi iqlim maryut-misr." *ri'ayat al-badw wa-tahdirahum wa-tawtinahum,* vol. 2, 1–31.

Havakook, Yaacov. 1986. *From Goat Hair to Stone: Transition in Bedouin Dwellings.* Tel Aviv: IDF.

Haviland, William. 2002. *Cultural Anthropology.* New York: Harcourt Brace College Publishers.

Hawting, G. R. 1989. "The Development of the Biography of al-Harith ibn Kalada and the Relationship between Medicine and Islam." In *The Islamic World, from Classical to Modern Times,* edited by C. E. Bosworth, Charless Issawi, Roger Savory, and A. L. Udovitch. Princeton, NJ: Darwin Press.

Healy, Judith, and Martin McKee. 2004. "Delivering Health Services in Diverse Societies." In *Accessing Health Care: Responding to Diversity,* edited by Judith Healy and Martin McKee. Oxford: Oxford University Press.

Hernandez, Francisco. 1992. "How Mexican Women Give Birth and the Double Bath for Children." In *Medical Practices in Ancient America,* edited by Miguel Guzman, 152–53. Apartado, Mexico: Ediciones Euroamericanas.

Higgins, A. J. 1983. "Observations on the Diseases of the Arabian Camel (*Camelus dromedarius*) and Their Control: A Review." *Veterinary Bulletin* 53 (12): 1089–100.

Higgins, Rosalyn. 1969. *The Middle East,* vol. 1 of *United Nations Peace Keeping, 1946–1967, Documents and Commentary.* London: Oxford University Press.

Hilf, Ahmad ibn Muhammad. 1985. *al-tib fi turathina al-sha'bi (al-badawi fi al-shamal).* taḥrir 'Alī Hrib.

Hilton-Simpson, M. W. 1922. *Arab Medicine and Surgery: A Study of the Healing Art in Algeria.* London: Oxford University Press.

Hitti, Philip. 1951. *History of the Arabs.* 10th edition. London: Macmillan.

Hitti, Yusuf. 1984. *Hitti's Medical Dictionary.* English-Arabic. Beirut: Librairie Du Liban.

Hobbs, J. 1989. *Bedouin Life in the Egyptian Wilderness.* Austin: University of Texas Press.

Hodes, Richard. 1997. "Cross-cultural Medicine and Diverse Health Beliefs. Ethiopian Abroad." *Western Journal of Medicine* 166: 29–36.

Hodgson, Marshal. 1974. *The Venture of Islam*. Chicago and London: University of Chicago Press.

Holbeche, S. 1989. *The Power of Gems and Crystals*. London: Judy Piatkus.

Hooper, David. 1937. *Useful Plants and Drugs of Iran and Iraq*. Vol. 9, no. 3. Chicago: Field Museum of Natural History.

Hughes, Charles, and John Hunter. 1970. "Disease and Development in Africa." *Social Science & Medicine* 3: 443–93.

Huleilhel, Ahmad. 2005. "Demographic Changes in the Arab Population in Israel since the Nineteen Fifties." In *Arab Society in Israel: Population, Society and Economy*, edited by Aziz Haidar. Jerusalem: Van Leer Jerusalem Institute/Institute of Israeli-Arab Studies.

al-Hunaydi, Muhammad. 1965. "al-Qita' al-badawi wa-shibh al-badawi wa-wasai'l tawtinahum zirai'yan fi al-mamlaka al-urduniya al-hashimiya." *ri'ayat al-badw wa-tahdirahum wa- tawtinahum*, vol. 1, 61–106.

Hurtado, Magdalena, Carol Lambourne, et al. 2005. "Human Rights, Biomedical Science, and Infectious Diseases among South American Indigenous Groups." *Annual Review of Anthropology* 34: 639–65.

Ibhanesebhor and Otobo. 1996. "In Vitro Activity of Human Milk against the Causative Organisms of *Ophthalmia neonatorum* in Benin City, Nigeria." *Journal of Tropical Pediatrics* 42 (6): 327–29.

Ibn Abi Usaybi'ah. 1965. *Kitab 'uyun al-anba' fi tabaqat al-tibbā'*. Baiyrut: Manshurat dar Maktabat al-hayat.

Ibn al-Baytar, Abd Allah ibn Ahmad. 1992. *al-Jami' li-Mufradat al-Adwiya wa'l-Aghdhiya*, (Compendium of Simple Drugs and Food), vols 3–4. Baiyrut: Dar al-Kutub al-'Ilmiya.

Ibn-Manzur, Abi al-Fadl. 1956. *Lisan al-'Arab*. Tome XIII. Bayrut: Dar Sader.

Ibn 'Uthaymin, Muhammad. 1991. *Fatawa*. Riad: Dar 'Alam al-Kutub.

Ibn Zuhr, 'Abd al-Malik. 1992. *Kitab al-Aghdhiyah*. Madrid: al-Majlis al-Ala'a lil-Abhath al-'Ilmiyah.

Ibrahim, M.A. 1986. "Veterinary Traditional Practice in Nigeria." In *Livestock Systems Research in Nigeria's Subhumid Zone*, edited by R. von Kaufmann, S. Chater, and R. Blench, 189–203. Proceedings of the 2nd ILCA/NAPRI Symposium. Addis Ababa: ILCA.

Imperato Pascal. 1974. Nomads of the West African Sahel and the delivery of health services to them. *Social Science and Medicine* 1974, 8: 443–457.

Inhorn, Marcia C. 1994a. "*Kabsa (Mushahara*) and Threatened Fertility in Egypt." *Social Science & Medicine* 39: 487–505.

———. 1994b. *Quest for Conception: Gender, Infertility, and Egyptian Medical Traditions*. Philadelphia: University of Pennsylvania Press.

———. 1996. *Infertility and Patriarchy: The Cultural Politics of Gender and Family Life in Egypt*. Philadelphia: University of Pennsylvania Press.

———. 2003. *Local Babies, Global Science: Gender, Religion, and In Vitro Fertilization in Egypt*. New York and London: Routledge.

———. 2005. "Healing and Medicine: Popular Healing Practices in Middle Eastern

Cultures." *Encyclopedia of Religion*, 2nd ed. Lindsay Jones, ed. New York: Macmillan. Pp. 3834–39.

———. 2012. *The New Arab Man: Emergent Masculinities, Technologies, and Islam in the Middle East*, Princeton University Press.

International Labour Organization (ILO). 1964. *Cooperation régionale et Internationale dans le domaine de la sedentarisation*. TMNS/1964/2. Geneva: ILO.

Ismail, Faruq. 1976. *al-Taghayyur wal-tanmiyah fi al-mujtama' al-sahrawi* (Change and Development in Desert Society). Alexandria: Alexandria University Press.

Israeli Defense Forces (IDF). 1954. *The Negev Bedouin*. Tel Aviv: Israeli Defense Forces Publisher.

Israel State Comptroller. 2001. Paragraph 421.

Izhaki, Rika. 1993. "The Ophtalmic Hospital of the Order of St. John (1882–1948)." *Cathedra* 67: 114–35. (In Hebrew.)

Jabbur, Jibrail. 1995. *The Bedouins and the Desert: Aspects of Nomadic Life in the Arab East*. Albany: State University of New York Press.

Jacquart, Danielle. 1996. "The Influence of Arabic Medicine in the Medieval West." In *Encyclopedia of the History of Arab Science*, 3 vols, edited by Roshdi Rashed, 3: 963–71. London: Routledge.

Jaddou, Hashem, Anwar Bateila, Mohammed al-Khateeb, and Kamel Ajlouni. 2003. "Epidemiology and Management of Hypertension among Bedouins in Northern Jordan." *Saudi Med. Journal* 24 (5): 472–76.

Janzen, John M. 1978. *The Quest for Therapy in Lower Zaire*. Berkeley: University of California Press.

al-Jawziyya, Ibn Qayyim. 1998: *al-Tib al-Nabawi*= Medicine of the Prophet. Translated by Penelope Johnstone. Cambridge: The Islamic Texts Society.

Jehovah's Witness case. 1964. *Application of the President and Directors of Georgetown College, Inc., Federal Reporter, second Series*, vol. 331: 1000–1018, decided by the Federal Court of Appeals for the District of Columbia in 1964.

Johnstone, Penelope. 1975. "Tradition in Arabic Medicine." *Palestine Exploration Quarterly*: 23–37.

———. 1998. *Ibn Qayyim al-Jawziyya, Medicine of the Prophet*. Translated and edited by Penelope Johnstone. Cambridge: Islamic Texts Society.

Joseph, Suad .1996. "Gender and Citizenship in Middle East." *Middle East Reports*, no. 198 (January–March): 4–10.

Kahana, Yael. 1985. "The Zar Spirits: A Category of Magic in the System of Mental Health in Ethiopia." *Journal of Social Psychiatry* 31: 134–43.

Kain Z. 1985. "Ischemic Heart Disease among the Negev Bedouins." MD thesis, Ben-Gurion University of the Negev, Beer Sheba.

Karakrah, Muhammad. 1992. "Development of Public Health Services to the Palestinians under the British Mandate 1918–1948." Master's thesis, University of Haifa. (In Hebrew.)

Kark, Sidney. 1962. *A Practice of Social Medicine, A South African Team's Experiences in Different African Communities*. Edinburgh: E. & S. Livingstone.

Katakura, Motoko. 1977. *Bedouin Village: A Study of a Saudi Arabia People in Transition*. Tokyo: University of Tokyo Press.

Kay, Shirley. 1978. *The Bedouin*. New York: Crane, Russak & Company.

Kazaz, Nissim. 1990. "Circumcision among the Bedouins: Traditional and Change." *Israel—People and Land* 5–6 (23–24): 305–14.

Keenan, Jeremy. 2006. "Sedentarization and Changing Patterns of Social Organization among the Tuareq." In *Nomadic Societies in the Middle East and North Africa: Entering the 21st Century,* edited by Dawn Chatty, 916–39. Leiden: Brill.

Kennedy, J. 1987. *The Flower of Paradise: The Institutionalized Use of the Drug Qat in North Yemen.* Dordrecht and Boston: D. Reidel.

Khan, M. S. 1986. *Islamic Medicine.* London: Routledge & Kegan Paul.

al-Khatib, Ahmad. 1982. *Chihabi's Dictionary of Agricultural and Allied Terminology.* English-Arabic. Beirut: Librairie Du Liban.

Kirby, William. 1856. *Introduction to Entomology; or Elements of the Natural History of Insects.* London: Longman, Brown, Green, and Longmans.

Kligler, Israel Jacob, A. Geiger, S. Bromberg, and D. Gurevich. 1931. "An Inquiry into the Diets of Various Sections of the Urban and Rural Population of Palestine." *Bulletin of the Palestine Economic Society* 5 (3): 72–92.

Kocache, Riad, trans. 1982. *The Journey of the Soul, the Story of Hai bin Yaqzan as told by Abu Bakr Muhammad bin Tufail.* London: Octagon Press.

Koenig, Harold. 2002. *Spirituality in Patient Care: Why, How, When, and What.* Philadelphia and London: Templeton Foundation Press.

Korf, L., and J. Malan. 2002. "Threat to Ethnic Identity: The Experience of White Afrikaans- Speaking Participants in Postapartheid South Africa." *Journal of Social Psychology* 142 (2): 149–69.

al-Krenawi, Alean. 2000. *Ethno-Psychiatry among the Bedouin-Arab of the Negev.* Tel Aviv: Hakibutz Hameuchad.

al-Krenawi, Alean, and John Graham. 1997. "Spirit Possession and Exorcism in the Treatment of a Bedouin Psychiatric Patient." *Clinical Social Work Journal* 25 (2): 211–22.

Krispil, Nissim. 1986. *Medicinal Herbs.* Jerusalem: Cana.

———. 2000. *Medicinal Plants in Israel and Throughout the World: The Complete Guide.* Or Yehuda: Hed Arzi.

Kunitz, Stephen. 2000. "Public Health Then and Now: Globalization, States, and the Health of Indigenous Peoples." *American Public Health* 90: 1531–39.

Kunz, George Frederick. 1915. *The Magic of Jewels and Charms.* Philadelphia: J. B. Lippincott.

al-Labadi, 'Abd al-'Aziz. 1992. *Tarikh al-Jiraha 'ind al-'Arab.* 'Amman: Dar al-Karmel.

al-Labbadi, A. 1986. *Al-ahwal al-sihhiya wal-ijtima'iya lil-sha'b al-Filastini, 1922–1972.* Amman: Dar al-Karmil.

Lane, E. W. 1981. *Manners and Customs of the Modern Egyptians.* London: East-West Publications.

Lawrence, Thomas Edward. 1979. *Seven Pillars of Wisdom.* Harmondsworth, UK: Penguin Books.

Layne, Linda. 1994. *Home and Home Land: The Dialogic of Tribal and National Identities in Jordan.* Princeton, NJ: Princeton University Press.

Lehninger, A. L. 1975. *Principles of Biochemestry.* New York: Worth.

Lev, Efraim. 2002. "Reconstructed Materia Medica of the Medieval and Ottoman al-Sham." *Journal of Ethnopharmacology* 80: 167–79.

Lev, Efraim, and Zohar Amar. 2000. "Ethnopharmacological Survey of Traditional Drugs Sold in Israel at the End of the 20th Century." *Journal of Ethnopharmacology* 72 (1–2): 191–205.

Levi, Shabtai. 1978. *refu'ah, higyenah ve-beri'ut etsel ha-Bedvim be-drum Sinai*. Bayt sefer sadeh, marumi sinai.

———. 1987. *The Bedouin in the Sinai Desert* (*ha-Bedvim be-Midbar Sinai*). Tel Aviv: Schocken. (In Hebrew.)

Lévi-Strauss, Claude. 1963. *Structural Anthropology*. New York: Basic Books.

Levy, Amalia, Drora Fraser, Hillel Vardi, and Ron Dragon. 1998. "Hospitalization for Infectious Diseases in Jewish and Bedouin Children in Southern Israel." *European Journal of Epidemiology* 14: 179–86.

Levy, Nissim. 1998. *The History of Medicine in the Holy Land: 1799–1948*. Haifa: Hakibbutz Hameuchad and the Bruce Rappaport Faculty of Medicine. (In Hebrew.)

Lewis, I. M. 2003. *Ecstatic Religion: A Study of Shamanism and Spirit Possession*. London and New York: Routledge.

Lewis, I. M., Ahmed al-Safi, and Sayyid Hurreiz, eds. 1991. *Medicine: The Zar-Bori Cult in Africa and Beyond*. Edinburgh: Edinburgh University Press for the International African Institute.

Lewis, Norman N. 1987. *Nomads and Settlers in Syria and Jordan, 1800–1980*. Cambridge: Cambridge University Press.

Lipsky, George. 1959. *Saudi Arabia, Its People, Its Culture*. New Haven, CT: HRAF Press.

Lithwick, Harvey. 2000. *An Urban Development Strategy for the Negev's Bedouin Community*. Beer Sheba: Center for Bedouin Studies and Development, Ben Gurion University.

Lloyd, Geoffrey Ernest Richard. 1950. *Hippocratic Writings*. London: Penguin.

Lowenthal, M. N., and S. Shany. 1994. "Osteomalacia in Bedouin Women of the Negev." *Israel Journal Medical Sciences* 30(7): 520–23.

Lozoff, Betsy, K. Kamath, and R. Feldman. 1975. "Infection and Disease in South Indian Families: Beliefs about Childhood Diarrhea." *Human Organization* 34: 353–58.

Luke, Harry Charles, and Edward Keith-Roach. 1930. *The Handbook of Palestine and Trans-Jordan*. London: Macmillan.

Lust, John. 1980. *The Herb Book*. New York: Bantam Books.

Maclagan, Ianthe. 2011. "Food and gender in Yemeni community." In Richard Tapper & Sami Zubaida 2011, Introduction, in *A Taste of Thyme: Culinary Cultures of the Middle East*, London: Tauris Parke Paperbacks.

Maclean, Una. 1971. *Magic Medical: A Nigerian Case Study*. London: Allen Lane, Penguin Press.

Maclennan, Norman. 1935. "General Health Conditions of Certain Bedouin Tribes in Trans-Jordan." *Transactions of the Royal Society of Tropical Medicine and Hygiene* 29 (3): 227–48.

al-Maḍi, Munib, and Sulaiyman Musa. 1959. *Tarikh al-Urdun fi al-qarn al-'ishrin*. 'Amman: Publishing rights reserved for the authors.

Madi, S. A., R. L. al-Naggar, S. A. al-Awadi, and L. A. Bastaki. 2005. "Profile of Major Congenital Malformations in Neonates in al-Jahra Region of Kuwait." *Eastern Mediterranean Health Journal* 11 (4): 1–8.

Makris, G. P. 2000. *Changing Masters: Spirit Possession and Identity Construction among Slave Descendants and Other Subordinates in the Sudan.* Evanston, IL: Northwestern University Press.

Mandaville, James. 1990. *Flora of Eastern Saudi Arabia.* London and New York: Kegan Paul International.

Marshal, Carter. 1972. "Some Exercise in Social Ecology: Health, Disease, and Modernization in the Ryuku Islands." In *The Careless Technology: Ecology and International Development,* edited by M. T. Fraver and J. P. Milton. 5–18. Garden City, NY: Natural History Press.

Marx, Emanuel. 1967. *Bedouin of the Negev.* Manchester: University of Manchester Press.

——. 1973. "Circumcision Feasts among The Negev Bedouin." *Int. J. Middle East Studies* 4: 411–27.

——. 1977. "Bedouin Pilgrimages to Holy Tombs in Southern Sinai." *Notes on the Bedouin* 8: 14–22.

Marx, E. 1990 Advocacy in a Bedouin Resettlement Project in the Negev, Israel. Pp. 228–244 in *Anthropology and Development in North Africa and the Middle East,* eds. M. Salem-Murdock and M.M. Horowitz. Boulder, Colorado: Westview.

Marx, Emanuel, and M. Sela. 1980. "The Situation of the Negev's Bedouin, Appendix No. 1." In *Ben-Mayer's Team for Evacuation and Resettlement of the Bedouin.* Tel Aviv: TAHAL.

McDermott, M. T. 2004. "Health Care among the Sinai Bedouin." *Military Medicine* 149: 442–45.

McElroy, Ann, and Patricia Townsend. 1996. *Medical Anthropology in Ecological Perspective.* Boulder, CO: Westview Press.

Meir, Avinoam. 1987. "Nomads, Development and Health: Delivering Public Health Services to the Bedouin of Israel." *Geografiska Annaler* 69B: 115–26.

——. 1997. *As Nomadism Ends, the Israeli Bedouin of the Negev.* Boulder, CO: Westview.

Meir, A. and Ben-David, Y. 1991. "Socio-economic Development and the Dynamics of Child Mortality among Sedentarizing Bedouin in Israel," Tidjschrift voor Economische en Sociale Geographie, Vol. 82, pp. 139–147.

Melling, Joseph, and Bill Forsythe, eds. 1999. *Insanity, Institutions, and Society, 1800–1914: A Social History of Madness in Comparative Perspective.* London and New York: Routledge.

Meyerhof, Max. 1928. *The Book of the Ten Treatises on the Eye Ascribed to Hunain Ibn Ishaq.* Cairo: Government Press.

——. 1931: "Science and Medicine." In *The Legacy of Islam,* edited by T. Arnold and A. Guillaume. Oxford: University Press.

Miller, Arthur Selwyn. 1984. *A "Capacity for Outrage": The Judicial Odyssey of J. Skelly Wright.* Westport, CT: Greenwood Press.

Miller, Max. 1973. "Industrialization, Ecology and Health in the Tropics." *Canadian Journal of Public Health* 64: 11–16.

Ministry of Health Report 2008, Jerusalem, Israel

Moed, Lisa, Tor A. Shwayder, and Mary Wu Chang. 2001. "Cantharidin Revisited: A Blistering Defense of an Ancient Medicine." *Arch Dermatol.* 137: 1357–60.

Mohammed, M. J. 1981. "Planning Policy and Bedouin Society in Oman." In *The Future of Pastoral People,* edited by John G. Galaty, Dan *Aronson,* Philip *Salzman,* and Amy Chouinard. Ottawa: IDRC.

Morgenstern, Julian. 1966. *Rites of Birth, Marriage, Death and Kindred Occasions among the Semites.* Cincinnati: Hebrew Union College Press.

Morsy, Soheir. 1978. "Sex Differences and Folk Illness in an Egyptian Village." In *Women in the Muslim World,* edited by Lois Beck and Nikki Keddie. Cambridge, MA: Harvard University Press, 599–616.

——. 1980. "Body Concepts and Health Care: Illustrations from an Egyptian Village." *Human Organization* 39: 92–96.

——. 1982. "Childbirth in an Egyptian Village." In *Anthropology of Human Birth,* edited by Margarita Artschwager Kay, 147–74. Philadelphia: F. A. Davis.

Muhsam, Helmut Victor. 1966. *Bedouin of the Negev: Eight Demographic Studies.* Jerusalem: Jerusalem Academic Press.

al-Munjid fi al-Lugha wal-'Alam. 1975. Beirut: Dar El-Mashreq Publishers. 22nd edition.

Murad, A.S. 1966. *Lamhat min tarikh al-tibb al-qadim* (Glimpses from the History of Early Medicine). al-Qahira: Maktabat al-naṣhr al-haditha. (In Arabic.)

Murray, George William. 1935. *Sons of Ishmael. A Study of the Egyptian Bedouin.* London: George Rutledge & Sons.

Mursi. Amin. 1966. *Dirasatt fi'l-Shi'ūn al-tibbiyah al-'arabiyah* (Studies on Arab Medical Affairs). al-Iskandariya: al-ma'arif. (In Arabic.)

Musil, Alois. 1926. *The Northern Hegaz.* New York: American Geographical Society.

——. 1928. *The Manners and Customs of the Rwala Bedouins.* New York: American Geographical Society.

Mustafa, Muhammad. 1965. "tawtin al-badw fi al-muhafazat al-sahrawiyah-misr." *ri'ayat al-badw wa-tahdirahum wa-tawtinahum,* vol. 2, 70–80.

Myntti, Cynthia. 1993. "Social Determinants of Child Health in Yemen." *Social Science of Medicine* 37 (2): 233–40.

al-Najjar, Amer. 1994. *Fi tarikh al-tib fi al-Dawlah al-Islamiya* (History of Medicine in the Islamic Empire). al-Qahira: Dar al-Ma'arif. (In Arabic.)

al-Nasiri, Muhammad. 1965. "Mushkilat al-badawah wa-mashru'at al-tawtin fi al-maghrib." *ri'ayat al-badw wa-tahdirahum wa-tawtinahum,* vol. 2, 249–78.

Nasr, S.H., 1968: Science and Civilization in Islam. Cambridge, MA: Harvard University Press.

Nathan, Hilel. 1980. "Uvula Amputation among the Bedouin." *Madà* 24 (3): 156. (In Hebrew.)

Nathan, Hilel, I. Hershkovitz, B. Arensburg, Y. Kobyliansky, and M.Goldschmidt-Nathan. 1982. "Mutilation of the Uvula among Bedouin of the South Sinai." *Israel Journal of Medical Sciences* 18: 774–79.

Nathan, M. A., E. M. Fratkin, and E. A. Roth. 1996. "Sedentism and Child Health among Rendille Pastoralists of Northern Kenya." *Social Science and Medicine* 43 (4): 503–15.

Nations, Marilyn, and Sharmenia Nuto. 2002. "Tooth Worms, Poverty Tattoos and Dental Care Conflicts in Northeast Brazil." *Social Science & Medicine* 54 (2002): 229–44.

Nesbitt, Mark. 1995. "Plants and People in Ancient Anatolia." *Biblical Archaeologist* 58: 2.

Nejidat 'Ali. 1981a. "About Some Medicinal Plants of the Nejidat Tribe." *Israel Land and Nature* (Fall): 17.

———. 1981b. "'al tsimhi refu'ah ahadim etsel shevet Njidat." *Teva' ve-arets* 23 (4): 163.

———. 1984. "mirkahat bedvit, 'al tsimhi refu'ah etsel kamah mi-shevti ha-bedvim be-tsfun ha-arets." *Teva' ve-arets* 26 (6): 29–30.

Nicholson, Reynold. 1975. *The Mystics of Islam*. London: Arkana.

al-Nimr, Ihsan. 1961. *Tarikh Jabal Nabulus wa-l-Balqa'*. Nabulus: Matba'at Jam'iyat 'Ummal al-Matabi' al-Ta'awuniya.

Nissenbaum, Arie. 1978. "Dead Sea Asphalt-Historical Aspects." *American Association of Petroleum Geologists* 62: 837–44.

Omran, Abdel Rahim. 1992. *Family Planning in the Legacy of Islam*. London: Routledge.

Osborn, Dale. 1968. "Notes on Medicinal and Other Uses of Plants in Egypt." *Economic Botany* 22 (2): 165–17.

Osol, Arthur, and George M. Gould. 1972. *Blakiston's Gould Medical Dictionary*. 3rd edition. New York: McGraw-Hill.

Ozaydin, Zuhal. 2002. "The Establishment and Activities of the Ottoman Red Crescent Society." In *History of Medicine Pharmacology Veterinary Medicine in Anatolia and Turkish Culture*, ed. Nil Sari. Istanbul: Nobel Yayıncılık.

Palevitch, Dan, and Zohara Yaniv. 2000. *Medicinal Plants of the Holy Land*. Tel Aviv: Modan.

Palmer, E. H. 1871. *The Desert of the Exodus*. Vol. 2. Cambridge: Deighton, Bell.

Panter-Brick, Catherine. 1991. "Parental Responses to Consanguinity and Genetic Disease in Saudi Arabia." *Social Science & Medicine* 33: 1295–302.

Peredo, Miguel Guzman. 1992. *Medical Practices in Ancient America*. Mexico City: Ediciones Euroamericanas.

Peters, Emrys. 1990. *The Bedouin of Cyrenaica: Studies in Personal and Corporate Power*. Cambridge: Cambridge University Press.

Philby, John. 1933. *The Empty Quarter*. New York: Henry Holt.

Philips, D., and Y. Verhasselt. 1994. *Health and Development*. London: Routledge.

Phillips, E. D. 1973. *Greek Medicine*. London: Thames and Hudson.

Philips, Jane. 1958. *Lebanese Folk Cures*. Ann Arbor, MI: University Microfilms.

Pillsbury, B. L. K. 1978. *Traditional Health Care in the Near East*. Washington, DC: U.S. Agency for International Development.

Pink, Pinhas. 1991. "Beersheba Conquest in the World War I." In *Beersheba Sights*, edited by Gideon Biger and Ely Schiller. Jerusalem: Ariel.

Pinczuk, Shira. 1994. "Pregnancy and Delivery among the Negev Traditional Society." Paper submitted to the Environmental High School at Sde Boqer.

Pisharoty, P. R. 1993. "Notes from Kerala." *Honey Bee* 4 (4): 12, 17.

Prince, Raymond. 1974. "Indigenous Yoruba Psychiatry." In *Anthropology and Community Action*, edited by E. Hegeman and L. Kooperman. Garden City, NY: Anchor Books.

Qaramani, Muhammad. 1965. "*ri'ayat al-badw al-ruhhal wa-tawtinahum* ijtima'aiyan fi muhafazat sina'." *ri'ayat al-badw wa-tahdirahum wa-tawtinahum*, vol. 1, 513–29.

Quran. 1930. Translated by Mohammed Marmaduke Pickthall. Karachi: Taj.

al-Qurtubi, Ahmad. 1993. *al-Jami' li-ahkam al-Quran*. Bairut: Dar al-Kutb al-'Ilmiya.

al-Radihan, Khaled. 2006. "Adaptation of Bedouin in Saudi Arabia to the 21st Century: Mobility and Stasis among the Shararat." In *Nomadic Societies in the Middle East and North Africa: Entering the 21st Century*, edited by Dawn Chatty, 840–64. Leiden: Brill.

al-Rajib, Hamd. 1965. "al-batrul ka-wasilatun li-tawtin al-badw fi al-kuwait." *ri'ayat al-badw wa-tahdirahum wa-tawtinahum*, vol. 2, 157.

Rasmussen, Susan. 1995. *Spirit Possession and Personhood among the Kel Ewey Tuareq*. Cambridge: Cambridge University Press.

Raswan, Karl. 1935. *Black Tents of Arabia: My Life among the Bedouin*. Boston: Little, Brown.

Raz, Aviad. 2005. *The Gene and the Genie: Tradition, Medication and Genetic Counselling in a Bedouin Community in Israel*. Durham, NC: Carolina Academic Press.

Read, Margaret. 1966. *Culture, Health, and Disease: Social and Cultural Influences on Health Programmes in Developing Countries*. London: Tavistock.

Reilly, Benjamin. 2013. "Revisiting Consanguineous Marriage in the Greater Middle East: Milk, Blood, and Bedouins." *American Anthropologist* 115 (3): 374–85.

Reiss, Nira. 1991. *The Health Care of the Arabs in Israel*. Oxford: Westview.

Reynolds, Vernon, and Ralph Tanner. 1995. *The Social Ecology of Religion*. New York: Oxford University Press.

al-Rihani, Amin. 1928. *Tarikh Najd wa-mulhaqatihi*. Bairut: dar al-Rihani li-tiba'at wal-nashri.

Ring, M. 1998. *Historia ilustrada da odontologia*. Sao Paulo: Manole.

Rispler-Chaim, Vardit. 1992. "The Siwak: A Medieval Islamic Contribution to Dental Care." *Journal of the Royal Asiatic Society* 2 (1): 13–15.

———. 1996. "Islamic Law of Marriage and Divorce and the Disabled Person: The Case of the Epileptic Wife." *Die Welt des Islam* 36 (1): 90–106.

Roboff, Farron Vogel. 1977. "The Moving Target: Health Status of Nomadic Peoples in Coping with Desertification." *Economic Geography* 53 (4): 421–28.

Roemer, Milton. 1960. *Henry Sigerist on the Sociology of Medicine*. New York: MD Publications.

Romem, P., H. Reizer, Y. Romem, and S. Shvarts. 2002. "The Provision of Modern Medical Services to a Nomadic Population: A Review of Medical Services to the Bedouins of Southern Sinai during Israeli Rule 1967–1982." *J. Israel Medical Association* 4 (4): 308–8.

Rosen, Lawrence. 1998. *The Anthropology of Justice: Law as Culture in Islamic Society*. Cambridge: Cambridge University Press.

Roth, Eric, A., Martha Nathan, and Elliot Fratkin. 2005. "The Effect of Pastoral Sedentarization on Children's Growth and Nutrition among Ariaal and Rendille in Northern Kenya." In *As Pastoralists Settle: Social, Health and Economic Consequences of Pastoral Sedentarization in Marsabit District, Kenya*, edited by Elliot Fratkin and Eric Abella Roth. New York and London: Kluwer Academic.

Rouget, Gilbert. 1985. *Music and Trance*. Chicago: University of Chicago Press.

Rubin, Nissan. 1995. *Reshit ha-hayim: tiksi ledah, milah u-fidyon ha-ben bi-mekorot Hazal* (The Beginning of Life: Birth Rituals, Circumcision and Redemption of a

Male First Born in the Literature of the Blessed Sages (HAZAL). Tel Aviv: Ha-Kibuts ha-meuhad.

———. 2008. *Time and Life Cycle in Talmud and Midrash: Socio-Anthropological Perspectives.* Boston: Academic Studies Press.

Ruperez, P. 2002. "Mineral Content of Edible Marine Seaweeds." *Food Chemistry* 79: 23–26.

Sabir, Muhyi al-Din. 1965. "tawtin al-badw wa-tahdirahum fi jumhuriyat al-Sudan." *ri'ayat al-badw wa-tahdirahum wa-tawṭinahum,* vol. 1, 243–374.

Sabih, Hasan. 1965. "al-buhuth al-'ilmiya wa-qimatuha bil-nisbati li-'amaliyat al-tawtin fi al-jumhuriya al-'Arabiya al-Muttahidah." *ri'ayat al-badw wa-tahdirahum wa-tawtinahum,* vol. 1, 491–511.

Sadalla, Edward, and David Stea. 1982. "Nomads, Behavioral and Psychological Adjustment to Sedentarization." *Geographical Research Forum,* no. 5: 3–14.

al-Said, M. S. 1997. "Medicine in Islam." In *Encyclopedia of the History of Science, Technology, and Medicine in Non-Western Cultures,* edited by Helaine Selin. Dordrecht, Boston, and London: Kluwer Academic.

al-Sayyad, Muhammad. 1965. "al-tawtin wal-khuttatu al-qawmiyatu li-tanmiyatu al-ijtima'iyatu wal-iqtisadiyatu." *ri'ayat al-badw wa-tahdirahum wa-tawtinahum,* vol. 1, 409–24.

Salah al-Din Basha. 1965. "asalib al-tawttun wa-anmatihi wa-imkaniyatihi wa-mutatalabatihi wa-mushkilatihi." *ri'ayat al-badw wa-tahdirahum wa-tawtinahum,* vol. 2, 279–92.

Salazar, Francisco Cervantes. 1992. "Physicians and Sorcerers." In *Medical Practices in Ancient America,* edited by Miguel Guzman Peredo. Mexico City: Ediciones Euroamericanas.

Salim, Shakir. 1970. *Echibayish—an Anthropological Study of a Marsh Village in Iraq.* Baghdad: al-Ani Press. (In Arabic.)

Saliternik, Z. 1978. "Reminiscences of the History of Malaria Eradication in Palestine and Israel." *Journal of Medical Sciences* 14 (56): 518.

Salzman, Philip. 1980. "Processes of Sedentarization as Adaptation and Response." In *When Nomads Settle,* edited by Philip Salzman. New York: Praeger.

Sanders, Paula. 1991. "Gendering the Un-gendered Body: Hermaphrodites in Medieval Islamic Law." In *Women in Middle Eastern History,* edited by Nikki Keddie and Beth Baron, 74–95. New Haven, CT: Yale University Press.

Sarnelli, T. 1940. "Resection of Uvula in Native Medicine of Arabia, Kordofan and Ethiopia." *Riv. Med. Trop.* 4: 288–93.

Savage-Smith E. 1996. "Medicine." In *Encyclopedia of the History of Arabic Science,* vol. 3., edited by Roshdi Rashid in collaboration with Regis Morelon. London and New York: Routledge.

Scotch, Norman. 1963. "Socio-cultural Factors in the Epidemiology of Zulu Hypertension." *American Journal of Public Health* 53: 1205–13.

Scudder, Thyer. 1973. "Human Ecology of Big Projects: River Basin Development and Resettlement." *Annual Review of Anthropology* 2: 45–55.

Seaman, John, Julius Rivers, John Holt, and John Murlis. 1973. "An Inquiry into the Drought Situation in Upper Volta." *Lancet* (6 October): 774–78.

Seligman N, Rosensaft Z, Tadmor N, Katzenelson J, Naveh Z. 1959. *Natural pasture of Israel. Vegetation, carrying capacity and improvement.* Merhavia: Sifriat Poalim (in Hebrew).

Senatorea Felice, Nelly Apostolides Arnold, and Franco Piozzic. 2004. "Chemical Composition of the Essential Oil of *Salvia multicaulis Vahl. var. simplicifolia Boiss.* Growing Wild in Lebanon." *Journal of Chromatography* A, 1052: 237–40.

Serour Gamal.I, editor. 1992: Islamic views. In: *Proceedings of the First International Conference on Bioethics in Human Reproduction Research in the Muslim World;* 1991 Dec 10–13; Cairo: International Islamic Center for Population Studies and Research, Al Azhar University.

———. 1997. "Islamic Development in Bioethics." In *Bioethics Yearbook,* vol. 171, edited by B. Andrew Lustig. Dordrecht: Kluwer Academic Publishers for Baylor College of Medicine.

———. 1998. "Reproduction Choice: A Muslim Perspective." In *The Future of Human Reproduction: Ethics, Choice and Regulation,* edited by John Harris and Soren Holm, 191–202. Oxford: Clarendon Press.

Shani, J., Joseph, B., Sulman, F.G. 1970. Fluctuations in the hypoglycaemic effect of *Poterium spinosum L.* (Rosaceae). Archives Internationales de Pharmacody- namie et de Therapie 185, 344–349.

Sharaf, ʿAbd Al-ʿAziz. 1965. "tawtin al-badw wa-tahdirahum fi Libiya." *ri'ayat al-badw wa-tahdirahum wa-tawtinahum,* vol. 2, 177–247.

Sharif, Y. 1970. *Tarikh al-tibb al-'arabi* (History of Arab Medicine). al-Qahira: matba'at sijil al-'arab. (In Arabic.)

Sharp, Lesley. 1993. *The Possessed and the Dispossessed: Spirits, Identity, and Power in a Madagascar Migrant Town.* Berkeley and Los Angeles: University of California Press.

———. 1994. "Exorcists, Psychiatrists, and the Problems of Possession in Northwest Madagascar." *Social Science and Medicine* 38 (4): 225–42.

al-Shartuni, Sa'id. 1992. *Aqrab al-mawarid fi fush al-'arabiya wal-shawarid.* Bayrut: Maktabat Lubnan.

al-Shatti, A. S. 1970. *al-ʿArab wal-tibb* (The Arabs and Medicine). Dimashq: Manshurat Wazarat al-Thaqafa. (In Arabic.)

Sheets, P. D. 1987. "Dawn of a New Stone Age in Eye Surgery." In *Archeology: Discovering Our Past,* edited by R.bJ. Sharter and W. Ashmore. Palo Alto, CA: Mayfield.

Shiloah, Amnon. 2001. *Music in the World of Islam.* Jerusalem: Institute for Israeli Arab Studies.

Shiloh, Ailon. 1961. "The System of Medicine in Middle East Culture." *Middle East Journal* 15: 277–88.

Shimkin, Nahum. 1926. "Trachoma in Palestine; Its Epidemiology and a Review of Measures for Dealing with It." *British Journal of Ophthalmology* (May): 247–79.

———. 1936. "Eye Diseases and Their Causes in Canaan." *Harefuah* 9 (5): 315–41. (In Hebrew.)

Shimoni, Yacob. 1947. *The Arabs of Palestine.* Tel Aviv: 'Am Oved.

Shinar, Pessah. 1982. "Elements of Magic in Modern North African Jewelry, *Yesodot magiyim ba takhshitanut ha-Maghribit ba-'et ha-hadashah.*" *Pe'amim* 11: 29–42.

Shinnawi, Mustafa. 1982. *refu'ah 'amamit ve-ha-Bedvim ba-negev.* Beer Sheba: Medical School.

Shorter Encyclopedia of Islam. 1974. Leiden: Brill.

Shuqayr, Na'um. 1916. *Tarikh Sina al-qadim wal-hadith wa-jughrafiyatuha.* al-Qahira: matba'at al-ma'aref.

Shvarts, S. 1987. *Kupat-Holim Haclalit, The General Sick Fund.* Sede Boqer Campus: The Ben-Gurion Research Center, The Ben-Gurion University of the Negev Press, 1987 (in Hebrew).

Sibai, Zuhayr. 1981. *The Health of the Family in Changing Arabia: A Case Study of Primary Health Care.* Jedda: Tihama.

Sibai, Z. and W., Reinke 1981. Anthropometric measurements among pre-school children in Wadi-Turba, Saudi Arabia. *J. Trop. Pediatr.* 27: 150–154.

Sider, Gerald. 2008. "The Construction and Denial of Indigenous Identities: Recognition, Misrecognition, and the Question of Nativein Nation-States and Anthropology." *Dialect Anthropology* 32: 275–95.

Sincech, Francesco. 2002. *Bedouin Traditional Medicine in the Syrian Steppe: Al-Khatib Speaks: An Interview with a Hadidin Traditional Doctor.* Rome: FAO.

Singer, Amy. 1996. Ottoman Palestine (1516–1800): Health, Disease, and Historical Sources. In: Manfred Waserman and Samuel Kottek *(editors), Health and Disease in the Holy Land,* Lewiston: The Edwin Mellen Press.

Smith, T. 1990. "Poverty and Health in the 1990s." *Br. Med. J.* 301: 349–50.

Smith, Robertson. 1903. *Kinship and Marriage in Early Arabia.* Boston: Beacon Press.

Sohar, Ezra. 1980. Adam ve-'Aklim, Jerusalem: Keter.

Spicer, Neil. 2005. "Sedenterization and Children's Health: Changing Discourses in the Northeast *Badia* of Jordan." *Social Science & Medicine* 61 (2005): 2165–76.

Spoer, A. M. 1927. "Sickness and Death among the Arabs of Palestine." *Folk Lore* 38: 116.

Stavi, Moses. 1946. *ha-Kefar ha-'Arvi: pirki havai.* Tel Aviv: 'Am 'oved.

Stedman, Thomas Lathrop. 2000. *Stedman's Medical Dicionary,* 27th edition. New York and London: Lippincott Williams & Wilkins.

Stillman, Norman. 1983. "Women on Folk Medicine: Judaeo-Arabic Texts from Sefrou." *Journal of the American Oriental Society* 103 (3): 485–93.

Strathearn, John, C. 1933. "The Problem of Blindness in Palestine." *Folia Ophthalmologica Orientalia* 1: 121–42.

Strathearn's Report. 1932. Jerusalem: Government of Palestine.

Sufian, Sandy. 1999. "Healing the Land and the Nation: Malaria and the Zionist Project in Mandatory Palestine." PhD diss., New York University.

Sufian, Sandra. 2002. "Arab Medical Systems in the British Mandate 1920–1947." In *Separate and Cooperate, Cooperate and Separate: The Disengagement of the Palestine Health Care System from Israel and Its Emergence as an Independent System,* edited by Tamara Barnea and Rafiq Husseini. Tel Aviv: Am Oved.

Suhrawardi, Abu-Hafṣ 'Umar ibn Muhammad. 2005. *'awarif al-ma'arif.* al-Qahirah: maktabat al-iman.

al-Suyuti, Jalal ad-Din. 1899. *al-Rahma fi al-tibb wal-hikma.* Bayrut: al-Maktaba al-thaqafiya.

Swift, Jeremy, C. Toulmin, and S. Chatting. 1990. "Providing Services for Nomadic People." UNICEF Staff Working Papers No. 8. New York: UNICEF.

Syrian Delegation. 1965. "al-nashāṭu al-mabdhūlu bi-majāli al-badāwati fī al-jumhūrīyah al-'Arabīyati al-Sūrīyati." *ri'āyat al-badw wa-taḥḍīrahum wa-tawṭīnahum,* vol. 1, 479–83.

al-Tabari, Ibn Jarir. 1992. *Tafsir al-tabari.* Bayrut: Dar al-Kutb al-'Ilmiya.

al-Tabari, 'Ali ibn Sahl Rabban. 1928. *Firdaws al-hikma.* Berlin: Buch Kunstdruckerei.

al-Taher, 'Ali. 1965. "dirasah maiydaniya litawtin al-badw fi al-mamlakah al-urduniya al-hashimiya." *ri'ayat al-badw wa-tahdirahum wa-tawtinahum,* vol. 1, 1–59.

Tal, Pnina. 1981. *Medicinal Plants.* Tel Aviv: Rshafim. (In Hebrew.)

Tal, Sigal. 1995. *The Negev Bedouin Woman in an Era of Changes.* Lahav: Joe Alon Center. (In Hebrew.)

al-Tamimi, Abu-Abd Allah, M.1976. *Kitab al-Murshid.* Freiburg: Schwarz.

Tamir Oren, Roni Peleg, Jacob Dreiher, Talab Abu-Hammad, Yunis Abu Rabia, Mohammad Abu Rashid, Alex Eisenberg, David Sibersky, Alex Kazanovich, Elbedour Khalil, Daniel Vardy and Pesach Shvartzman. 2007. "Cardiovascular Risk Factors in the Bedouin Population: Management and Compliance." *IMAJ* 9: 652–55.

Tekce, B. 1990. "Households, Resources, and Child Health in a Self-Help Settlement in Cairo, Egypt." *Soc. Sci. Med.* 30: 929–40.

Thesiger, Wilfred. 1959. *Arabian Sands.* London: Penguin.

Thomas, Bertram. 1932. "Anthropological Observations in South Arabia." *Journal of the Royal Anthropological Institute of Great Britain and Ireland* 62 (Jan.–June): 83–103.

Thomson, W. 1979. *Black's Medical Dictionary,* 32nd edition. London: A & C Black.

Tifashi, Ahmad ibn Yusuf. 1977. *Azhar al-afkar fi Jawahir al-ahjar.* al-Qahira: al-haya'h al-misriyah al-'ammah lil-Kitab.

Topp, Sonia, Judith Cook, W. W. Holland, and A. Elliot. 1970. "Influence of Environmental Factors on Height and Weight of School Children." *British Journal of Preventive and Social Medicine* 24: 154–62.

Townsend, C. C., and Evan Guest. 1980. *Flora of Iraq,* vol. 4 no. 1–2. Baghdad: Ministry of Agriculture and Agrarian Reform.

Tryoler, H. A., and John Cassel. 1964. "Health Consequences of Culture Change—II. The Effect of Urbanization on Coronary Heart Mortality in Rural Residents." *Journal of Chronic Diseases* 17: 167–77.

Tsikhlakis, Rana. 1997. "Diet and Nutrition Report." In *Pastoralists of the Lower Danan Reserve Area: Attitudes to and Prospects for Integration into Reserve Management Strategy,* edited by Alan Rowe, Rebecca Salti, Shahin Sirhan, and Aish Audi. Unpublished report. Royal Society for the Conservation of Nature, Amman.

Turner, Victor. 1967. *The Forest of Symbols: Aspects of Ndembu Ritual.* Ithaca, NY: Cornell University Press.

Ullmann, Manfred. 1970. *Die Medizin im Islam.* Leiden: Brill.

——. 1978: *Islamic Surveys—Islamic Medicine.* Edinburgh: University Press.

Underwood, Jane. 1975. *Biocultural Interactions and Human Variation.* Dubuque, IA: W. C. Brown.

Urkin Jacob, Hana Shalev, Sofer Shaul, and Alen Witztum 1991. "Henabane (*Hyoscyamus reticulatus*) Poisoning in Children in the Negev." *Harefuah* 120 (12): 714–16.

Valdes, Gonzalo Fernandez. 1992. "The Herb or Plant called *Perebecenuc* and Its Excellent and Proven Properties." In *Medical Practices in Ancient America,* edited by Miguel Guzman Peredo. Mexico City: Ediciones Euroamericanas.

Van Balen, Frank, and Marcia C. Inhorn. 2001. "Introduction—Interpreting Infertility: View from the Social Sciences." In *Infertility Around the Globe: New Thinking on Childlessness, Gender, and Reproductive Technologies,* edited by Marcia Inhorn and Frank van Balen, 3–32. Berkeley: University of California Press.

Wehr, Hans. 1994. *The Hans Wehr Dictionary of Modern Written Arabic.* 4th edition. Ithaca, NY: Spoken Language Services.

Weiner, J. S. 1977. "Human Ecology." In *Human Biology, an Introduction to Human Evolution, Variation, Growth and Ecology,* edited by G. Harrison, J. S. Weiner, J. M. Tanner and N. A. Barnicot. Oxford: Oxford University Press.

Weir, Shelagh. 1985. *Qat in Yemen: Consumption and Social Change.* London: British Museum Publications.

———. 1990. *The Bedouin.* London: British Museum Publications.

Weiss, A. 1961. "Epidemiological Studies on the Incidence of Coronary Heart Diseases in the Bedouin of the Negev." MD thesis, Hebrew University Medical School.

Weitzman, S., E. E. Lehmann, and Y. Abu-Rabiah. 1974. "*Diabetes mellitus* among the Bedouin Population in the Negev." *Diabetologia* 10: 391.

Weitzman, S., and S. Rosen. 2001. "Health Needs of the Negev Population." Report of the Working Group, Goldman Foundation.

Westermarck, Edward. 1926. *Ritual and Belief in Morocco,* 2 vols. London: Macmillan.

World Health Organization. Farid, M.A., 1954. "Ineffectiveness of DDT residual spraying in stopping malaria transmission in the Jordan Valley. WHO Bulletin, vol. 1954, No. 4–5, pp. 765–784. WHO(05)B936.

World Health Organization. 2000. *The World Health Report 2000. Health Systems: Improving Performances.* Geneva: World Health Organization.

Yasin, Shihab al-Badri. 2003. *al-tadawi bi-alban wa-abwal al-ibil* (Treatments by Camel Milk and Urine). Macca: dar tibbiyat al-khadra. (In Arabic.)

Zamir M. 1972. "Myocardial Infarction in the Bedouin Population in the Negev (a Survey of 35 Cases)." MD thesis, Tel Aviv University Medical School, Ramat Aviv.

Zimmerman, J. E. 1964. *Dictionary of Classical Mythology.* London and New York: Harper & Row.

Zubaida, Sami, and Richard Tapper. 2011. *A Taste of Thyme: Culinary Cultures of the Middle East.* London: Tauris Parke Paperbacks.

Index

Printed in the USA
CPSIA information can be obtained
at www.ICGtesting.com
LVHW020928140124
768964LV00042B/1865